RETHINKING SOCIAL WORK IN A GL

Rethinking Social Work in a Global World

Gai Harrison and Rose Melville

First published 2010 by
PALGRAVE MACMILLAN

Palgrave Macmillan in the UK is an imprint of Macmillan Publishers Limited,
registered in England, company number 785998, of Houndmills, Basingstoke,
Hampshire RG21 6XS.

Palgrave Macmillan in the US is a division of St Martin's Press LLC,
175 Fifth Avenue, New York, NY 10010.

Palgrave Macmillan is the global academic imprint of the above companies
and has companies and representatives throughout the world.

Palgrave® and Macmillan® are registered trademarks in the United States,
the United Kingdom, Europe and other countries.

ISBN: 978–0–230–20135–4

This book is printed on paper suitable for recycling and made from fully
managed and sustained forest sources. Logging, pulping and manufacturing
processes are expected to conform to the environmental regulations of the
country of origin.

A catalogue record for this book is available from the British Library.

A catalog record for this book is available from the Library of Congress.

10 9 8 7 6 5 4 3 2 1
19 18 17 16 15 14 13 12 11 10

Printed and bound in Great Britain by
CPI Antony Rowe, Chippenham and Eastbourne

For Norman and Alison Melville
and
Bablu Singh

Acknowledgements

We would like to thank the following social work students who contributed their ideas to the book: Frances Cheverton, Christine Gardiner, Keirnan Fitzpatrick, David Meddings, Lawrence Massaquoi, Lorraine O'Reilly, Thomas Pritzler, Kyoko Ishigure and Timothy Carroll.

Thanks also to Vikas Gora and Aastha Malhotra for sharing their reflections on life in the field.

Contents

Glossary of Terms and Abbreviations

AHRC	Asian Human Rights Commission	www.ahrchk.net
BASW	British Association of Social Workers	
BIHR	British Institute of Human Rights	
CAFTA-DR	Dominican Republic–Central America–United States Free Trade Agreement	
CEDAW	Convention on the Elimination of All Forms of Discrimination against Women	
CFCs	chloro-fluorocarbons	
Christian Aid	International Aid Charity	www.christianaid.org.uk
COSW	Commonwealth Organization for Social Work	
DCA	Department for Constitutional Affairs	
DSM	*Diagnostic and Statistical Manual of Mental Disorders*	
EPAs	Economic Partnership Agreements	
EU	European Union	http://europa.eu/index_en.htm
FAO	Food and Agricultural Organization	www.fao.org
FAST	Families and Survivors of Tsunami	
GDP	gross domestic product	
Global North	This is a term used to describe developed or industrialized countries	
Global South	This is a term used to describe developing countries	

GNP	gross national product	
G7	Composed of finance ministers from the following countries Canada, France, Germany, Italy, Japan, United Kingdom & United States	
G8	Composed of heads of governments of the following countries: Canada, France, Germany, Italy, Japan, United Kingdom & United States, Russia	
G20	Membership consists of finance ministers and central bank governors of 19 world largest economies and the EU	
GRAMEEN BANK	Bank offering credit to poor people residing in rural Bangladesh – these micro credit schemes have spread around the world	www.grameen-info.org
HDI	Human Development Index	
HREOC	Human Rights and Equal Opportunity Commission	
HPI	Human Poverty Index	
HRC	Human Rights Council – part of the UN system to monitor human rights	www2.ohchr.org/english/bodies/hrcouncil
HRW	Human Rights Watch – an independent NGO that monitors human rights around the world	www.hrw.org
IASSW	International Association of Schools of Social Work	www.apss.polyu.edu.hk/iassw
ICCPR	International Covenant on Civil and Political Rights	
ICD	International Classification of Diseases	
ICESCR	International Covenant on Economic, Social and Cultural Rights	

ICSW	International Council on Social Welfare	www.icsw.org
ICT	Information and Communication Technology	
IDS	Institute of Development Studies	www.ids.ac.uk/ids/
IFSW	International Federation of Social Workers	www.ifsw.org
ILO	International Labour Organization	www.ilo.org
IMF	International Monetary Fund	www.imf.org
IPCC	Intergovernmental Panel on Climate Change	www.ipcc.ch
MDGs	Millennium Development Goals	
NATSIEC	National Aboriginal and Torres Strait Islander Ecumenical Commission	www.ncca.org.au/natsiec
NGOs	Non-government organizations	
NSPCC	National Society for the Prevention of Cruelty to Children	
OECD	Organization for Economic Cooperation and Development	www.oecd.org
OXFAM	A non-government relief and development organization	www.oxfam.org.uk
PCI	Per capita income	
PPP	Purchasing power parity	
PRGF	Poverty Reduction and Growth Facility	
PTSD	Post-traumatic stress disorder	
SST	Social shaping of technology	
Structural adjustment	A range of economic strategies imposed on countries by the World Bank and IMF as conditions of loans	
TNCs	Transnational Corporations	
TRAIDCRAFT	Fair trade development charity	www.traidcraft.co.uk
TRIPS	Trade-Related Aspects of Intellectual Property Rights	

UDHR	Universal Declaration of Human Rights	www.un.org/en/documents/udhr
UN	United Nations	www.un.org
UNDP	United Nations Development Programme	www.undp.org
UNFCC	UN Framework Convention on Climate Change	
UNFPA	United Nations Population Fund	
UN-Habitat	The United Nations Human Settlements Programme	www.unhabitat.org
UNHCHR	United Nations Office of the High Commissioner for Human Rights	www.ohchr.org
UNHCR	United Nations High Commissioner for Refugees	www.unhcr.org
UNIFEM	United Nations Development Fund for Women	www.unifem.org
WCC	World Council of Churches –international organization of churches from over 110 countries	www.oikoumene.org
WDM	World Development Movement	www.wdm.org
WFP	World Food Program	www.wfp.org
WHO	World Health Organization	www.who.org
WSF	World Social Forum is a large alliance of non-government organizations and social movements	www.wsf.org
WTO	World Trade Organization	www.wto.org

Chapter 1

Introduction

Over the past two decades we have witnessed what could be termed a 'global' turn in social work. This trend is evidenced by a growing number of published texts and edited collections on how global processes interact with social work practice (e.g. Cox and Pawar, 2006; Dominelli, 2007a; Healy, 2001; Hokenstad and Midgley, 1997; Ife, 2001; Lyons, Manion and Carlsen, 2006). In some ways, this trend is not surprising. Globalization is an influential discourse in a variety of associated disciplines, including sociology, political science, economics and cultural studies and social work has lent heavily on these disciplines in constructing its own knowledge base. Global frames of reference have similarly infiltrated social policy and promoted new understandings of governance, citizenship and the role of the state, which are also key concerns in social work. However, the question remains as to why, at this particular point in history, the 'global' resonates with a growing number of writers in social work. In particular, discourses on globalization have struck a chord with many of these writers, although they have not always been endorsed in an uncritical manner.

Perhaps one reason why the global has emerged as a prominent theme in social work is because via a number of influential institutions such as the media, government and financial markets, we are continually reminded of our interconnectedness with the rest of the world. As we are writing, news of a 'credit crunch' in the United States that is fuelling a deepening global financial crisis has saturated both the local and international media. Reports suggest that its effects will reverberate around the world, in turn having a negative impact on many local economies and causing financial market turmoil. At the same time, the International Monetary Fund (IMF) has issued a press release claiming that China is now the biggest contributor to global growth and that the world is becoming increasingly dependent on the continued robust performance of the leading developing countries: China, India and Russia (Elliott, 2007). The dominant discourse that pervades both these reports is that happenings on one side of the world can have significant implications for locations on the other side of the world. Moreover, they both foreground the issue of interdependency, or, put more simply and crudely, the idea that what happens to 'them' has implications for 'us'.

Climate change and environmental degradation are issues that have similarly featured significantly in both the local and international media. In

1

fact, it seems that rarely a day goes by where the environment and related concerns do not feature in media reports. More recently, we have witnessed an acute interest in how factors such as soil damage, pollution, depleted water supplies, rising temperatures linked to increased green house emissions and contaminated waterways have compromised the livelihoods of people who are dependent on the physical environment for their economic survival. Because the bulk of the world's poor people – including many indigenous groups – live off the land, this has serious implications for their welfare. At the same time, global warming and urbanization are reducing the amount of land available for agriculture. All these factors combined have further threatened the food supplies of those already at risk of malnutrition and starvation. These developments have in turn fuelled concerns that millions of 'climate refugees' will attempt to enter the European Union over the course of the next ten years (Traynor, 2008).

This theme of global interdependence similarly resonates with media reports of a global food crisis. In 2008, the United Nations (UN) warned that a dramatic increase in the price of basic foodstuffs such as wheat and rice had severely compromised the ability of the World Food Programme (WFP) to feed the world's poor, putting millions of people at risk of malnutrition (Borger, 2008a). Environmental factors associated with climate change, such as flooding, drought and severe winters, coupled with higher fuel and transport costs are, in the main, responsible for depleted global food reserves and higher prices. The quest to produce alternative forms of energy has further compounded this problem as more and more land is given over to the production of grain and sugar for biofuels. The fact that food prices are soaring around the world reflects the global dimensions of the problem and will arguably have implications for the practice of many social workers. At the same time, the effects of this food crisis will be variable depending on one's geopolitical location and socio-economic status.

Clearly, such issues need to be placed in a global context in order to, first, understand the extent and interlinked nature of the problem and, second, to come up with viable strategies to address such food shortages. Such developments pose considerable challenges for meeting the millennium development goal on hunger – halving the number of people in the world who go hungry every day – and require a coordinated approach that goes beyond the local level (UN, 2008). For some readers, the millennium development goals may appear to be lofty ideals far removed from the realities of day-to-day practice in social work. On that level, we are prepared to concede the possibility that meeting these goals have questionable practical relevance for clients' immediate needs, while acknowledging the limits of what is realistically achievable in social work!

However, on another level, it is not unusual for social workers to come across increasing numbers of people who are struggling to make ends meet and who find that a significantly large proportion of their disposable income must now be set aside for the purchase of food. Unprecedented protests about the rise in costs for basic food items have been witnessed in countries as diverse as Italy, France, Mexico, Indonesia, Morocco, Uzbekistan, Yemen, the Philippines, Guinea, Mauritania and Senegal (Lemaître, 2008). This issue has not only garnered attention in poorer countries in the global South but has also been identified as a concern for the rural and urban poor in the global North. Australia, for example, has experienced prolonged drought, which has drastically reduced grain production and depleted reserves. Farming communities suffering from drought-related poverty and associated social problems have come to the attention of many Australian social workers, and mental health workers have noted a rising number of suicides in rural areas (Hall and Scheltens, 2005).

For some social workers then, perhaps one reason why they have identified with the global turn is because they are seeking a new analytical lens (or lenses) to understand the social problems they encounter, particularly when they are constantly reminded of their interconnectedness with the rest of the world. Moreover, seeing social problems in this light invites us to reframe our understanding of social justice in terms of global justice.

According to the International Federation of Social Workers (IFSW), 'social workers, by the nature of their work, tend to meet those who are more likely to have suffered the damaging consequences of some aspects of globalization' (IFSW, 2005a). This statement would suggest that the IFSW, a key institution in social work, subscribes to the idea that not only is there a phenomenon called globalization but that it also influences the work of practitioners. The IFSW go on to suggest that globalization affects everyone in the world and that while some people have benefited from a more pronounced sense of interconnectedness that manifests on an economic, technological, cultural, social and political level, for other people this has exacerbated or even created new social problems. Accordingly, globalization is seen to be experienced locally and variably, and it is these aspects of globalization that are one of the key concerns of this book.

One of our main aims in writing this book is to explicate the relationship between the global and the local in relation to a range of social issues and populations and to explore how such an analysis may assist us to 'rethink' social work. By electing to use the term 'global' in our book title, we are aware that we run the risk of creating expectations that this book will provide global coverage of social work! Clearly, such an endeavour would be highly ambitious. It would also run the risk of providing a very superficial account of social work in all its various guises around the world. However, providing a global overview of social work is not our intention. This is not a book about comparative social work and how social work is practised in different countries. Equally, it is not a book about international social work, although in Chapter 2 we do briefly explore this coupling of 'international' with 'social work' as an evolving and contested domain of practice. By locating social work in a global context, our purpose is to promote the idea that local concerns need to put in a global, spatial and historical context, and, in doing so, we draw on a range of local examples. In particular, we are interested in exploring how adopting such a lens to look at social work and social problems can provide new insights into practice that go beyond while also incorporating a local frame. Further, we wish to foreground the issues and challenges utilizing such a lens may pose for social work.

Despite the IFSW's endorsement of globalization, we acknowledge that 'globalization' is a controversial term in that it has been the topic of considerable debate and contestation. As an analytic construct, it is somewhat ambiguous in that it has been defined and employed in a multitude of ways in the literature, and this is a topic we return to in Chapter 2, where we examine some different theoretical approaches to globalization. The 'unsatisfactory' nature of the term is aptly summarized by Tomlinson (2007, p. 148), who suggests that as a predominantly Western discourse, it 'invites overstatement and smacks of an overweening tendency to universalize', while most of the phenomena associated with globalization are rarely ever '*literally* global in their reach'. Yet Tomlinson (2007) also goes on to defend globalization as an analytical construct by asserting that despite its shortcomings, it still has significant explanatory potential while also disrupting many of our conventional ideas about how we contextualize the social, economic, political and cultural domains in which we operate.

Writers who endorse the idea of globalization have been subjected to further criticism on the basis of confusing causation with association. In other words, there is some confusion around whether particular factors such as the rapid diffusion of Information and Communication Technologies (ICT), the development of globalized production chains where the production process is dispersed across a number of different countries and the liberalization of trade and investment have 'caused' globalization or are just associated features of globalization. Similarly, there is substantial slippage between description and prescription in the literature, whereby writers move seamlessly from describing processes and events purported to be associated with globalization to then prescribing a particular ideological response to the issues or problems raised (Yeates, 2007). Alternatively, many writers make unsubstantiated claims about globalization and its impact on people's welfare, where globalization is conceptualized in a reductionist manner as 'something that is done by "them" to "us"' (Yeates, 2007, p. 643). Such deterministic accounts are similarly evident in the social work literature, for example:

> Globalization has redefined communities, changed boundaries, fused cultures and altered social relations within and between communities to create

players with access to markets and choices, and non-players who are excluded. (Dominelli, 2007b, p. 7)

Similarly,

Globalization enhances productivity and economic growth and encourages the interflow of money, resources and people. However, it also upsets the existing regional and international equilibrium, causes distress in the underprivileged, activates fierce competition and heightens tensions among different interest groups. (Man Ng and Chan, 2005, p. 79)

Regardless of the truth or otherwise of these accounts, what is clear is that for some writers in social work globalization has come to be associated with reconfigured spaces, cultural shifts, competiveness, social divisiveness and increasing inequality. We return to this idea of globalization as contested terrain in Chapter 2. However, historically, it is important to note that locating social work in a global context is not necessarily a new or radical idea, particularly if we think about how the welfare state has developed in many countries in the context of colonization. For example, Yeates (2007) points out that Britain's former status as a colonial power has long been implicated in the exporting of particular welfare models and ideologies to its former colonies. Moreover, in what follows, she describes the importance of these colonies to the development of the British welfare state itself:

[Britain's] colonies – Ireland, Australia, Canada, India, Hong Kong, and many African countries – sustained Britain's economic foundations, constituted a destination to which criminal classes and other socially deviant groups and individuals could be exported and formed a labour pool from which Britain drew to staff its welfare services. (Yeates, 2007, p. 636)

Notwithstanding this observation, most contemporary accounts of welfare tend to privilege the role of the nation state in shaping welfare systems rather than pointing to the role of colonial expansion and other transnational influences. This in turn brings us to another key contention of this book – processes of colonization and decolonization are still prominent influences in the lives of many people around the world. Many of these people reside in former colonies that have been granted independence and are now engaged in the often fraught process of nation building while attempting to integrate into a globalized economy. Others are residents of countries that constitute former colonial powers such as Britain, France, Spain and Portugal, some of whose governments are still trying to extricate themselves from their responsibilities in their former protectorates, or alternatively, dealing with the legacy of colonialism, such as migration flows from former colonies. In the meantime, it has been suggested that new forms of imperialism have emerged in the global era under the guise of capitalist expansion and political domination, in turn replicating the power relations of colonialism.

Although colonial rule has been commonly portrayed as a one-way relationship of conquest and domination, postcolonial critics have contested this deterministic version of events, suggesting that both the *colonizer* and the *colonized* were transformed by the experience. Moreover, colonization was often actively resisted. In this sense, postcolonial criticism is concerned with unpacking such representational practices, particularly in terms of how they continue to inform contemporary writings on global relations and reproduce the stereotypes and power relations of the colonial era (see Chapter 2). Such colonial constructions are not only evident in the First World–Third World dichotomy but also evident in other spatial references such as 'East' and 'West'. Alternatively, they surface in other dichotomous representations of social relations such as the native/non-native speaker (Harrison, 2006).

Using the lens of colonization to position and locate ourselves, both of us are descendants of European settlers who either freely immigrated or were forcibly transported as convicts to Australia. The arrival of our ancestors effectively displaced the local Indigenous population, and European colonization of Australia was accompanied by much violence and loss of life. Today, Aboriginal Australians continue to live with the legacy of colonization, dispossession and the loss of their land. The relationship between Indigenous Australians and the descendants of European settlers remains an uneasy one – punctuated by themes of loss, exploitation and denial on the part of many white Australians – and these fraught social relations form the backdrop for much social work practice with the Indigenous Australian population. By way of example, Indigenous children are significantly over-represented in the Australian child protection system and are six times more likely to be placed in care than other Australian children (Stanley, Tomison and Pocock, 2003). In comparison with the non-Indigenous population, Aboriginal Australians also experience poorer levels of health, higher rates of incarceration and significantly lower life expectancies (Australian Human Rights Commission, 2006).

Such trends are evident in many countries around the world where Indigenous populations or First Nations peoples are contending with the legacy of colonization and dispossession, including Canada, East Timor, Kenya, New Zealand, Northern Ireland, Palestine, South Africa, the United States and Zimbabwe. In order to fully understand the reasons for child abuse, neglect and poor health in many of these communities, practitioners must understand how colonization continues to impact the lives of Indigenous individuals and families. In other words, 'the trauma experienced by

Indigenous people is not only historic, but continues today' and manifests in the form of a range of social problems such as alcohol and drug abuse, poverty and family violence (Stanley et al., 2003, p. 7).

The IFSW (2005b) similarly recognizes that the needs and interests of Indigenous peoples 'have been historically undervalued' and 'at times deliberately marginalized by the State and other interests'. Nevertheless, it would be a mistake to see colonized groups solely in terms of a victim discourse. Indigenous perspectives on social work have contributed significantly to forging innovative forms of practice (e.g. see Gray, Coates and Yellow Bird, 2008; Ling, 2007; Lynn, 2001). We return to these themes in the following chapter, where we explicate our understanding of postcolonialism and how it links to a global perspective in social work.

A word on language

In our research for this book we have come across a complex array of terms on offer for mapping the world. For example, while some writers continue to map the world in terms of 'East–West' or 'North–South' lines, others prefer to divide up the world in terms of perceived level of development, which has manifested in dualisms such as 'developed–developing' world or 'overdeveloped–underdeveloped' countries. Alternatively, some writers in social work have elected to portray global relations in terms of the 'majority–minority' world or the 'two-thirds' world (IFSW, 2003). These writers seek to draw attention to the fact that the vast majority of people in the world are in fact from poorer countries or what has traditionally been called the Third World. The latter term is seen to have negative connotations and reconceptualizing the world in terms of majority–minority relations is seen to serve a political purpose in that it reverses the hierarchal dualism inherent to the 'First World–Third World' construction.

Arguably then, the representational function of language is seen to be of some importance in social work. Indeed, it has become commonplace in many social work texts to set clear parameters around the language to be used and to offer rationales for electing to use certain terms instead of others. However, in this book we have not adopted this practice and instead have opted to use a variety of terms. There are several reasons for doing this. First, we concur with Bakhtin (1981) that meaning is not invested in language itself but, rather, is a product of social interaction. In other words, meaning is negotiated and open to contestation. Moreover, all terms and their definitions have their limitations and will evoke different cultural and social meanings. In this sense, whatever terminology we elect to use will be inadequate in at least some people's eyes! Second, in recognition that meaning is context dependent, we see value in using a variety of terms that can illuminate different dimensions of the subject matter under consideration. For example, while many people see the 'Third World' as an outdated expression that has negative connotations, other writers – particularly those who identify with the postcolonial tradition – have purposively elected to use the term for political, strategic or ironic purposes (Darby, 2006, pp. 4–5).

By virtue of the fact that we have written this book in English – with all its attendant cultural constructs – arguably it is likely to be of most interest to those social work professionals and students who hail from Anglophone countries. Our current location in a Western, Anglophone academy is obviously a key factor here, and, in this sense, we do not claim to be representative of the social work profession across the globe. Indeed, we recognize that *social work* itself is an English term that does not have universal applicability. In recognizing that social work can be called many things, some writers have forged new labels such as 'the social professions' in an attempt to be inclusive of the diversity of titles used across the world (Lyons et al., 2006). Nonetheless, Lorenz (2008, p. 8) points out that, at least in the broader European context, 'English terminology continues to play a significant levelling role' in social work.

However, this observation also raises an interesting point in terms of the key themes covered in this book in that colonization and globalization have both contributed to the situation where English now constitutes a global language. In fact, it has been estimated that nearly one-third of the world's population use English in one form or another and that the vast majority of these speakers are not from the traditional Anglophone countries but from those locations where English has a colonial legacy or where it is learnt for economic, social or educational purposes (Fishman, 2000). There are now four times as many 'non-native' speakers of English as so-called 'native' speakers, which raises interesting questions in terms of whether the traditional Anglophone countries can claim ownership of English anymore (Harrison, 2006). For social workers then, we suggest that one of the challenges of locating the profession in a global, postcolonial context pertains to the politics of language use and whether English can continue to serve as the 'de facto' lingua franca of social work on an international level.

Clearly, our geopolitical location, linguistic affiliations and sociocultural environment will have a bearing on how we understand, experience and write about the global. However, this observation is consistent with our thesis that global processes are experienced locally and will mean different things to different people in different places at different times in history. In this sense, we see this book as just one account of social work in a global, postcolonial world, while acknowledging that there could be many more and varied accounts.

Guarding against making prescriptions and predictions for practice

In the process of engaging with a text such as this one, it is likely that the reader will have an expectation that a book *about* social work *for* social workers will contain some prescriptions for practice. Or if such a book does not contain prescriptions, then at least it should discuss implications for practice. However, in this book we have guarded against making too many concrete prescriptions for practice and similarly have not speculated too much about the future of social work in a global world. There are several reasons for this, which we outline as follows.

The first reason why we are reluctant to make prescriptions or predictions for social work is because of the dynamic and changeable global environment in which social work operates. By way of example, when we first planned this book some years back there were a multitude of references in both the social work and broader literature to US global dominance and its perceived political, cultural and economic authority over many other countries. However, during the process of writing this book we heard many political commentators allude to the end of US power and the need to re-theorize global power relations to take account of the rising power of emerging economies such as China, India and Brazil. At the time of writing, security experts are predicting the end of US global dominance and the stalling of the spread of Western-style democratic capitalism (Borger, 2008b). In this constantly changing environment, we contend that prescriptions and predictions for practice can become quickly outdated.

Some writers seek to align globalization with complexity theory (e.g. see Urry, 2003, 2005) and point to the impossibility of making predictions in a complex, non-linear, open-ended global system – that in fact comprises multiple criss-crossing systems – and is continually evolving and changing. According to this theoretical perspective, we can explain events but not predict them. Given this complexity, it is not possible to observe straightforward cause–effect relationships. The dynamic interaction that occurs between the macro and micro levels means that we cannot categorically state what the outcomes for people will be at the local level. Moreover, the actions of individuals themselves also have transformative effects upon the world (Urry, 2005).

This observation leads us to the second reason why we have guarded against making concrete prescriptions for practice. We argue throughout this book that globalizing forces need to be grounded in local contexts, as global processes are experienced locally and variably. While we refer to local examples of practice in various chapters, we clearly cannot generalize from these examples to other contexts given that social, political, economic and legal realities frame practice at the local level. For example, the situation of indigenous groups in Indonesia who are contending with the effects of both colonization and globalization will be specific to that context, thus different to the issues faced by indigenous groups subjected to the same processes in countries such as Canada. While there may be some commonalities across experiences, social work requires us to make context-specific assessments that take account of people's particular social and economic arrangements along with other local environmental factors that impact their lives. The global context of people's lives is clearly relevant here, but it needs to be factored into the assessment process in terms of how it interacts with local situations. We return to this issue of assessment in Chapter 10.

The third reason why we have guarded against making prescriptions for practice is because there is a vast difference between writing *about* social work and actually *doing* social work. Academics, practitioners and students have all commented on this disjuncture between theory and practice, and while we do not engage with this debate in any detail here, we do acknowledge a perceived practice–theory gap that does not pervade just social work but many other professions. Possibly, this book will raise more questions rather than provide answers about the relationship between the global and the local and the historical context of this relationship. Rather than offering a definitive account of social work, we suggest that the main contribution of this book is to assist social workers contextualize their work with regard for these broader dimensions and how they interact with local elements of practice. To this end, at the end of each chapter we pose questions to assist you to reflect on how the information presented may relate to your particular local context.

Structure of the book

Chapter 2 lays out the conceptual framework for the book with specific reference to the two key topical themes of globalization and postcolonialism. In this chapter we also briefly explore the idea of international social work as a related discourse.

The next six chapters focus on particular issues and populations that we believe have special relevance for social work in a global world. Chapter 3 takes up the issue of globalized economic structures and institutions, patterns of global poverty and the challenges this poses for social work. In Chapter 4, we explore immigration and people movement, with particular regard to contemporary patterns of migration in the world and how this impacts our understanding of practice with immigrant and refugee populations. This chapter further considers how conventional understandings of citizenship in the context of the nation state are being contested in a global, post-colonial era and what the implications of this may be for social work practice.

In Chapter 5, we turn our attention to the impact of globalization on women and examine the significant economic, social and political inequality still experienced by women and girls on a global level. Following on from this discussion, Chapter 6 takes up the issue of health in the global era. Mental health is explored in some depth as an example of a global health issue that has been relatively neglected in both the national and international arenas. Factors such as unemployment, migration, poverty and social change are risk factors for a range of mental health problems, and globalization has been implicated in the exacerbation of these problems. In this chapter, we also track the emergence of a new global mental health movement which has arisen to raise the profile of mental health and challenge major inequities that exist between countries in the provision of services. Chapter 7 then takes up the interconnected themes of the telecommunications revolution, global networking, the electronic context of social work practice, social activism and representational practices that are employed on the Internet. We suggest that these developments not only pose particular challenges for social workers but also offer opportunities to develop innovative forms of practice.

In Chapter 8, we turn to the topic of the environment and sustainable development. Here we make a case for social workers' active involvement in the movement towards sustainable development which, increasingly, is recognized as being consistent with the profession's holistic 'person-in-environment' approach. In Chapter 9 we turn to the issue of human rights and social work and critically analyse the embedded discourses underlying the notion of universal human rights. In this chapter, we also consider the strengths and limitations of using rights-based frameworks for practice in social work. Finally, in Chapter 10 we attempt to pull all of these themes together, revisit our ideas about working locally within a global context and summarize what we see as the major issues and challenges faced by social work in a global, postcolonial world.

Rethinking Social Work in a Global, Postcolonial World

Introduction

In this chapter, we explore two of the prominent themes or reference points in this book – globalization and postcolonialism – and present an argument as to why we believe there is a need to position social work in these particular contexts. Although our principal aim is to locate social work in a global context, we believe that linking globalization with a postcolonial perspective can enhance existing understandings of global processes. Rather than offering solutions or prescriptions for action, we invite readers to consider some of the issues and challenges posed by globalization and postcolonialism for social work. We also foreground how these concepts may assist in not only rethinking the range of social issues and problems that social workers encounter but also the domain of social work itself. In particular, we examine the debate concerning whether social work is a local concern – an activity that is particular to the nation state – or whether it has a rightful place on the global stage in the guise of international social work.

Globalization as a contested and contentious term

Globalization is a somewhat contentious term that provokes considerable debate in terms of, first, whether it actually exists and, second, what it actually is. In general, the literature tends to highlight the compression of time and space as the driving force behind globalization. This in turn is said to engender a sense of greater interconnectedness between people and places, signified by the increased flows of people, money, goods, services and information across the globe. However, often there is a lack of clarity and specificity about just what it is that is globalized and the term globalization has been subjected to critique because it is seen as a vague, ill-defined concept. Indeed, one prominent writer in the field has observed that 'there are few terms that we use so frequently but which are in fact as poorly conceptualized as globalization' (Giddens, 1996, cited in Scholte, 2008, p. 1473).

Some sceptics contest the actual existence of globalization, suggesting that globalization is just a manifestation of contemporary internationalization

(Hirst and Thompson, 1996). For other writers, globalization is in danger of becoming a catch-all – and thus meaningless – term that encompasses a diverse array of processes associated with the idea of global interconnect-edness. Alternatively, critics argue that, as a social theory, globalization has failed to adequately account for contemporary social change (Rosenberg, 2005). For others, globalization is seen to be just a dressed-up term for imperialist-capitalist development (Sparks, 2007). Yet again, some social commentators have observed a 'post-globalist' turn and point to terms and expressions such as 'sinking globalization' or 'the end of globalism' which have started to emerge in the literature (Held and McGrew, 2007).

Regardless of these debates, it cannot be denied that globalization is a prominent discourse that has become associated with a broad range of domains spanning the media, business, economics, politics, welfare, development, education and even sport. Moreover, key global institutions such as the United Nations (UN), the International Monetary Fund (IMF) and the World Bank have all employed globalization as an analytical tool in conducting research and developing policy, with particular regard to the impact of globalization on developing countries. For example, according to the UN Millennium Declaration, globalization has resulted in uneven development and exacerbated poverty in many parts of the world (UN, 2000). Similarly, the interconnectedness of globalization and inequality featured significantly in a recent report produced by the IMF on the world economic outlook (IMF, 2007).

Some critics, however, contest the relevance of this discourse for the 'majority world', claiming that globalization is a preoccupation of those from wealthier countries in the 'global North' who have overgeneralized its significance and reach (Connell, 2007). Nonetheless, since the English term 'globalization' first made an appearance in the middle of the twentieth century, equivalent terms have emerged in a diverse range of languages including Arabic, Chinese, French, Russian, Spanish, Swahili, Finnish, Nepalese and Timorese, suggesting that globalization is not just a discourse unique to the richer Anglophone countries (Scholte, 2008).

Of particular interest in this book is how globalization has come to be linked with a range of social problems. For many people, globalization is associated with inequality, poverty and a host of other social ills. Indeed, this is the position adopted by the UN, who developed the Millennium Development Goals as a strategy to reduce global poverty and improve standards in education, gender equality, health and the environment around the world. A contrasting perspective, however, is that globalization holds the promise of overcoming social and economic disparities via economic growth and the income generated from free trade (Wolf, 2004). Debates also rage about globalization's sphere of influence and impacts, with some critics suggesting that the role of globalization has been radically overstated. For these writers, the nation state still plays a significant role in shaping domestic affairs and regulating its economic, political and social domains. Alternatively, the view is put forward that a small number of dominant nation states, via institutions such as the G8 (Group of Eight) nations or the UN Security Council, exert considerable control over global economic, legal and political arrangements (Hardt and Negri, 2004).

Accordingly, we can see that the dynamics and consequences of globalization are subjected to endless debate and speculation. These debates encapsulate a wide range of concerns, from the power and influence of transnational corporations, to climate change and environmental degradation, to the global spread of AIDS. Alternatively, they cover issues such as the perceived 'Americanization' of the world through media giants such as CNN and fast-food outlets such as McDonalds. The deepening divide between the rich and the poor has also been attributed to a global economy where international bodies such as the World Bank regulate the affairs of financially strapped developing nations. Globalization has been similarly implicated in disputes over the introduction of genetically modified seeds into developing countries by big corporations, despite their questionable benefits for poor farmers. What these examples demonstrate is how as a multifaceted discourse, globalization has come to be associated with a host of disparate social issues.

The position we adopt in this book is that social workers need to have a critical awareness of globalization not only as a prominent discourse that operates both within and beyond the profession but also as a lens that offers new insights into and possibilities for practice. We believe this critical awareness is necessary for two reasons. First, globalization has been linked with a range of social problems that have traditionally garnered the concern of social workers, and as a theoretical perspective it holds the possibility for furthering our understanding of these problems. Viewed in this way, globalization has particular salience for assessment purposes, especially when trying to make sense of global issues such as environmental degradation and climate change and the impact they have on people's lives. Second, like all theoretical perspectives employed in social work, we suggest that globalization needs to be subjected to critical scrutiny in terms of both its explanatory power and its utility for practice. Although we endorse the value of a global perspective in social work, we are acutely aware of its perceived limitations. For this reason, later on in this chapter we suggest that a postcolonial lens is a useful adjunct for viewing globalization, particularly in terms of offering a historical perspective on global processes and broadening our understanding of how colonization has shaped global relations.

In the remainder of this chapter, we examine some key theoretical positions on globalization, before moving on to explore how a postcolonial lens can complement existing understandings of globalization. We then examine our own positioning in a global, postcolonial world. Following this discussion, we turn out attention to how the 'global' connects to social work and also consider some critiques of this relationship. In the final part of the chapter, we explore the idea of international social work as both a contested and an evolving concept.

Some key theoretical perspectives on globalization

In the following discussion, the writings of the sociologist, Roland Robertson (1992); the social theorist, Anthony Giddens (1990, 2002a); and the cultural theorist, Arjun Appadurai (1996) are discussed in terms of how they illuminate different dimensions of globalization. Consideration is also given to how these global dimensions might intersect with social work. There is, of course, a huge array of writings on globalization. However, we have chosen to focus on these particular authors because their work represents seminal writings on globalization, which in turn have informed the later literature – and debates – on globalization.

For Robertson (1992), the most salient feature of globalization is the transformation of time and space leading to 'the compression of the world'. While acknowledging that globalization is often equated with modernity, Robertson argues that globalization is much broader than that. According to his reading of *globalization*, the world is a more accessible place and we are able to more readily interact with other people, cultures and ideas. In such a mobile world, we are able to take things from the global and accommodate them to local conditions, a process he terms glocalization (Robertson, 1992, pp. 173–4). Instead of being a one-way flow that promotes homogeneity, the global is seen to interact with the local to produce hybrid cultural practices and products. Similarly, we can see this process occurring in social work. For example, while American models of practice have been exported to other parts of the globe, they have not been uncritically applied in a 'pure' fashion. Rather, they have been modified and indigenized according to local needs (Nimmagadda and Cowger, 1999). Globalization, therefore, just does not change local cultures but is also acted upon by the local.

Robertson (1992, p. 132) defines 'globality' as an awareness of the world as a 'single space', which refers to one's subjective awareness of being part of a global entity. This involves having a level of consciousness of our collective identity as global citizens, rather than seeing ourselves as solely affiliated with an ethnic group or the nation state. The benefits of having a 'global consciousness' include the potential to act collectively to address social injustices such as violations of human rights. For example, global social movements such as the anti-globalization lobby have heightened awareness of the cross-border nature of many social problems. Arguably, such a 'global awareness' of social problems is equally important for social workers.

Similar to Robertson, Giddens (1990) sees the compression of time and space as being central to globalization. At the same time, he argues that globalization is not a unitary process, but a 'complex set of processes' (Giddens, 2002a, p. 12). While recognizing the importance of economic globalization – a topic we return to in Chapter 3 – Giddens sees global-ization as not solely driven by the integration of the world market but, to a large degree, as brought about by advances in communications. For Giddens, the new global order is signified by the spread of institutions asso-ciated with modernity, including capitalism, industrialism, administrative/ surveillance powers and militarization. He argues that the collapsing of time and space in the contemporary era has pre-empted a rethinking and restructuring of many of our basic social institutions, such as the econ-omy, government, family, gender and sexuality. For example, advances in communication systems have seen the proliferation of international social movements as well as less desirable outcomes such as the global network-ing of terrorist cells. In some contexts, family caregiving practices have similarly been transformed. Aided by new communication technologies, more people who relocate to another country are caring for older family members or children 'across borders', and we return to this issue of trans-national care in Chapters 4 and 5.

Giddens (1990, p. 64) sees globalization as being underpinned by the theme of the 'intensification of worldwide social relations'. In part, the freeing-up of trade and capital has fuelled this interdependence. Globalization, therefore, calls into question the continued relevance of the nation state. Proponents of Gidden's thesis point to the role of powerful regulatory institutions such as the World Bank, the World Trade Organization (WTO) and the IMF. At the same time, the role of long-standing international bodies such as the UN have been called into question in a climate of rapid global change and instability. For example, critics of the UN argue that given the cur-rent political and economic uncertainty accompanying globalization and escalated levels of conflict around the world, this institution is well overdue for a fundamental overhaul of its charter, role and policies (Hagen, 2003). Arguably, these debates surrounding the roles and practices of these supra-national bodies are of relevance to social workers concerned with issues of poverty, the environment, social development and human rights.

Another key writer on globalization, Appadurai (1996), puts forward the view that the most salient feature of globalization is increased diversity. Appadurai (1996) describes five dimensions of globalization, which he calls ethnoscapes, technoscapes, financescapes, mediascapes and ideoscapes.

Respectively, these 'scapes' refer to the movements of people, technology, money, information and ideologies that go beyond territorial, linguistic or cultural borders. Cultures are interacting in new and varied ways, and in a 'deterritorialized' world, Appadurai (1996, p. 158) argues, that it is necessary to think 'beyond the nation'. This increased global mobility has in turn accentuated the issues of difference and diversity, which have traditionally constituted key concerns in social work, especially in terms of how difference may be ascribed to certain groups or individuals to signify their inferior status or exclude them.

It is claimed that, to some degree, all countries are affected by cross-border flows of capital, labour, information, power, values and imagery, particularly via influential institutions such as Hollywood, CNN, Starbucks and McDonalds. In this New World Order, debates rage about the perceived influence of the United States and European cultures on developing countries. However, these institutions not only transform local practices but they themselves are also transformed by indigenous cultures (Appadurai, 1996). For example, Bollywood, while often portrayed as India's version of Hollywood, is now a global cinema that has evolved in its own right to merge 'tradition with modernity' and attracts a wide audience that goes well beyond the Indian diaspora (Punathambekar, 2005).

Moreover, Appadurai (1996) contests cultural imperialism theory, which envisages Western values and ideas being transferred via a one-way process to poorer countries on the periphery and instead highlights how cultural influences flow in multiple direction. The notion of cross-border movement, epitomized by flows, networks and reconfigured social relations is, therefore, key to Appadurai's understanding of globalization. He further points to its indeterminate and irregular nature by arguing that depending on one's history, language and place in the world, globalization will be experienced differently. Such subjective experiences of globalization will be further mediated by one's affiliations, whether that be with 'nation-states, multinationals, diasporic communities, as well as subnational groupings and movements...and even intimate face-to-face groups, such as villages, neighbourhoods and families' (Appadurai, 1996, p. 33). This situated understanding of the world resonates with Robinson's delineation of globality or what is sometimes referred to as globalism. For social workers then, Appadurai's work offers a new lens for understanding people's processes of identification, their complex social relations and their subjective experiences, which are all key areas of concern for practice.

Clearly, all of the foregoing perspectives on globalization offer useful insights into global processes and their impact on local institutions as well as how they have reconfigured social relations. Nonetheless, contemporary understandings of globalization have been subjected to critique on the basis of assuming the 'newness' of globalization while also failing to adequately consider the role of colonization in creating global relations of power. In the following section, we consider how theoretical insights from postcolonial studies can complement existing understandings of globalization.

Linking globalization with a postcolonial perspective

The term 'postcolonial' – and its derivatives – is somewhat confusing in that it tends to be used in a variety of ways in the literature. Postcolonial theory has been employed in a diverse range of disciplines, including literary studies, international studies, history, anthropology and geography. For the purposes of this book, we have deployed some of the terms associated with postcolonial studies in the following way. The hyphenated term 'post-colonial' is used to refer to countries that have formerly been under colonial rule or have experienced the effects of imperial expansion. In contrast, postcolonialism refers to a broad range of critical scholarship that seeks to rewrite colonial relations in order to offer alternative insights into the complexity of these relationships in both their historical and continuing forms. Like globalization, postcolonialism constitutes a broad, contested and diverse scholarship, and the discussion that follows is of necessity focused on a selective reading of the literature. However, we have again chosen to focus on some seminal works in the area (Ashcroft, Griffiths and Tiffin, 1989; Bhabha, 1994; Loomba, 1998; Moore, 2001; Narayan, 1997; Ngugi wa Thiong'O, 1981; Pratt, 1992; Said, 1978, 1981, 1993; Spivak, 1988, 1990; Young, 2001) as well as writers who have written specifically on the links between globalization and postcolonialism (Behdad, 2005; Darwin, 2007; Robertson, 2003, 2004).

While some writers use the terms colonization and imperialism interchangeably, Young (2001) makes a conceptual distinction between these terms. Imperialism implies government control from the metropolitan centre and the expansion of state power, where empire serves ideological as well as financial purposes. Colonization, on the other hand, involves the establishment of colonies for settlement or commercial purposes and historically has manifested in a diverse range of forms and practices in different countries. The key difference here is that colonization is usually associated with the invasion and physical occupation of a country, while imperial power may be exercised by one country over another without direct occupation.

Postcolonial critics argue that, in the main, accounts of colonization have been constructed from the perspective of the colonizers and often fail to recognize the multiple forms of resistance employed by indigenous populations (Ashcroft et al., 1989; Bhabha, 1994; Ngugi wa Thiong'O, 1981; Said, 1993). Rather than putting colonized peoples and countries yet again under the 'colonial gaze', postcolonialism is more concerned with critically examining existing accounts of colonization and posing new questions. By doing so, postcolonial critics seek to decentre or contest colonial accounts that define their subjects in simplistic cultural terms and have provided justification for past and ongoing colonization practices (Said, 1978, 1993).

Postcolonial critics are similarly sceptical of accounts of globalization that minimize the role of colonization in creating the contemporary global order. Writers who are affiliated with the postcolonial tradition argue that it is important to understand the continuities and links between older forms of colonialism and neocolonial manifestations of global inequalities and hierarchies. In other words, postcolonialism assists us to site the historical links between colonialism and globalization and the parallels between former periods of colonization and the contemporary era of expansionist imperialism (Behdad, 2005). Accordingly, postcolonialism can be conceptualized as a way of understanding or thinking about the present that is informed by the past. At the same time, this knowledge is not fixed as our ideas about the present evolve in accordance with the passage of history and unfolding events. These new understandings of the present may in turn lead us to ask new questions about the past (Darwin, 2007).

In this sense, many postcolonial writers are concerned with the historical dimensions of globalization and how they have shaped contemporary geopolitical conditions and global social relations. Rather than being a recent phenomenon, globalization can be seen as a long-term historical trend dating back over at least five centuries. For some writers, globalization has been a dominant force in the world since the era of sixteenth-century colonial expansionism, which saw the opening up of regional trade (Robertson, 2003). Loomba (1998, p. xiii) notes that by the early part of the twentieth century, European colonialism had left its mark on nearly 85 per cent of the world. Colonization entailed not only economic development and military invasion but also cultural and social reformation, along with population displacement. However, while the origins of globalization are commonly traced back to the era of European expansionism, empire building has not been the sole province of the European states. Middle Eastern, North African and Asian empires have similarly played a part in laying the foundations for contemporary patterns of globalization (Darwin, 2007).

Although the colonial era of European military invasion and expansion has more recently given way to the age of decolonization, postcolonial writers argue that processes of colonization and decolonization continue to impact nearly all countries and populations of the world (Moore, 2001). For many countries that have gained independence in the post-colonial era, the legacy of colonization continues to hinder their development and destabilize their communities while creating new social divisions and forms of inequality. Robertson (2004, p. 562) claims that colonialism not only compromised the ability of newly independent countries to survive in a globalized world but that a residual colonialism is evident in the modernization programmes imposed on poorer countries by the richer industrial nations as a precondition for aid or debt relief. Such modernization programmes commonly include deregulating and opening up markets, privatizing public utilities and reorienting local economies traditionally reliant on subsistence farming to export production – a subject we return to in Chapter 3, where we examine global poverty and economics.

As noted in Chapter 1, colonization continues to impact the lives of many indigenous groups around the world. Johnson (2000, p. 153) describes as follows some of the effects of different patterns of colonization on indigenous populations:

> ...in the 'settler societies' of Canada, Australia, New Zealand and South Africa, European populations came, saw, conquered and stayed on to dominate and enrich themselves but not the indigenous populations. In contrast, for example, in India and Africa, colonisation involved the calculated incorporation of the two societies, and a withdrawal by the colonial powers which often resulted in political and economic chaos.

Many of these indigenous groups continue to live with the legacy of colonization and are engaged in ongoing struggles for recognition, self-determination, reparation and land rights. Paradoxically, this quest for independence has at times reinscribed the influential position held by the ex-colonial powers. For example, in Australia, a significant number of Aboriginal and Torres Strait Islander people are still grappling with the effects of being part of the 'stolen generation', when children were removed – often forcibly – from their families and placed in institutional care or with white families. Such paternalistic welfare policies remained in place right up until the 1970s, and despite an official inquiry into these practices, repeated calls for the Australian government to apologize were initially met with considerable resistance.

Social workers were similarly implicated in some of these practices or at least bore witness to them (Gilbert, 2005). At the same time, ongoing colonization and dispossession have seriously compromised the health and welfare of the Indigenous population. Life expectancy for Indigenous Australians is on average 17 years less than that for non-Indigenous Australians, while in some areas infant mortality rates are three times the national rate (Thomson et al., 2007). Accordingly, an understanding of Indigenous history and colonization is critical to meaningful social work practice with Aboriginal and Torres Strait Island people (Gilbert, 2005).

Postcolonialism disrupts the perception of the West as being the primary reference point for globalization. Some postcolonial writers contest the framing of global social relations in terms of colonialism's legacy of core-periphery binarisms or the hegemonic 'global North' and the dominated 'global South' (Behdad, 2005). According to this standard reading of colonization, which is similarly evident in much of the early social work literature, 'the all-but-irresistible force of Western colonialism radiated outwards from a European or American metropolis, moulding and shaping a passive Third World 'other' in its own image, and to its own ends' (Sweeting and Vickers, 2005, p. 114). For example, Midgley (1981, 1990) has long argued that academic imperialism continues to infiltrate social work through the exporting of knowledge to Third World countries that is often inappropriate for their needs and stage of development. Similarly, we have seen the emergence of discourses on neo-imperialism and debates about whether social work itself is a part of this project (Cox and Pawar, 2006; Gray, 2008; Haug, 2005). Such debates tend to pit 'Western' styles of social work against Indigenous forms of knowledge, claiming that the imposition of the former style of social work on developing countries represents a new form of imperialism. However, this assumes that there is a monolithic body of Western social work knowledge, which is highly debatable (Yan and Tsui, 2007).

In contrast to this deterministic version of events, postcolonial writers seek to demonstrate not only how the subjectivity of Indigenous inhabitants was constructed through processes of colonization and othering but also how the colonizer was similarly constituted under the 'native gaze' and shaped by these same practices. In other words, colonizers were equally transformed by their experiences, especially in the face of challenge or resistance (Johnson, 2000, p. 154). Postcolonial writers describe how colonization was in fact resisted on many levels, such as the refusal to speak the imposed language or the appropriation of the colonizer's language for subversive purposes (Memmi, 1967; Ngugi wa Thiong'O, 1981). Alternatively, resistance took the form of irony, mimicry or parody of the stereotypical behaviours expected of colonized subjects (Bhabha, 1994).

Pratt (1992) defines 'transculturation' as a process of cross-fertilization of cultural and representative practices that occurs when the colonizer and colonized come into contact with each other. This contrasts with conventional ideas about the colonizer–colonized relationship, where it is assumed that periphery cultures undergo a one-way process of acculturation by dominant cultures (Pratt, 1992, p. 6). Applying this perspective to social work, postcolonial theorists would recognize the possibilities for social work to be a productive site of intercultural exchange, borrowing and mixing of ideas. For example, in a study that examined the experiences of overseas-born social workers working in Australia, one participant from India, Tejal, described how social workers from developed countries have appropriated forms of practice commonly used in community development projects in India and modified them for their own purposes (Harrison, 2007, p. 81). Below, Tejal elaborates on this process:

> Like now, social enterprise is a big thing...working with small groups, micro finance and all that. I mean I was working in India six or seven years back with all those sort of things.

On one level then, postcolonialism encompasses a range of critiques of the processes surrounding the production of knowledge pertaining to 'the other'. Holliday (1999, p. 245) defines 'othering' as 'the process whereby the "foreign" is reduced to a simplistic, easily digestible, exotic or degrading stereotype'. The foreign is then translated into 'them' or 'other', inadvertently furthering the process of cultural imperialism. For example, Said (1978, 1981, 1993) has written extensively on how Western media, governments and academia sustain a negative portrayal of the Orient, Islam and Arab people via a process of othering. Such a portrayal serves the purpose of either exoticizing or demonizing certain countries and their religious beliefs, such as the case where Muslims who carry out acts of violence are primarily identified by their religion and cast as Islamic fundamentalists. Said (1978) demonstrates how this 'othering process' sustains a negative portrayal of Islam and Arab people through a discourse of orientalism that in turn rationalizes Western intervention.

This pervasive tendency to construct subordinated populations within the confines of colonial discourses in turn negates people's agency. For example, in what follows, Narayan (1997, p. 185) talks about how such representations of 'otherness' may promote a view of the passive victim that further reifies a one-dimensional view of identity:

> Part of what worries me about these representations is their overly uniform representations of 'Other cultures' as the 'victims of Western culture' – victims either of 'Western consumerism' or of other rapacious and corruptive inroads by 'Western culture'. The agency of 'Others' often gets completely effaced in these representations. ... Part of what worries me too is an underlying tendency to see both 'Western culture' and a great many 'Other cultures' as simpler and less hybrid than they already are.

Accordingly, postcolonial theorists have sought to destabilize the hierarchical structure inherent in the self–other distinction and expose the power differential inherent to this relationship while drawing attention to the complex nature of identity. Critics such as Said (1978), Spivak (1988) and Bhabha (1994) contend that the inclination of Western writers to represent colonized populations as the 'other', the non-Western binary opposite of themselves, has distorted and oversimplified intercultural relations. Similar to post-structural accounts of subjectivity which have more recently been employed in social work (see Fook, 2001), postcolonial writers recognize the existence of multiple, contradictory and shifting identities. In contrast to viewing culture as a unifying and homogenizing force, the relationship between an individual and his or her culture is envisaged as dynamic and ambivalent rather than stable and certain (Bhabha, 1995, p. 208). This dynamism is particularly evident when individuals traverse two or more different cultural and linguistic spaces (Williams, 2007).

A postcolonial perspective highlights not only the significance of the 'social' but also the spatial and historical dimensions of people's lives. We contend that reconceptualizing identity in this way is particularly important not only for social workers working with international populations but also for those working with displaced indigenous populations who are dealing with the legacy of colonization. It also allows us to better understand the diasporic experience of the migrant who negotiates a new linguistic and cultural identity. Below, Young (2001, p. 317) uses the biography of Mahatma Gandhi to illustrate this perspective on identity:

> Gandhi was a diasporic product: he left India when he was eighteen and did not return to settle there until he was forty-six. Completing his legal education in Britain, and spending twenty-one years of his life in South Africa, he, like many diasporic individuals, came to his understanding of his own culture, and developed the basis of his politics, abroad.

Postcolonial writers argue that we need to recognize the limitations associated with thinking in simplistic dichotomies such as First World–Third World peoples and to engage in a process of reflexivity about our constantly changing subjectivities and positions. Moreover, on a global level, the growing strength of some Asian economies and the existence of 'Third World' conditions in some developed countries have forced us to rethink traditional ideas about these classificatory schemes. For example, more recently we have seen China emerge as a strong economic contender on the world stage, replacing the United States as the biggest contributor to global growth in 2007. Indeed, China, India and Russia were responsible for half of global growth in 2007 (IMF, 2007).

In other words, there is a need to move beyond the binary of the West and 'the rest' (Loomba et al., 2005). Similarly in social work, Martinez-Brawley and Brawley (1999, p. 33) argue that identity is complex and that neither the majority nor the minority can define the 'other as they did in the past'. Sewpaul (2007) further contends that we need to challenge essentialized thinking that produces dichotomies such as the 'North and the South' or the 'East and the West'. As she points out, 'With the diversities and inequalities of capital accumulation and consumption, much of the North exists in the South, and vice versa' (Sewpaul, 2007, p. 399). Accordingly, it is important to remember that there are both commonalities *between* East and West and differences *within* East and West (Doel and Penn, 2007).

In summary then, difference – and how it is conceptualized – is a key concern of postcolonial writers, who have attempted to challenge traditional understandings of identity and social relations based on the outdated binary opposition of the colonizer and the colonized. These theoretical developments have in turn invoked a politics of representation in terms of who is allowed to speak about difference. For example, is it the case that Anglophone social workers from working-class backgrounds in the global North should only speak on behalf of their own reference group? Similarly, should Francophone social workers from middle-class backgrounds in the global South limit their representational practices to French-speaking middle-class people from this location? There are, of course, clear problems with such representational practices in that they privilege certain aspects of identity such as language, class and geographical location while failing to recognize that people have multiple affiliations.

The intent of postcolonial critics, however, is not to proscribe speaking practices but rather to direct our attention to a critical examination of how the 'other' is constructed and represented in terms of one's own reference group (Johnson, 2000, p. 168). This is important for two reasons. First, it requires us to consider the ways in which subjugated groups have often been represented in a negative light, or alternatively, as powerless victims. Second, reflecting on our own representational practices reveals as much about us as it does about others. Clearly, some form of essentialism is unavoidable when representing the subject; according to Spivak (1990, p. 109), 'it is not possible to be non-essentialist.' It is, however, possible to reflect on our own part in these representational practices and to consider their effect on social relations. For example, sometimes it serves a strategic or political interest to use terms such as 'East' and 'West', especially when trying to draw attention to social problems such as poverty or the inequitable distribution of wealth. On other occasions, however, the use of such terms may serve to reify existing power relations.

In this way, postcolonial critics not only interrogate colonial discourses but also turn an 'autocritical' gaze on discourses that have emanated from postcolonialism itself, debating and reappraising the utility of key ideas and frames of reference for a constantly changing world (Moore, 2001). This is perhaps not unlike the critical reflective tradition employed in social work, where practitioners are encouraged to identify and question assumptions and discourses that underpin their work, which in turn may illuminate new ways of thinking about practice. In this sense, we suggest that social workers also need to critically reflect on the utility of postcolonial accounts for practice.

Our own positioning in a global, postcolonial world – thinking beyond the nation state

Adopting a global, postcolonial perspective requires us to rethink traditional links between physical location and social space, which in turn has implications for our identification processes. While many of use may assume a national identity, it is important to remember that the nation state is in fact a relatively new phenomenon. In the past, rulers tended to exert control over people rather than clearly delineated territories. For many countries granted independence in the post-colonial era, attempts at 'nation building' are still 'in process' or have floundered as they have also sought to contend with globalization and integrate into a highly competitive global economic market (Robertson, 2004). On one level then, the nation state is a rather nebulous concept.

While it has been suggested that globalization will make the nation state less relevant, paradoxically, in some quarters of the world, the nation state has assumed even more importance, and this has coincided with the rise of nationalism and a renewed preoccupation with maintaining local traditions and culture. However, regardless of these debates about the continued relevance of the nation state, what is clear is that it is now possible to participate in multiple communities, some of which transcend the nation state. For example, one of the authors – Gai – has resided in Australia, Japan and the United Kingdom, and at the same time, maintains a strong connection with India because her partner is from Punjab. This situation is even more complex when we take into consideration the Indian diaspora that indirectly forms part of her social space. In other words, because of residing in both England and Australia – two countries which host sizable Indian communities – her networks have expanded to include members of Indian communities in these countries along with India itself. These links are not only of a social nature but also of a financial nature, where money is regularly sent to family members residing in India. Such practices are no longer unusual in a globalized world. Indeed, remittances are now a more important source of income than overseas aid in some countries, and in 2006 India received more remittances from migrant workers than any other country in the world (Migration News, 2007).

Rose, the other author, spent five of her formative years growing up in a remote village in the Highlands of Papua New Guinea, where she lived in a timber frame house with a thatched roof with a dirt floor covered with sawdust. Rose's family survived on the local diet of sweet potatoes, vegetables and home-baked bread, supplemented by meat from a small herd of goats and chickens. Rose became proficient in Tok Pisin – a pidgin English which serves as a lingua franca in Papua New Guinea – and Enga, the local dialect. Later, she attended a local boarding school, where she studied an American-based curriculum and every morning swore allegiance to the flag of the United States of America. She recalls being totally confused about her own citizenship and, rather than identifying with Australia – the country of her birth – saw herself as Papua New Guinean and American. These identities in turn were acted out differently according to the social space she occupied. When Rose did eventually return to Australia to live, she had a difficult time adjusting to Australian life and school; was teased for having a 'strange' accent; and felt like a migrant in her own country.

These sorts of identification processes force us to rethink the notion of identity as relational rather than fixed. In an age of increased global mobility, where there is not only unidirectional but also multidirectional movement of people, identification processes become more fluid and people may have multiple affiliations that go beyond traditional ideas about national identity. Indeed, Roudometof (2005) contends that 'glocalization' or the reconfiguration of local conditions via globalization has produced 'transnational social spaces'. Similarly in social work, Poole and Negi (2007) argue that this intensification of global links has challenged traditional ideas about national territorial boundaries as more and more individuals, communities and organizations interact across borders. Accordingly, greater global interconnectedness has transformed our spatial notions of communities and groups.

The perceived impact of globalization on social work

Social work is always subjected to the influence of the broader social and politico-economic context in which it operates. Yet it has been claimed that 'social welfare is the least studied dimension of globalisation' (Poole and Negi, 2007, p. 1). The previous discussion on globalization highlighted a contemporary global context marked by increased flows of money, people and ideas around the world due to factors such as trade liberalization, the internationalization of economic exchange and the growth of global communication systems and media. Accordingly, some see globalization as a significant factor in shaping contemporary social work systems and practices in that the increased rate of cultural, social and economic exchange has the potential to transform social work at the local level.

George and Wilding (2002) argue that the workings of the welfare state have been profoundly influenced by neoliberalism, the dominant, although not the only, ideology accompanying globalization. While there is no direct causal relationship, they argue that 'globalization expresses, promotes and legitimates' neoliberal policies (George and Wilding, 2002, p. 56). Neoliberalism emphasizes individual autonomy, self-reliance at the expense of state-sponsored welfare, minimal regulation of markets and the value of competition. Proponents of neoliberalism favour decreased public expenditure and borrowing, lowering taxes, paring down public services and privatizing social services and public utilities. This translates into practices such as the rationalization of state-provided social security, the establishment of mutual obligation welfare arrangements, the deregulation of the workforce, the weakening of unions and the casualization of labour (Reiger, 2002). Neoliberalism is also consistent with the mindset of powerful global institutions such as the World Bank, the IMF and the WTO, which, to varying degrees, mediate the affairs of nation states.

Transnational neoliberalism has seen a 'decentring' of the nation state, where national governments no longer have as much control over economic growth, social expenditure and employment, and global competition dictates greater job market flexibility (Mishra, 1999). In particular, the global migration of skilled labour – particularly from developed to developing countries – has been a significant trend that is similarly reflected in social work (Welbourne, Harrison and Ford, 2007). This in turn has fuelled concerns that richer nations are responsible for a 'brain drain' in poorer countries that can ill-afford the loss of their trained personnel.

A further factor influencing employment practices is the internationalization of labour, whereby the production process is broken up and dispersed across several locations to save costs and to bolster efficiency (Cohen and Kennedy, 2000, pp. 136–7). For example, by utilizing cheap labour in developing countries, transnational corporations can make huge savings on production costs. Alternatively, technological advances in global communication systems have enabled some companies to make substantial savings by outsourcing services such as call centres to lower-wage countries such as India (Ritzer and Lair, 2007). This in turn has resulted in job losses and promoted job insecurity in developed world economies.

In this 'New World Order', the power of unregulated capital rivals that of the state. However, the effects of globalization are uneven, and rather than just bearing the brunt of its impact, the nation state also shapes globalization via its actions. Some nation states are clearly more powerful than others. Midgley (2007a), therefore, argues that social workers need to appreciate the nature of global power relations in order to fully understand economic inequalities and the issues faced by groups marginalized by their ethnic, gender, religious or cultural affiliations. In particular, he is critical of the part successive American governments have played in promoting the values of neoliberal free market capitalism throughout the world.

Lyons, Manion and Carlsen (2006) claim that regardless of the organizational context that social workers practise in, it is highly likely that on some level globalization will impact their work. In particular, the deregulation and liberalization of markets along with the new global division of labour driven by multinational corporations has concrete implications for people's socio-economic welfare in terms of employment opportunities and access to affordable goods and services. Moreover, one of the key impacts of globalization on social work service delivery and welfare provision has been the penetration of market forces and global competition into the welfare state. In particular, it has paved the way for the privatization of welfare services, which in turn has favoured the development of a managerialist and technocratic culture in many social work agencies (Carey, 2008; Dominelli, 1997).

These developments have also had exclusionary effects on recipients of state welfare, and globalization has brought about a fundamental change in thinking about people's right to access publicly funded welfare provision (Dominelli, 1997). George and Wilding (2002, p. 57) claim that neo-liberalism now constitutes 'the dominant international belief system within which debates about the provision of public services take place'. Advocates of this welfare regime see the market as the best and most efficient means to redistribute resources, ultimately providing for everyone's needs. In reality, however, what has happened is that inequalities have widened; more people are experiencing poverty; and pockets of extreme poverty have evolved in certain sectors of the world. For writers such as Ife (2001), global processes are significant because of their potential for perpetuating inequitable social relations. Globalization is implicated in the increased social divisiveness between the so-called haves and the have-nots, which is marked by unequal access to power and material resources, and this is a topic we return to in Chapter 3.

Writers from a range of countries around the world have foreground the importance of a global perspective in social work. In the United States, Finn and Jacobson (2003) claim that issues of social justice – a core value in social work – can now only be comprehensively understood from a global perspective. Likewise, Hokenstad and Midgley (1997) emphasize the theme of 'global interdependence', arguing that social workers need to have some understanding of the global picture in order to practise effectively at the local level. In the United Kingdom as well, Lyons (1999) contends that social issues such as poverty, migration and the environment must be conceptualized in terms of their global connections rather than just viewed within the confines of the nation state. Similarly, in Australia, Ife (2001) underscores the importance of seeing social work within a context of global relations, particularly in relation to human rights and social justice. Writing from South Africa, Sewpaul (2007) argues that redistributive justice must be re-envisaged in terms of the global-local dialectic, especially when global structural factors are responsible for poverty and exclusion at the local level. What is common to all the views of social work described previously is the theme of global interconnectedness. A second common theme is increasing global inequalities and what we, as social workers, should be doing about it.

Many writers who employ globalization as an analytical lens to examine social problems urge social workers to become more politically active rather than just being service oriented in their quest to address uneven development and global poverty (Dominelli, 1997, 2007b; Healy, 2007a; Midgley, 2007a; Sewpaul, 2007; Wagner, 1997). These writers claim that globalization is a significant factor in shaping contemporary practice and that, at the very least, social workers need to have a critical awareness of global processes. For example, Dominelli (1997; 2007b) argues that it is at the community level that local manifestations of global processes are clearly evident in the everyday lives of the people who are denied the economic resources necessary for a decent standard of living. In a similar vein, Midgley (2007a) proposes that social workers must contribute to debates that examine the role of international relations in promoting social welfare (or 'social ilfare') while also forming coalitions with international agencies that promote social justice and human rights.

Nonetheless, globalization and the role of social work globally are contested issues in the social work literature. For example, Pugh and Gould (2000) critique the social work literature on globalization on the basis of being overdeterministic. They also point to the vagueness of the definitions used, the presumption that transnational activity is something 'new' and how some authors make unsupported claims about the 'fragmentation' of social work. Other writers argue that a preoccupation with the 'global' denies the still active role of the nation state in mediating local welfare regimes that shape social work practices (McDonald, Harris and Wintersteen, 2003).

On another level, Webb (2003a) argues that social workers do not have a legitimate mandate to intervene at the global level and that writers who embrace global discourses are trying to reinvent social work for their own purposes. He further argues that such an imagined global project reeks of imperialist intent, particularly when social workers act on their own ideas about who are the 'socially excluded' and construct their perceived plight in terms of their own spatial understandings. Webb (2003a) claims that for most front-line practitioners, the global context of social issues will not be a relevant concern in their day-to-day work. He concludes his critique by arguing that rather than talking about global social work in the singular, realistically we can only refer to social work in a plural sense in that it encompasses multiple practices. Accordingly, social work cannot be imagined in terms of a core set of values that are transferable across the globe. Local social work practices evolve in line with particular historical, social and cultural conditions, which in turn produce 'situated' clients.

International social work as a contested and evolving concept

The idea of 'international social work' is somewhat controversial in that some writers either refute the existence of such a practice or delimit it to a literal translation of the term to mean social work that occurs 'between nations' (Healy, 2001, p. 5). Historically, the term has been loosely used to denote a variety of practices and discourses that transcend the national level, including information exchange, education, community development, human rights-based practice and work with diverse populations (e.g. see Cox and Pawar, 2006; Healy, 2001; Ife, 2001; Lyons, 1999; Lyons et al., 2006; Midgley, 1990). Given the multiple definitions accorded to international social work, it can be seen as a contested, evolving and indeterminate project. Nonetheless, as evidenced by the birth of a variety of international professional forums such as the International Federation of Social Workers (IFSW), and the introduction of a set of international standards for social work education, the prefacing of social work with the term 'international' constitutes a prominent discourse in the contemporary era.

In this book, internationalization is used to refer more to a *context* for and *way of seeing* social work where global processes are implicated rather than the delineation of clearly discernable cross-national activities. It is used to signify the idea that social work is located in a context of progressive globalization of social, political and economic affairs, whereby broader sociocultural, political and economic conditions interact on a dynamic level with local contexts. Ife (2001, p. 74) maintains that 'all social work must be concerned with the global, and all social work in this sense is international social work.' Rather than seeing this domain of social work in the traditional sense of being a specialized field of work outside the realm of mainstream practice, he contends that in a context of globalization an international perspective permeates all social work practice. He argues that globalization affects all social workers and the populations whom they work with. Moreover, in order to 'make sense' of the issues faced by the people they seek to assist, social workers need to think about the broader international perspective.

Healy (2001) puts forward a similar argument for a global focus in social work and delineates four dimensions of international social work: domestic practice in a global context, professional exchange of ideas, international development work and international policy formation. In this book, we are particularly concerned with the first dimension of international social work as delineated by Healy (2001) – domestic practice in a global context. In other words, we believe that it is important to view social work *contextually*, where global factors are implicated in local manifestations of social conditions, which in turn shape domestic social work practices. This idea is consistent with Healy's (2001, p. 7) delineation of 'internationally related domestic practice and advocacy'. For example, it signifies a context where social workers are working with increasingly diverse populations through multifaceted patterns of global mobility where a range of diasporic relationships extend beyond national boundaries.

The understandings of international social work offered by both Healy (2001) and Ife (2001) presume an interrelationship between the domestic and global that permeates all social work to varying degrees. Their ideas resonate with the 'dual configuration' model of international social work proposed by Penna, Paylor and Washington (2000, p. 109), which is both 'idiosyncratic to the culture of the nation states' and 'has a dynamic which incorporates an impulse to include broader supranational concerns'. Accordingly, the local cultural context is also a significant factor in this view of social work, as it has a bearing on how international social work is experienced at the local level.

Midgley (1994, p. 178) refers to the idea of promoting an international perspective in social work as 'an ideological approach', which requires thinking and acting beyond locally endorsed values and practices and recognizing the reality of global interdependence. Yet he adopts an air of pessimism by suggesting that few social workers move beyond seeking to enhance their understanding of an international perspective in social work. Arguably, the need to understand the international dimensions of social work is particularly important in a context where the profession is no longer strictly confined by boundaries of nation, geography or culture. However, at the same time, this broader understanding of social work needs to be translated into practice, and this is the challenge that practitioners currently face.

In summary then, we suggest that while the global context is an important consideration in social work, the influence of the nation state and the importance of understanding local conditions must not be subordinated to broader, all-encompassing global discourses on social work. Moreover, social workers must guard against dressing up imperial practices in new clothes by uncritically electing to intervene at the global level. Perhaps at this stage the first step in coming to grips with the global-local nexus is to broaden our understanding of the perceived impact of globalization on social problems and how this translates to the local level, along with the potential of globalization for both producing and ameliorating uneven development. In the following chapters, attention will be turned to a number of key social issues that are seen as being intricately bound up with global process.

Summary

This chapter has highlighted some significant points of intersection between globalization and social work. In addition, it has drawn attention to the ways in which a postcolonial lens may complement existing understandings of global processes and the implications of this for social work. It has further considered the idea of international social work as a contested and evolving project. In the following chapters, we consider a range of social issues and populations that we consider have particular salience for social workers in a global, postcolonial world.

Discussion points

1. In what ways do you think your own location, the language(s) you speak and your sociocultural environment influence the way you understand and experience globalization?
2. Can you identify any transnational influences on the contemporary welfare arrangements in your own state or country that shape social work practice at the local level?
3. What is meant by the idea that identity is 'relational'? Think about the communities that you currently participate in. Do any of them transcend the nation state?
4. What do you see as the benefits of having a global consciousness in social work practice?
5. Given that there are multiple understandings of international social work, how do you understand this concept? What are some examples of this form of practice?

Chapter 3

The Global Economy, Poverty and Social Work

Introduction

Ameliorating the impact of poverty has long been the focus of day-to-day social work intervention with people at the local level. In recent years, poverty has received increasing attention at the global level. Global inequality and poverty are increasing more than at any other time in our history. Given continual environmental degradation and its links to health and education inequalities, we suggest that global poverty is likely to become a more pressing issue. The United Nations Development Programme (UNDP, 2007, p. 25) estimates that over 1 billion people live 'at the margins of survival'. The global food crisis referred to earlier in Chapter 1 threatens to push millions more people back into extreme poverty as the cost of food staples such as rice and wheat rise. Ironically, while global poverty is on the rise, global wealth is also increasing. However, this wealth is held by a small number of elites and not benefiting those most in need.

In this chapter we first explore different understandings of poverty before briefly examining the extent of global poverty. We then examine the perceived role of economic globalization in exacerbating poverty. Given the persistence of high levels of poverty in developing countries, we also consider how global capitalism and neoliberal market-driven policies have transformed power relations between the global South and North. Next, we consider the relationship between nation states, transnational corporations and international institutions such as the World Bank before turning to examine the role of trade in perpetuating global inequality. In the final section, we provide an overview of the role of social work in addressing poverty to create a more inclusive and equitable world, with particular reference to the ideas of global redistributive justice and global citizenship.

What is poverty?

Poverty is a very complex phenomenon as well as being a socially, politically and culturally contested notion. In an attempt to differentiate extreme poverty and material deprivation at a global level, the World Bank adopted the international benchmark known as purchasing power parity (PPP). For the purposes of measuring global poverty, this gives us an indication of differences in people's purchasing power across income groups and locations using a common currency. In 1990, the level set for 'extreme' poverty was US$1.00 a day, while for middle-income developing countries the poverty line was fixed at US$2.00 (Chen and Ravallion, 2007). The significance of these measures is that they are used to quantify how many people are living in poverty by calculating how many people fall below these thresholds. However, these benchmarks were initially set very low and did not necessarily reflect the consumption patterns and spending priorities of poor people. The international poverty line has only recently been adjusted to US$1.25 to reflect standards of living in 2005 (World Bank, 2008a). Even so, these measurements grossly underestimate the number of people living in poverty around the world (Pogge, 2004).

In Western nations, poverty has been defined in various ways. The most common approach has been to use an arbitrary statistical figure – or poverty line – as a set minimum amount of income/expenditure. Poverty has also been conceptualized in absolute and relative terms. *Absolute poverty* describes the situation of people who are deemed to lack the basic resources needed to maintain health and subsistence living. By contrast, *relative poverty* compares how different groups are faring in the same population. It is seen as less extreme deprivation and is based on normative beliefs about disparities in income distribution. Other measures of poverty used include the gross domestic product (GDP) of countries and per capita income (PCI). However, there are many criticisms of the adequacy of using income measurements to estimate poverty levels. They tell us very little about how poverty impacts personal aspirations, the quality of people's social relationships, their degree of political participation and their access to education (Shaffer, 2008). In other words, they tell us very little about the non-material dimensions of people's lives. All of these are important regardless of where we live in the world.

The notion of social exclusion and the capability approach developed by Sen (2000) provide a more comprehensive understanding of the spatial, participatory and relational experiences of poverty. Rather than just viewing poverty in terms of income deprivation, the capability approach recognizes that poverty is also a form of capability deprivation, whereby people may be prevented from being able to take part in their community, receive an education, work and share the same opportunities enjoyed by others. Accordingly, there have been attempts to broaden the view of poverty from one that focuses solely on monetary measures to one that recognizes 'the disadvantages that arise from being excluded from shared opportunities enjoyed by others' (Sen, 2000, p. 44).

In an attempt to provide a more holistic understanding of poverty, the UNDP developed the human poverty index (HPI) – one for industrialized countries and one for developing countries – which uses statistical measures such as life expectancy, literacy rates, economic provisions and social exclusion based on measures of long-term employment (UNDP, 1997). Beitz (2008, pp. 114–16), however, suggests that in order to fully understand poverty we must factor in not only income inequality and different forms of social inequality but also the subjective experience of being relegated to a lower social ranking and status. In contrast to traditional psycho-individualistic perspectives on poverty, social workers have similarly been urged to adopt structural analyses of poverty (Mubangizi, 2008). These expanded definitions of poverty have moved the focus to the social justice and human rights dimensions of poverty as well as highlighting its structural causes, all of which are key concerns in social work.

In 2000, the United Nations (UN) established the Millennium Development Goals project outlining eight key objectives with projected targets aimed at reducing the worst excesses of poverty and inequality within a 15-year time frame. The focus of the first Millennium Development Goal is to halve the proportion of people living on less than $1 a day by 2015. However, of some concern is the observation that at the midway point the world community is still a long way from achieving many of the targets in this time frame, with some countries actually experiencing a drop in their standard of living and on the key human development indexes – HDI (UNDP, 2007, pp. 225–6; UN, 2008). In the following section, we examine the extent of global poverty in more detail with reference to groups who are at particular risk of poverty.

The extent of global poverty

There is a highly skewed distribution of wealth and inequality between regions and countries. South Asia and sub-Saharan Africa have the highest rates of poverty, whereas in China, India and Latin America the number of poor people has been decreasing (World Bank, 2007). Another group of countries that are affected by high levels of poverty include newly independent nations such as East Timor, which have previously experienced a long history of external domination and exploitation. Similarly in South America, several countries with a prior history of colonization have large sections of their populations entrapped in poverty (Gilbert, 1997).

It is important to remember that significant economic inequalities are evident not only between countries but also *within* countries. Despite an increase in wealth in OECD (Organization for Economic Cooperation and Development) countries, poverty and inequality is becoming more deeply entrenched. Ironically, one of the world's richest nations, the United States, has higher levels of inequality than any other industrialized nation. Similarly Australia, which has a HDI ranking of 3, has a poverty rate of 14 per cent (Saunders, 2005, pp. 2–3). Despite its rapid move up the global economic ladder, India too is becoming more unequal as the gulf between the rich and poor expands (UN-Habitat, 2008).

The extent of global poverty is quite alarming. As mentioned earlier, over 1 billion people are living at survival poverty rates on less than US$1 per day. However, another 2.6 billion people live on less than US$2 a day, which constitutes 40 per cent of the world's population (UNDP, 2007, p. 25). Other important indicators of well-being include access to education, housing, sanitation and food, and the following statistics reveal some of the more salient aspects of human deprivation and poverty:

- Estimates suggest that 28 per cent of children residing in developing countries are malnourished and are either underweight or stunted, while another 10 million children under the age of five die each year from poverty and malnutrition (UNDP, 2007, p. 25).
- Nearly 1 billion people do not have access to secure sources of clean water, while 2.5 billion people live without adequate sanitation (UN, 2008, p. 4).
- More than one-third of the urban population in developing countries lack durable housing and live in slum-like conditions (UN, 2008, p. 5).
- There are still around 75 million children who do not go to primary school, and over half of them are girls (UN, 2008, p. 5).

The population groups most impacted by global poverty include women, older people, child-headed households and orphans, the unemployed, young people with limited or no education and people with disabilities (Cox and Pawar, 2006; Filmer, 2008; Lyons, 1999; see also UN, 2008). Women are disproportionally impacted by poverty, and we return to this theme in Chapter 5 where we look more specifically at the 'feminization of poverty'. A comparative study of the relationship between poverty, disability and schooling across 13 developing countries revealed that children with disabilities were less likely than their peers to start school or complete the whole cycle of primary school. Disability, as a barrier to school attendance, was found to be more important than geographic location, gender or economic status (Filmer, 2008, p. 19). These findings are particularly disturbing in the context of developing countries, as they suggest that disability is associated with chronic poverty in adulthood.

Indigenous peoples are among the poorest people in the world. In Mexico, for example, those states populated predominantly by indigenous people experience much higher levels of poverty than those with few indigenous people (Gilbert, 1997, p. 324). Similarly in Myanmar (Burma), indigenous groups are among the poorest in South Asia. Although the poverty rates have improved since the 1970s, Indigenous Australians have an income poverty rate twice as high as non-Indigenous Australians (Hunter, 2001). Poverty has implications for indigenous health and is linked to high mortality and morbidity rates and missed educational opportunities (Morrissey, 2003). Nonetheless, the Millennium Development Goals make no specific mention of indigenous populations, despite the fact that it is these groups who are often ranked at the bottom of many social and economic indicators of poverty. Moreover, indigenous groups have not been consulted about their particular experiences and understandings of poverty (National Aboriginal and Torres Strait Islander Ecumenical Commission [NATSIEC], 2007).

The previous discussion has highlighted both the extent and entrenched nature of global poverty and how certain groups and regions of the world are disproportionately affected by poverty and growing inequality. Both globalization and colonization have been implicated in the uneven social and economic development that has occurred around the world, and in the following section we examine how these factors have changed the face of global poverty.

Economic globalization and poverty

We are now said to live in a globalized economy characterized by greater economic interdependence between nations. Mishra (1999), however, suggests that it is more realistic to talk about international influences impacting domestic economies rather than a globalized economy per se, pointing out that the national economy still constitutes a distinct unit of analysis. Perhaps what we can say is that a distinguishing feature of many (but not all) domestic economies today is a greater degree of openness, particularly in relation to trade and investment.

George and Wilding (2002, p. 23) identify four factors that have contributed to this situation: (1) the heightened mobility of capital, goods and services across borders; (2) a greater degree of foreign investment; (3) a significant increase in the number of transnational corporations; and (4) the consolidation of a global trading market. As noted in Chapter 2, economic globalization has intensified over the past few decades. Advances in technology coupled with 'borderless capitalism' have allowed money to circulate more readily and speedily around the world (Giddens, 1999). This has facilitated the emergence of a new form of 'global capitalism', much less encumbered by national laws and regulations.

Sklair (2004) asserts that global capital has in fact replaced older forms of imperialism. Postcolonial writers suggest that this new form of global capitalism has changed the dynamics and power relations between the North and South. It is claimed that for the first time global capitalism has become unhinged from its European origins and no longer has a specific centre. Instead, it is much more fragmented and driven by transnational capital (Dirlik, 2005).

There are several important implications of this change. First, it foregrounds the role of the transnational corporation as one of the main drivers of economic activity in the global economy. Second, narratives about the history of global capitalism must now include non-European nations actively engaged in making their own histories and not simply being absorbed as the 'other' into one single European form of capitalism. Third, the new fragmentation of capitalism has been accompanied by the collapse of the three worlds into the global North and South (Dirlik, 2005). These terms are not strictly geographical referents. On a symbolic level, the global North refers to those locations where networks of global capitalism are largely concentrated, while the global South refers to populations marginalized by these developments. In what follows, Dirlik (2005, p. 579) describes this new configuration of global capitalism and its differential impacts:

> Parts of the earlier Third World are today on the pathways of transnational capital and belong in the 'developed' sector of the world economy. Likewise, parts of the First World marginalized in the new global economy are hardly distinguishable in way of life from that used to be viewed as the Third World.

As mentioned in Chapter 2, increasing integration of the global economy coupled with technological innovation has led to the internationalization of production and labour, characterized by dispersed production, flexible labour and new work routines. Effectively, this means the production process is now broken up and dispersed across several locations to save costs and to bolster efficiency. What is particularly noteworthy is the shift in manufacturing jobs from the global North to the global South which has been taking place for some time. By the end of the twentieth century, half of all manufacturing jobs were located in developing countries and manufactured goods constituted 60 per cent of these countries' exports to richer nations (UNDP, 1998, cited in Held and McGrew, 2000, p. 24).

What we are seeing is a major shift in employment patterns across countries and regions. In industrialized nations, low-skilled and unskilled workers are losing jobs and employment opportunities as transnational corporations move to find cheap and expendable labour in developing countries. However, it is not just blue-collar manufacturing jobs that are being relocated offshore. Service work such as telemarketing, software development and debt collection, along with legal work, health care and military aid are also being outsourced (Ritzer and Lair, 2007). Accordingly, it is clear that supranational economic practices are currently influencing local employment in ways we have not seen previously.

For some, this change in global labour and production signals a new form of 'imperialism', one in which the developing world is further marginalized. In the following quote, Sivanandan (1999, p. 8) describes how the site of domination between labour and capital has now moved to the developing nations:

> Its assembly lines are global, its plant is movable, its workforce is flexible. ...And, instead of importing cheap labour, it can move to the labour pools of the Third World, where labour is captive and plentiful – and move from one labour pool to another, extracting maximum surplus value from each, abandoning each when done.

In contrast, those who champion neoliberal globalization believe that the expansion of the economy with the accompanying growth in financial investment and trade will promote wealth, create employment and reduce poverty. However, while wealth has grown, the evidence so far would suggest that the expected outcome of poverty reduction has not materialized. Instead, we have seen uneven development with those from developing nations paying the highest price in the new global economy. It is estimated that 50 per cent of the world's population are excluded because they are not seen as useful either as producers or consumers in the global market place (Hoogvelt, 2007, p. 26). Furthermore, it is no longer necessary for global capital to 'colonize' this group, since they are peripheral to the global economy (Dirlik, 2005).

Global capital has been concentrated in high-income countries such as the United States, the United Kingdom and other OECD countries. The exception to this trend occurred during the expansionist period of colonization when up to a third of capital investment was spent in Third World countries (Hoogvelt, 2007, p. 21). The majority of capital investment is concentrated in three global regions: North America, Europe and East Asia. This centralizing trend is starting to reverse, albeit slowly with more capital flowing into developing countries. However, this investment is unevenly spread across developing countries with investors favouring high-technology industries rather than natural resources (World Bank, 2007, p. 35). Accordingly, emerging economies such as China have been able to take advantage of this trend, while many Latin American and African countries lose out on increasing employment and trade opportunities (Hoogvelt, 2007, p. 21). Nonetheless, in 2008 the flow of capital to developing countries 'seized up' in the face of a global financial crisis that sent many countries – both rich and poor – into recession (World Bank, 2009, p. 15).

Transnational corporations, supranational institutions and the nation state

In a globalized economy, the authority and sovereignty of the nation state has come under closer scrutiny. The nation state is often portrayed as having less control over its economic and social expenditure, while being more subservient to global capital and transnational corporations (Held and McGrew, 2000). This is due to several factors. First, the nation state has to relate to a more complex and interconnected economic system than it has in the past. In particular, governments are now in the position of having to make their policies appealing enough to attract foreign capital and trading partners and ensuring greater job market flexibility in order to retain a competitive edge in the global economy (George and Wilding, 2002). Second, increased competition in the global market place, reinforced by neoliberal and free market ideologies, has led to the rolling back of social, industrial and economic protection measures in Western welfare states. Effectively, this means that many governments have favoured deregulation, reducing the power of labour and unions, lowering taxes and expanding the role of the private sector at the expense of the public sector. These policies are similarly in line with many of the structural adjustment programmes advocated by supranational bodies such as the IMF (International Monetary Fund) and the World Bank.

Earlier in this chapter, reference was made to how transnational corporations are believed to constitute the core of the new capitalist global order. Contemporary estimates suggest that some 61,000 transnational corporations are engaged in production in over 900,000 foreign locations, who in turn are responsible for 10 per cent of global GDP (Dicken, 2007). These corporations are seen as major players in many economies of the world, generating massive wealth and pressuring governments to reshape their public policy for their own corporate ends (Sklair, 2004). In industrialized nations they have been accused of exerting pressure on governments to reduce taxation, create flexible workforces and minimize industrial and social protection measures available to workers. In poorer nations they may exert considerable power due to the fragile governance structures of many of these countries (Christian Aid, 2004). As a consequence, transnational corporations have been accused of taking advantage of lower taxation and financial regulatory environments while extracting concessions from governments that compromise the environment, reduce wages and lower working conditions.

Nonetheless, global capital has not overtaken the authority and autonomy of the nation state and nation states are not passive victims of economic globalization or transnational corporations. Rather they have a complex symbiotic relationship with the world economy, where capital drives globalization but at the same time capital needs the state (George and Wilding, 2002). Moreover, governments may employ the rhetoric of globalization for their own purposes, such as justifying cuts in domestic public funding in health, education and social services on the basis of needing to be a competitive player in the world economy. It is, therefore, important to remember that rather than just bearing the brunt of its impact, the nation state also shapes globalization via its actions (Mishra, 1999, p. 14).

On the other hand, the governments of many developing countries have struggled to assert their sovereignty in the face of structural adjustment programmes imposed by supranational bodies such as the World Bank and the IMF. Many of these programmes advocate the privatization of public utilities, the diversion of overseas aid away from essential social services, such as education and health care, to debt servicing and cuts in government spending. These policies had devastating economic consequences for Southeast Asian, African and Latin American countries during the latter part of the twentieth century (Gilbert, 1997; Jordan, 2008). Many of these countries were plunged further into greater levels of poverty during the financial credit crisis of the late 1990s (Foreign Policy, 2001).

Despite evidence that pro-market neoliberal policies, the basis of many structural adjustment programmes, are not effective anti-poverty measures, they were rigidly adhered to for over two decades. This policy failure did not prevent the World Bank from repackaging structural adjustment programmes under a different pretext known as the Poverty Reduction and Growth Facility – PRGF (Bretton Woods Project Update, 2001). Ironically, the World Bank finally admitted that these policies had negative consequences in some regions following intense criticism from developing nations and anti-poverty campaigners (Hall, 2007). It is primarily the Asian tiger economies, the newly industrializing economies of India and China and some Latin American countries that have made economic progress during the past decade. Despite debt-relief projects, many sub-Saharan countries are still repaying large debts, have less money available for infrastructure projects and social services and are marginalized in the global trading economy (World Bank, 2007).

The belated recognition by the World Bank of the need to balance economic development with social development in order to stem the growing inequalities fuelled by unregulated capitalism has had a devastating impact on many poorer countries. It is these countries whose fate has been pinned to the whims of the global market. Accordingly, those campaigning for socially responsible global policy want to make supranational organizations such as the World Bank more democratically accountable and fair in their global governance. In addition, they seek to highlight the inequitable social and economic arrangements between the richer North and poorer South countries and how current global governance benefits the former group of nations. For example, Elliott (2003, p. 12) poses the question: 'How is it that the G7 [France, Germany, Italy, Japan, the United Kingdom, the United States and Canada] can export neoliberal economic policies to Africa, yet the United States would not dream of accepting "structural adjustment" for its own malfunctioning economy?'

There is still disagreement about whether economic globalization has the potential to play a positive role in the eradication of poverty or whether it actually causes and exacerbates income inequalities and poverty both within and between countries. The UN, however, appears to have come down firmly on the side of globalization. In the UN Millennium Declaration, reference is made to the need 'to ensure that globalization becomes a positive force for all the world's people' (IMF, 2000, p. 351). Those who support this view claim that one way in which poor countries can benefit form globalization and reduce poverty is to play a more prominent part in the global trading system. This purported link between trade and poverty reduction is discussed in the following section, with reference to some of the more prominent critiques of the global trading system.

The link between trade and poverty

Developing nations have been encouraged to enter and compete in the global trading market as a major way to increase economic growth and reduce poverty (World Bank, 2007, p. 29). The rationale offered here is that those countries that are excluded from the world market do not reap the benefits of income generated from trade and cannot attract financial investment. Supranational bodies such as the WTO and the World Bank advocate liberalization of the terms and conditions of trade between nations – usually referred to as 'free trade'. However, while poor countries can potentially benefit from free trade, the global market place does not constitute a level-playing field. Instead, as Kofi Annan pointed out, current trade practices tend to benefit richer countries while seriously undermining the economies of poor countries:

> At present poor countries are under pressure from rich countries to liberalise their markets. Yet they find that many of their products are excluded from rich countries' markets by protective tariffs and quotas. That is not fair. Even less fair is the competition they face from heavily subsidised producers in those same rich countries. These subsidies push prices down, driving the farmers in poor countries out of business. (Annan, 2003, p. 2)

Even though world trade has grown enormously since 1980, the share of trade between countries is extremely uneven. Developed countries still control about 65 per cent of global trade. In recent times this pattern has started to shift. Over the past decade, China has increased its share of global trade and is now second to the United States, with India and Latin America also improving their position (World Bank, 2007). However, African countries have decreased their share of global trade from 5 per cent in the 1970s to

2 per cent in 2000 (World Bank, 2007). Wealthier nations control the larger share of trade as well as valuable commodities and post-production goods. By contrast, most developing countries rely heavily on the export of raw, unprocessed commodities that provide diminishing financial benefits.

Developing nations have traditionally relied on subsistence agrarian economies. For example, in China 50 per cent of the workforce are engaged in agriculture. In India this rises to 60 per cent, whereas a much smaller proportion of workers rely on farm income in rich countries (Polaski, 2005, p. 1). Many poorer countries have not benefited from trade liberalization in agriculture. A wide range of African, Latin American and Caribbean countries have suffered adversely in the pursuit of free trade policies advocated by the World Trade Organization (WTO) and the IMF. During the 1970s and 1980s, poorer countries such as Vietnam, Kenya and Mexico were advised by the IMF to stop growing food for consumption and to grow crops such as cocoa and coffee for export (Traidcraft, 2005). The IMF, through its structural adjustment packages and the urging of the WTO, also insisted that governments in low-income countries such as Malawi cease subsidising fertilizer and seeds for small-scale farmers (Bello, 2008). These policies resulted in food shortages in some African countries as well as the overproduction of certain crops and a dramatic drop in international prices. Overall, the value of agricultural products has dropped by 70 per cent over the past 20 years and the impact on developing countries has been enormous (Traidcraft, 2005). As a result, some poorer countries that were previously self-sufficient food producers become dependent on richer countries for more expensive food imports. Instead of trade providing an avenue out of poverty, such outcomes have plunged many low-income countries back into it.

What is clear from the previous discussion is that there is an asymmetry in trade liberalization, whereby poor countries are often pressured to tear down their protective barriers while many rich nations resist dismantling their own protectionist tariffs and reducing subsidies, particularly in the agricultural sector. Farmers in the West are subsidized to the tune of some $300 billion, which is six times the level of aid provided by rich countries to poor countries. Developing countries, on the other hand, lose around $700 billion in income from trade because of unfair trade rules (*The Guardian Weekly* in association with Traidcraft, 2003).

At the forefront of the trade liberalization push are the WTO and the World Bank. The WTO, established in 1995, is the main body regulating world trade. It is the sole international forum for trade negotiations, and its main roles are to monitor trade practices and mediate trade arrangements and disputes (WTO, 2008). The operations of this institution have attracted considerable attention and scrutiny, especially since many of its policies and practices appear to work in favour of richer nations. Some of these countries have been accused of manipulating trade rules and the arbitration system in their favour by, for example, switching between different regulations on tariffs and subsidies to circumvent WTO rules on reducing agricultural subsidies (Sharma, 2003). Both the European Union (EU) and the United States continue to maintain high subsidies for their agricultural sectors. In 2008, the US Congress passed a Farm Bill which not only increased existing subsidies for farmers but also provided them with new subsidies (*International Herald Tribune*, 2008). By contrast, India, the world's largest producer of milk, cannot export its dairy products because of competition from cheap, subsidized products from Canada and the EU. The WTO, in the meantime, ruled that the Indian government cannot subsidize its own farmers (Sharma, 2003).

More recently, the EU has been pursuing a new deal known as Economic Partnership Agreements (EPAs). Essentially, these are free trade deals that the EU is trying to negotiate with 77 of its former colonies in Africa, the Caribbean and Pacific region. These agreements are aimed at opening up these countries' markets to European goods, and concerns have been expressed that they will further undermine the development of poor countries by forcing them to liberalize their markets too quickly. While these countries previously enjoyed preferential access to European markets for their own goods, the WTO has now ruled that this practice is incompatible with WTO rules. Predictably, these developments will result in massive job losses and reduced government revenue as these countries' less secure industries struggle to compete with well-established European businesses (Traidcraft, 2008).

Some argue that the practices of the WTO perpetuate colonial practices and new forms of 'imperialism'. However, there are alternate discourses of resistance to unfair trade (Gills, 2000). The WTO has become the target of 'fair trade' and anti-globalization protests. A number of regional trading blocs have also been formed, such as the Dominican Republic–Central America–United States Free Trade Agreement (CAFTA-DR) in Latin America to resist the dominance of the US and EU stance in world trade (Abrahamson, 2007). In addition, a growing number of non-government organizations (NGOs) such as Traidcraft and Oxfam have been actively advocating for a more equitable trade system in the international arena. In particular, the idea of replacing free trade with fair trade has become a prominent mantra of these organizations. Essentially, fair trade entails paying poor farmers and other small producers a guaranteed fair price for their produce and eliminating intermediaries and purchasing directly from producers (McMichael, 2007). Although fair trade products still only account for a small proportion of global trade, the fair trade movement has been very successful in promoting the idea of a just trading system, and their products are well known to consumers in a range of countries.

There is an ongoing ideological debate among supporters and detractors of the WTO concerning the value of free trade in alleviating global poverty. Where the 'truth' lies is difficult to tell, as market forces are unpredictable and many economic theories of development have proven to be badly flawed in their implementation. Indeed, in the latter half of 2008 we witnessed this unpredictability, with many high-income OECD countries going into recession, suffering massive job losses and turning to the IMF for financial assistance (World Bank, 2009). During the same year, extreme weather conditions, high oil prices, water scarcity, poor harvests and food shortages compounded existing poverty in many developing countries. None of these outcomes were predicted by global research bodies such as the World Bank.

What is clear, however, is that a one-size-fits-all economic theory such as neoliberalism fails to recognize differences among states and is not going to benefit all countries. While economic liberalization and participation in the global trading market has reduced income inequalities and poverty in some locations, in others it has produced greater disparities of income and wealth. Arguably many poorer nations need both trade and aid (Page, 2007). In particular, those countries with fledgling industries need assistance not only to nurture these industries but to also diversify their economies in order to ensure long-term sustainable development. Moreover, governments cannot effectively buffer local populations from the unpredictable nature of global competition in the market place unless they have well-developed health, welfare and education systems. Many developing countries lack such systems, which places their populations at further risk of poverty.

A number of writers in social work support the view that globalization and its concomitant economic imperatives is contributing to a range of social problems and exacerbating existing inequities in the distribution of wealth (George and Wilding, 2002; Healy, 2001; Midgley, 1997; Seipel, 2003). Indeed, global poverty has been nominated as one of the greatest challenges to international social work and is seen to constitute the root cause of a range of other social problems (Healy, 2001). In the next section, we examine the role social workers play in tackling global poverty.

The role of social work in tackling global poverty

Poverty alleviation has been a front-line issue for social workers since the beginning of the profession. The twenty-first century presents a watershed in attempts to alleviate global poverty. We suggest that there is a greater moral imperative for social workers to address global poverty given the contemporary practice context. The UN (2008) has warned that the global food crisis and continual environmental degradation will result in higher levels of poverty, malnutrition and starvation worldwide. Global economic uncertainty coupled with the largest spike in oil prices since the 1970s has sparked widespread riots and blockades in many countries. The fallout from these macroeconomic concerns is being felt around the world, especially among the absolute poor living on less than US$1.00 per day.

The International Federation of Social Workers (IFSW, 2008a) has publicly stated its support for the Millennium Development Goals, with particular reference to the eradication of poverty. Social work responses to poverty will vary depending on the local context and will be informed by social, economic, demographic and cultural factors relevant to that context. In addition, social work interventions need to be respectful of local voices and practices (Laird, 2008). Nonetheless, given that poverty is a global concern, we suggest that social workers also need to adopt a global justice perspective on poverty and think and act beyond their local context. Globalization has moved social justice concerns of an economic, political and cultural nature beyond the confines of the nation state to a new international order (Fraser, 2007). This creates a space for a new politics of social justice to emerge involving respectful recognition of poor people and economic redistribution. The potential exists for social workers to now take advantage of this shift in focus.

The Western paradigm of social work has been subjected to critique on the basis that it promotes specialized remedial practices such as casework and group work, which Seipel (2003) claims have turned social workers into 'political illiterates'. As a result, social workers have given less emphasis to their central mission of social justice and have reduced their efforts to combat poverty. Sewpaul (2006, p. 431), among others, challenges social workers to embrace 'social activism, lobbying and advocacy', and work towards a world based on *redistributive justice* through building alliances with civil society organizations and various social movements. In order to be effective in this regard, social workers need to actively build coalitions with organizations such as trade unions, media and other institutions that share a mandate to end poverty (Seipel, 2003). In this way, they can be far more influential in their efforts to bring about policy change and the redistribution of wealth and resources necessary to end global poverty.

A global justice perspective necessitates proactive social work responses at the political and institutional level and not just individual and group interventions (Finn and Jacobson, 2003). This may involve, for example, lobbying governments and global institutions for debt relief for poorer countries and ensuring that they fulfil their overseas aid commitments. Alternatively, forming alliances with trade unions or civil society organizations to campaign for labour rights at a global level is another option open to social workers. There are also a number of prominent campaigns aimed at promoting fair trade referred to earlier that social workers can link up with. Given the disastrous outcomes of structural adjustment programmes in many developing countries, some social workers have been highly critical of the motives of supranational institutions such as the World Bank and the IMF and their capacity to reduce poverty (Jordan, 2008; Polack, 2004). However, Hall (2007) suggests that these powerful institutions should not be ignored and that we should continue to press for reforms to their processes and practices.

The history of social work's relationship with transnational institutions such as the UN reveals ambivalence in seizing opportunities in international forums (Healy, 2001). Indeed, some are sceptical of the profession's ability to be effective at the international level because of the particular location of social work within nation states (McDonald, 2006). However, there are increased efforts by social workers to work politically in international forums. The IFSW (2007) in a statement on the International Eradication of Poverty Day in 2007 wrote: 'It is a question of political will to create a world where people are no longer condemned to a life in poverty.' Clearly, this will also depend on the political will of social workers themselves.

For some social work writers, global poverty is a human rights issue. Ife (2008) argues that the discourse of human rights provides a bulwark against economic fundamentalism. In order to promote an alternative version of globalization based on 'human values, some idea of a common shared humanity, and a construction of global citizenship', Ife (2008, p. 24) urges social workers to exploit the potential of new communication technologies. In contrast to 'globalization from above', which in the main benefits wealthy and powerful groups, this involves a globalization accountable to the needs and preferences of ordinary people at the grass-roots level .This is referred to as 'globalization from below' and involves a political project in which democratic institutions are made more effective, and by implication decisions about the distribution of resources and goods within and between nations more equitable (Ife, 2008, p. 25). Sewpaul (2006, p. 429) argues that social workers need to be part of this 'global transformative project', which is just as much 'an ideological and intellectual endeavour as it is a pragmatic one'.

Although social workers practise in a wide range of settings in both the developing and developed world, across the board they work largely with people who are poor. Yet Engelbrecht (2008) argues that many social workers focus predominantly on the social and emotional well-being of poor people rather than their economic welfare. While acknowledging that social workers are unlikely to make an impact at the macroeconomic level, he suggests that social workers need to move beyond practical measures such as teaching clients how to budget more effectively. More specifically, Engelbrecht (2008) suggests that social workers need to employ strategies such as community education to enhance people's 'economic literacy' and link them into social and economic development projects. To be economically literate means having an understanding of the economy, recognizing that people are part of the economy and understanding its impacts on people's day-to-day lives. Thus, social development and education are seen to be pivotal to alleviating poverty.

Midgley (1997) argues that 'distorted development' arises when social development does not occur at a similar pace to economic development. He does not see economic development as a problem per se. Rather, he suggests that a lack of social development means that the fruits of economic progress are not equitably distributed and that this is the core of the massive poverty problem in many developing countries. In these countries, a significant number of people live in substandard housing, lack educational opportunities, face unemployment or underemployment and have access to very few social services. We equally see such poverty-related problems in highly industrialized countries, although they manifest in a different relative form.

In order to combat the problem of distorted development, Midgley (1997, pp. 14–24) outlines a developmental perspective as the key means to redress the imbalance between economic and social progress. A developmental perspective would in turn promote the health and welfare of the general population as a broad means of social protection. In this sense, development must be envisaged within the macro context. For example, some Asian and Latin American governments, acting against the advice of the World Bank and the IMF, have instituted (or re-instituted) a wide variety of social protection measures ranging from subsidies of staple food and fuel to universal primary education and basic health services. As a result, they can better protect their vulnerable and poor populations from the economic uncertainties of entering the global economy (Cook and Kwon, 2007).

In order to be integrated and inclusive, development must be carefully planned, dynamic rather than remedial and focused at the community level. In contrast to the 'top-down' structural adjustment programmes favoured by organizations such as the World Bank, a developmental perspective is 'bottom up'. Midgley (1997, pp. 14–24) outlines three key features of developmental strategy. First, organizational structures need to be established to coordinate and integrate social and economic growth, in line with policy development. Second, priority needs to be given to productive employment and income generation schemes, so that people can actively participate in their local economies and not be excluded from the benefits of economic growth. Third, in contrast to 'consumption-based services', workers need to encourage the development of 'productivist social welfare activities' that promote economic development and reduce dependency. On a more practical level, social development involves activities such as promoting sustainable economic growth, developing vital infrastructure, improving access to basic services such as sanitation and clean water and working towards reducing gender inequalities (Midgley, 2008).

Social workers in developing countries employ a wide range of community development strategies to combat poverty. Microcredit schemes, pioneered by the Grameen Bank, and social enterprise endeavours which aim to make people financially self-sufficient through small-scale employment projects and businesses have been transplanted to many Western countries. There are mixed reviews of the success of these projects (Midgley, 2008). However, we suggest that like any intervention that social workers employ, comprehensive assessment, consultation and a well-developed understanding of the local context are integral to effective outcomes and must precede intervention. Accordingly, the utility of such poverty reduction strategies will depend on the groundwork that is first carried out.

Krumer-Nevo (2008) claims that the middle-class bias of some social workers may lead them to assume that poor people come to accept and normalize their daily struggle with poverty. Yet action research with poor people has illuminated not only their sense of pain and humiliation but also their enormous drive and potential to improve their economic and social status (Krumer-Nevo, 2008). In order to work effectively with poor people, social workers need to recognize and validate their experiences and work in partnership with poor people to harness this potential. While the preceding discussion has highlighted some critiques of traditional social work methods such as case work and group work in the sense that they are ineffective methods for combating poverty, we suggest that these modes of working with people should not be discounted. They provide social workers with an opportunity to hear about people's experiences of poverty directly, to collect data and conduct case studies and to politicize this information. At the same time, the social work profession needs to adopt a holistic understanding of poverty and take an active stance in advocating for the adequate social protection of all people to ensure their well-being. Finally, social workers need to work collectively with other like-minded professional groups and community organizations in their efforts to eradicate poverty.

Summary

In this chapter we have explored definitions of and the extent of global poverty. We have examined the role of economic globalization in exacerbating income inequalities and offered a critical overview of the role of supranational institutions in addressing poverty. The social work profession has long been concerned with the livelihood, security and well-being of poor people, and practitioners have considerable expertise in recognizing the impact of poverty on people's lives. In addition to practical poverty alleviation strategies that practitioners employ on a day-to-day level, we suggest that social workers also have a moral obligation to work collectively with others to alleviate global poverty and advocate for global redistributive justice. In this sense, it is important for social workers to endorse the notion of global citizenship rather than seeing themselves solely affiliated with the nation state.

Discussion points

1. Given the range of meanings attached to poverty, how do you understand this concept? How does poverty translate into the day-to-day realities of people's lives?
2. Do you agree that social workers need to adopt a global lens when thinking about poverty? Why? What implications does this have for the way social workers understand and act on issues to do with redistributive justice?
3. It has been suggested that in order to effectively address poverty, social workers need to build alliances with social movements that have a mandate to end poverty. Can you identify any anti-poverty organizations or groups that social workers could potentially forge alliances with? How might you do this?
4. What opportunities exist locally for promoting fair trade in your area?
5. What methods of practice could you use to enhance people's economic literacy?

Chapter 4

Immigration and People Movement in a Global World

Introduction

In this chapter, we foreground some more recent trends in people movement on a global level and how this impacts our understanding of practice with immigrant and refugee populations. Migration is in fact a centuries-old practice and in that sense does not constitute a new phenomenon. However, what is noteworthy in the current context is the increased numbers of people moving around the world and the complex nature of these patterns of migration. In the first part of this chapter we briefly examine migration and globalization from both a historical and contemporary vantage point. Following on from this discussion we chart some more recent trends in people movement, before moving on to explore the vexed issue of border control. Next, we examine how traditional ideas about the links between citizenship and the nation state are being contested in a global, post-colonial era by those who seek to promote more inclusive forms of global citizenship. In this context, the increased movement of people across borders challenges state-centric notions of citizenship. Finally, we explore the implications of these migratory processes for social work practice, with particular reference to those countries where cross-border movement is strictly regulated. In this section we also consider the role of social work in addressing migration-related concerns.

Immigration in the era of globalization

Globalization has been implicated not only in the increased flows of capital, goods and ideas across borders but also in the increased movement of people across borders. Indeed, it has been suggested that border movements, both in terms of people moving around the globe and people adopting border identities, shape the local demographics of social work practice (Martinez-Brawley and Brawley, 1999). Many people frequently traverse two or more different cultural and linguistic spaces, and this form of mobility is similarly evident among social workers themselves. In this contemporary context, both social workers themselves and the populations they work

51

with constitute diverse groupings that are unstable and cannot be simply identified by cultural, ethnic or national affiliations.

It is difficult to categorically state how many people migrate each year, as there is no uniform method adopted by states for recording migration flows; furthermore, it is only possible to estimate the number of undocumented or 'irregular' migrants who cross borders. In 2005, the United Nations (UN) estimated that there were 191 million international migrants in the world, with women making up nearly half of this population (UN, 2006). Some 60 per cent of migrants currently reside in high-income countries, with the United States being the most popular destination. However, it is also note-worthy that approximately one-third of immigrants have relocated from one developing country to another and that, contrary to popular myth, South-to-South migration is nearly as common as South-to-North migration (UN, 2006).

An international migrant is defined by the UN as a person who resides outside his or her country of origin for a period of at least one year, and this represents approximately 3 per cent of the world's population (Seglow, 2005). However, migration affects nearly all countries and regions of the world either directly or indirectly and is inextricably bound up with issues of employment, poverty, development, security and human rights (Koser, 2007). For these reasons, migration and related concerns often feature cen-tre stage in domestic, regional and international politics. In many countries, issues relating to national identity (or a fear that too many migrants will dilute an imagined national identity) and concerns regarding social inte-gration and the economic impact of migration are preoccupations of both politicians and the public alike. These politics and debates are never far away from the realities of practice, where social workers may come across migrants or refugees who are not only experiencing transitional stress but may also be personally encountering these politics and related hostilities in their day-to-day lives. For these reasons alone, we believe that it is import-ant that social workers have a grasp of the politics of immigration and what potentially fuels anti-immigration sentiment.

It has been claimed that contemporary patterns of migration are sig-nificantly different than those that have occurred in previous eras due to the influence of globalization and decolonization (Appadurai, 1996). The end of the colonial era has seen the emergence of new nation states, many of which are experiencing civil strife and instability, which in turn has led to the internal displacement of its citizens. A growing recognition of 'global' citizenship and international human rights has meant that people whose rights are disregarded in their own countries are increasingly seek-ing asylum in other locations. At the same time, new forms of global media have propagated seductive Hollywood images of an 'ideal' life in the West, encouraging migration flows from developing countries to richer countries in the global North. Border movement has been further enhanced by innovations in technology and the compression of time and space that is said to characterize globalization, and migrants are now able to maintain closer contacts with family and friends in their country of origin (George and Wilding, 2002, pp. 144–9).

However, while the factors discussed previously have been implicated in promoting migration flows in the contemporary global era, it is important to remember that large-scale migration is not necessarily new or unprecedented. A key example here is the Trans-Atlantic slave trade, which coincided with the rise of European empire building and was integral to the maintenance of the British Empire and the economic prosperity of Britain. It has been estimated that in the period from 1500 till 1870, some 19 million Africans were enslaved and transported to the New World (Chandler, 1994 – cited in Ahluwalia, 2006, p. 542). Other forms of slavery that resulted in large-scale migration included the transportation of bonded or indentured labour to the colonies. Indian workers, for example, were imported as indentured labourers to work on white-owned plantations in Sri Lanka and Fiji. The ascendance of 'race thinking' and the construction of racialized identities, whereby 'white' signified superiority and 'black' signified inferiority, were used to justify the enslavement and forced transportation of these groups (Ahluwalia, 2006).

Slavery not only undermined the development of many African and Asian-Pacific countries but also promoted the social exclusion of black and minority ethnic groups in those countries where slaves were both transported and repatriated to in the wake of abolition. Despite the abolition of slavery, the racism that evolved during the colonial era continues to inscribe contemporary social relations in many Western countries. Münkler (2007) further contends that one lasting legacy of the slave trade, and subsequent attempts to end slavery, is the idea that people can be classified as 'illegal commodities'.

Indeed, this discourse on illegality resonates strongly today in contemporary debates on immigration, particularly as it applies to groups such as asylum seekers and refugees. More recently, the issue of asylum has been highlighted as an 'impending crisis' in the industrialized world – particularly across Europe – because of a perceived fear that the numbers of asylum seekers arriving without authorization is spiralling out of control. Many of these countries have subsequently developed policies to deter asylum seekers and have introduced rigorous tests for determining which applicants qualify for refugee status and which ones represent 'bogus' claims (Koser, 2007, pp. 84–7). Clearly, such policies give credence to the idea that hordes of bogus asylum seekers and illegal immigrants from poorer countries are trying to gain entry into the developed world.

The 1951 UN Convention Relating to the Status of Refugees defines a refugee as someone

> who owing to a well-founded fear of being persecuted for reasons of race, religion, nationality, membership of a particular social group, or political opinion, is outside the country of his nationality and is unable to, or owing to such fear, is unwilling to avail himself of the protection of that country. (UN High Commissioner for Refugees [UNHCR], 2007–8, p. 4)

This definition, however, excludes those individuals who are displaced within their own countries through civil wars or other disturbances and who are referred to as internally displaced persons. It also excludes those 'economic migrants' from poorer countries who are seeking a higher standard of living in the industrialized world, as well as 'stateless' persons or those who are not formally recognized as nationals by any state (UNHCR, 2007–8). Environmental refugees are another group who do not fit neatly within this definition. In 2006, along with the 10 million formally recognized refugees in the world, there were some 32.9 million 'persons of concern' identified by the UNHCR. This group included asylum seekers whose applications for asylum or refugee status are pending, environmental refugees who have been forced to leave their homes through environmental disasters and other internally displaced persons not included in official refugee statistics (UNHCR, 2007–8).

Hayes (2005) contends that while the language may change in terms of how we label migrants – asylum seekers, economic migrants and so on – essentially, such terminology reflects a political purpose in that it is deliberately deployed to constrain the movement of certain people and curtail their rights. Social workers themselves have been implicated in such practices. For example, in the United Kingdom some practitioners have found themselves in the position of having to ascertain the immigration status of clients in order to establish eligibility for services. More worryingly, such attempts to control and limit immigration are creating a 'divided globe', whereby there are now very few legal means available to poorer people who wish to immigrate to richer countries (Hayes, 2005, p. 184). In the following section, we examine in more detail how people are actually moving across the globe, with reference to both regular and irregular patterns of migration.

Contemporary patterns of migration

Giddens (2001, p. 259) outlines four models of migration that have influenced our understanding of people movement in the period since the Second World War. The classic model characterizes settler societies such as Australia, Canada and the United States. These countries were built on immigration, and immigration was actively encouraged in the initial stages of nation building. The colonial model of migration is associated with former colonial powers such as France, Holland and Britain, which have traditionally favoured immigration from ex-colonies such as India, Pakistan and some African countries. In contrast to migration for settlement, the guest worker model is characterized by temporary migration and is tied to the demands of the labour market. While initially prominent in countries such as Switzerland and Germany, more recently this model has gained popularity in a range of countries contending with an ageing workforce and labour shortages.

The final model identified by Giddens (2001) is the 'illegal' or irregular model, whereby people enter countries without official documentation or, alternatively, overstay their visas. One of the most prominent images associated with irregular migration that has garnered the attention of the global media is the movement of people across the Mexico–United States border. In the United States, the vast majority of all new arrivals from Mexico are believed to be undocumented; in 2006, it was estimated that some 6.6 million unauthorized Mexican migrants were living in the country (Batalova, 2008). However, there are other notable trends in irregular migration that tend to receive less media attention. For example, a significant proportion of irregular migrants in Australia are UK citizens, many of whom entered the country as students and stayed on after their visas expired (Koser, 2007, p. 57). Irregular immigration is believed to be on the increase, although as stated earlier it is difficult to predict just how many people migrate to other countries in this way. Advances in technology and transport have made it easier for people to cross borders, while making it harder for the state to patrol its borders. Somewhat ironically, irregular migration is further fuelled by many countries' attempts to tighten border security and limit immigration, as many would-be migrants find conventional channels of migration closed to them and, therefore, resort to illegal means.

Along with illegal or irregular migration, another contemporary pattern of people movement is what is known as the *diaspora*, which is where groups who are bonded together by ethnic ties or a shared history are dispersed throughout the globe rather than residing together in one geographical location. Thus, we have seen the birth of the Jewish diaspora, the African diaspora, the Cuban diaspora, the Indian diaspora and the Yugoslavian diaspora. Notably, many of these diasporic communities have evolved involuntarily through experiences of colonization, persecution and displacement (Giddens, 2001, pp. 260–3).

Patterns of migration are changing in that more people are moving to other countries temporarily for work and study purposes and then returning to their country of origin. As noted earlier, demographic decline and labour shortages have prompted a number of high-income countries along with some emerging Asian economies to actively recruit workers – both skilled and unskilled – from abroad. For example, many Thai workers cross the border to work in Malaysia, but with no intention of settling there (Hugo, 2003). Similarly, migration from Mexico to the United States is characterized by its circularity, whereby many workers move back and forth between the two countries. This type of circular migration, often based on existing transnational networks, appears to be a growing trend, along with the emergence of 'a nomadic global elite' (Seglow, 2005, p. 317).

In some parts of the world, the movement of professionals and other skilled labour from low-income to high-income countries has raised concerns about 'brain drain'. This is a particular concern for those poorer countries who can ill-afford the loss of their skilled workers to richer countries (Omaswa, 2008), and social workers themselves have been implicated in such practices. For example, the United Kingdom relies heavily on overseas workers to fill social work labour shortages, with significant numbers of practitioners coming from countries such as South Africa, India and Zimbabwe (Welbourne, Harrison and Ford, 2007). However, while concerns have been expressed that the emigration of skilled labour from developing countries may compromise the economic development of these poorer nations, equally, there are potential benefits to be derived from engaging in the international labour market. In particular, remittances sent home by workers constitute an important source of income for some of these countries, and when workers do eventually return home they often bring back new skills and knowledge (Welbourne et al., 2007).

In addition to the conventional forms of migration described previously, the digital revolution has enabled the development of a 'virtual' labour market, which has allowed people to participate in the global economy via working online while staying at home. In contrast to physical migration, Aneesh (2006) describes this phenomenon as 'virtual migration', which is a growing trend in post-industrial work settings where 'information work' is central to many organizations' operations. Virtual migration also represents a viable alternative for those who wish to move to another country for economic or work purposes, but who find that the country in question is antagonistic towards or not receptive to migrants.

While discussions on migration often tend to focus on movement out of countries, it is noteworthy that in recent decades internal migration has also occurred on a considerable scale. Industrialization, poverty and development-induced displacement have resulted in many people relocating – or sometimes being forcibly moved – from rural areas to cities. The UN predicts that by 2030, some 5 billion people or 60 per cent of the world's population will live in urban areas (UN Population Fund [UNFPA], 2007). This pattern of migration is particularly pronounced in countries such as

China, India, Russia, Brazil and some African countries such as Kenya and Nigeria. Such internal patterns of migration create their own challenges. For example, mass movement from the countryside to cities has contributed to slum growth and strained critical infrastructure, public utilities and social services. Many migrants end up working in the informal sector and are socially isolated from their families and communities of origin (UNFPA, 2007). The expansion of the urban perimeter has further implications for the environment in that it impinges on natural ecosystems and cuts into agricultural land. Poor people make up a significant proportion of this urban spread, and the need to address urban poverty and improve the living standards of slum dwellers has been recognized by the UN in its Millennium Declaration (UNFPA, 2007).

In summary, we can say that current patterns of migration in the world are characterized by both internal and external migration, adversarial relationships between sender and receiver countries, permanent relocation as well as circular movement, dispersed ethnic groups and irregular cross-border movement. In many countries, immigration policies are increasingly labour driven, and governments and transnational businesses alike recognize that in order to retain a competitive edge in the global labour market, they must open up their borders to foreign workers (Jordan, Stråth and Triandafyllidou, 2003). While previous theories of migration often failed to consider a gender analysis of cross-border movement, more recently the 'feminization' of migration has also become a prominent discourse (George and Wilding, 2002). Increasing numbers of women from developing countries are moving to industrialized locations for work, often providing for families left behind, and we return to this topic in Chapter 5, where we explore the impact of globalization on women.

The unprecedented levels of people movement in the world are in turn challenging traditional conceptions of political borders and shaping relations between nation states in new ways. At the same time, many richer countries have witnessed a rise in anti-immigrant sentiment, the manifestation of new forms of racism and a general unease with multicultural policies fuelled by fears that ethnic diversity represents a threat to social cohesion. In response to these social tensions, the governments concerned have, in the main, attempted to regulate and contain immigration while reinforcing their borders (Doty, 2003). These contemporary social trends are relevant to the day-to-day work of social workers, who have traditionally worked at the interface between migration and welfare while also advocating for the rights of those who are at risk of social exclusion on the basis of cultural, racial, ethnic and religious or language factors. In the following section, we examine this issue of border control in more detail with reference to some of the negative images of certain groups of migrants that are circulated in the public domain.

Immigration, border control and fear of the foreigner

While much attention is focused on immigration to richer countries such as the United States, Australia, Canada and the United Kingdom, less attention tends to be given to outward flows from these countries. For example, according to the Institute for Public Policy Research, nearly one in ten Britons now live overseas, and the implications of this trend are that Britain has more people living overseas than almost any other country (McVeigh, 2008). However, despite endorsing the right to emigrate, many richer countries tend to be preoccupied with reinforcing their own borders, particularly in the wake of the terrorist acts of 11 September 2001 (Doty, 2003). More recently this preoccupation has resulted in a host of surveillance activities being put in place to contain immigration. For example, in what follows, McVeigh (2008, p. 3) summarizes some of the strategies adopted by the British government to gain tighter control over people's border movements:

> The government is shaking up the immigration system: fingerprint checks for all visa applicants, on-the-spot fines for employers who don't check that their workers are entitled to work, the expansion of detention capacity, a points system for managing migration; compulsory ID cards for foreigners; and the counting in and out of arrivals.

In the case of groups such as asylum seekers, as pointed out earlier the governments of many richer countries have similarly adopted punitive but domestically popular policies. For example, up until 2008, Australia employed a policy of mandatory detention for asylum seekers who arrive by sea and who are more commonly termed 'boat people'. All asylum seekers – and their children – who 'illegally' entered the country were detained in detention centres until their applications for asylum were processed. Classifying asylum seekers as illegal arrivals effectively denied this group the benefits associated with citizenship and recourse to the justice system. A tangential development has been the government's declaration of a 'Migration Excision Zone' – ostensibly to deter people smugglers – but also to disqualify immigrants landing in these territories from being able to legally claim the right to asylum in Australia (Evans, 2003).

Likewise in the United States, immigration policies and border-control policies reflect a concern with containing migrants and asylum seekers who are seen as a threat to internal stability or security. In particular, mass migration from Latin America to the United States has met with hostility and resistance on the part of many locally born residents, prompting the US government to build a reinforced fence along parts of the US–Mexico border (Moses, 2006, pp. 120–1). Part of this resistance stems from the fear that an influx of migrants will increase demand for social services and place stress on existing infrastructure, schools and housing. Another commonly expressed fear is that undocumented migrants who perform jobs that local people are reluctant to do will further depress the wages of low-skilled workers. However, the evidence regarding the effects of immigration on wages is mixed, and migration is generally thought to contribute to overall economic growth (Koser, 2007).

Even in the European Union, where cross-border movement has more recently been enabled between member states and promoted labour mobility, recent research suggests that discriminatory attitudes towards migrants are widespread (Zick, Pettigrew and Wagner, 2008). Moreover, those seeking to immigrate to Europe from outside the continent still face formidable barriers, especially when seeking political asylum or a better lifestyle. This is particularly evident in media portrayals of African migrants attempting to cross the Strait of Gibraltar to mainland Spain, or alternatively, negotiating a hazardous sea journey to the Canary Islands in overloaded fishing boats, and the substantial loss of life that accompanies these migratory journeys (De Haas, 2007).

The prominence of these images in the media have fuelled fears that immigration from developing countries is out of control and that we are in the midst of a global refugee crisis precipitated by regional instability, poverty, civil conflict and war. These images belie the fact that refugees only make up a small proportion of global migration, although fears have been expressed that the number of environmental refugees will rise in the future (Seglow, 2005). While a common perception exists that refugees mainly seek asylum from the richer Western nations, the reality is that most refugees are living in makeshift camps in other developing countries closer to home. Hence, these poorer countries bear a disproportionate proportion of the cost of looking after the world's refugee population (Mupedziswa, 1997). In 2006 Pakistan hosted the single largest number of refugees, followed by Iran. Between them these countries provided asylum to 20 per cent of the world's refugees (UNHCR, 2007).

Irregular migration and human trafficking are other issues that have garnered much media attention and been the subject of intense public debate. In this way, migration is often seen in a negative light or comes to be associated with a host of social problems. However, such simplistic portrayals of migration tend to downplay the complexity of these issues. For example, while human trafficking is often equated with slavery, this tends to negate the motivations of the parties involved, and the fact that for some people, trafficking is the only means available to them to cross borders. Similarly, media portrayals of sex trafficking often deny the agency of the women and girls involved (Weitzer, 2007). While much effort has been directed towards criminalizing trafficking and apprehending traffickers, far less attention has been focused on the welfare of those being trafficked. Moreover, operating from a predominantly legal discourse, it is very easy to justify the deportation of those caught up in trafficking, including children, because they are ascribed the status of illegal immigrants (Moosa-Mitha, 2007). Consequently, trafficking is primarily understood within the dominant discourse of border control and illegal immigration, in turn marginalizing the human rights and citizenship claims of those caught up in this practice.

The previous examples suggest that for many richer countries in the global North, immigration and ethnic diversity have come to be seen as a potential threat to the territorial integrity of the nation. One commonly expressed fear is that migrants will compete with locals for scarce resources such as housing and jobs, and in this sense migration is constructed as a burden to the host community. However, not all migrants are perceived in a negative light, and as Tyler (2006, p. 186) wryly points out, 'some foreigners are more foreign and less desirable than others.' In particular, 'non-Western immigrants' are perceived as a threat to the social cohesion and security of these countries (De Haas, 2007). Attitudes towards migrants are shaped by contemporary race relations and a fear of 'the foreigner', and in this sense, immigration has become racialized. However, in contrast to older styles of racism based on a belief in white superiority, Jayasuriya (1998, pp. 24–30) argues that a new nationalistic version of racism has emerged where cultural differences are essentialized and conformity is measured by factors such as the ability to speak the national language. In more recent times this fear of the foreigner has also extended to certain religious groups such as Muslims, manifesting in Islamaphobia. Nonetheless, there is a denial of and silencing around racism of this kind, particularly when it is couched in the language of homeland security. It is this political climate that has fuelled the current concern with protecting 'the nation' from 'illegal arrivals' from other parts of the world, in turn creating what Evans (2003) calls 'border panic'. Moreover, constructing migrants as a threat rationalizes their exclusion from citizenship rights (Raijman et al., 2008).

In the following section, we consider this question of migration and citizenship in more detail, first, in terms of the right to enter and live in a new country, and second, in relation to the entitlements of migrants subsequently granted residency. These are important considerations for social workers, not only on a practical level in terms of determining immigrants' entitlements and legal standing but also on a social justice level in terms of ensuring that the resources and opportunities available to nationals are similarly available to migrants (International Federation of Social Workers [IFSW], 2005c).

Citizenship in the global, post-colonial era

In political theory, citizenship has been traditionally understood within the context of the individual's relationship with the state (Kabeer, 2002). The concept of 'national citizenship', however, is being called into question as more and more people cross borders in search of asylum or employment. The emergence of transnational communities, diasporas and a globalized workforce have further unsettled the idea of state membership because such groups are often positioned outside the conventional bounds of the state. Moreover, state-centric notions of citizenship may have little significance for those who identify with other forms of community based on commonalities such as cultural affiliation or politics. Such cosmopolitan notions of citizenship privilege multiculturalism rather than the nation state as the main frame of reference in which identities are forged (Roudometof, 2005).

Prior to the emergence of nation states, people were able to move about relatively freely, only constrained by the limitations of the transport and technology available to them. In other words, 'illegal migration' did not exist. The creation of the nation state has resulted in rigid boundaries being created between different groups of people, most notably those deemed to be national citizens and those deemed to be aliens or non-citizens (Doty, 2003). This in turn has resulted in the state attempting to regulate people movement via the introduction of policies that determine who can enter the country and who can claim citizenship status. In this way, 'citizenship is constructed as a defence, a barrier by which to keep non-citizens out' (Moosa-Mitha, 2007, p. 317).

Inequality between countries is one of the major factors prompting people to immigrate, and determining who has right of entry to a country clearly involves questions of justice. Moreover, it has been suggested that state-centric notions of justice and citizenship are inadequate for protecting the rights of migrants 'whose legal protection is only as strong as the laws that govern non-citizens' (Bagchi, 2008, p. 199). Jordan and Düvell (2002, p. 237) argue that if we subscribe to the idea of political justice inherent to liberal democracy, which encompasses 'the right to decide where to work and live', then 'it is border control, not free movement, that needs to be justified'. Cosmopolitan theories of justice similarly support this principle of more open borders, not only on moral grounds of freedom of movement but also in terms of global redistributive justice and welfare (Seglow, 2005). In other words, distributive justice must be conceptualized beyond state borders and rich states must ensure that poorer countries have a fair share of both resources and opportunities. Immigration policy, in particular, involves questions of justice because of its potential to constrain people's opportunities and life chances. In what follows, Seglow (2005, p. 329) elaborates on this understanding of cosmopolitan justice as it applies to immigration and the opening up of borders:

> Citizens – especially citizens in rich states – have powerful duties to help build a just global order, one in which all persons are able to lead decent lives. Once

achieved, this need not include completely open borders, although there are good reasons – not least to encourage the spread of cosmopolitan sentiment – for borders to be more open than they currently are. Until we realize that ideal, and perhaps even if we do, rich states have substantial duties to admit poor outsiders.

Clearly, the case for completely open borders can be easily overridden by counter-arguments made by the state in relation to concerns such as over-population, sustainability and security issues. Equally, however, the argument can be made that there needs to be constraints on the sovereignty of the state, especially if its policies regarding right of entry are discriminatory or curtail the rights of certain immigrants (Jordan and Düvell, 2002, p. 244). Refugees, asylum seekers and poorer migrant workers are not afforded the global mobility enjoyed by those with affluence and power, and Ife (2008) argues that social workers, therefore, need to take up the issue of global citizenship for these excluded groups. He goes on to suggest that the discriminatory treatment experienced by these groups is evocative of the British Poor Laws, 'when to be poor meant to have one's freedom of movement severely curtailed' (Ife, 2008, p. 84).

Even after being granted the right to live in a new country, migrants may still experience discrimination and social exclusion, especially if they are not granted the same access to public goods as those in the host society. Generally speaking, the notion of citizenship is tied up with ideas about what constitutes the rights, responsibilities and duties of community members. It implies the importance of being officially recognized as a *member* of a community along with being able to *participate* in society (Kabeer, 2002). In this sense, it ties into debates about who has the right to become one of 'us,' who is the 'other' and on what basis do we deny a person the right to become 'us' and relegate him or her to the category 'them'. Marshall defined citizenship as 'a status bestowed on those who are full members of a community' where 'all who possess the status are equal with respect to the rights and duties with which the status is endowed' (Marshall and Bottomore, 1992, p. 18). He claimed that the recognition of civil, political and social rights is a prerequisite for citizenship and argued that the state must take responsibility for the overall welfare of its citizens. However, the status of migrants is not so clear-cut in this regard, especially when there is one set of laws and policies for those deemed to be 'nationals' and another set for new residents derived from immigration (Raijman et al., 2008).

For those migrants denied access to citizenship, their prospects are likely to be rather limited in that they are more susceptible to being economically disadvantaged, culturally invisible and under-represented in the political domain. Accordingly, those granted residency also need to be afforded the social rights of citizenship, the right to work, the protection of the law, access to health and welfare services and the right to vote. Equally, they need to be afforded equality of opportunity. This is a position that is similarly endorsed by the IFSW (2005c) in their international policy on migration, which states that social workers should work towards ensuring migrants enjoy the same standards of rights, freedoms and responsibilities afforded to citizens of host nations. In the following section, we expand further on the potential of social work in this regard, as well as considering the role of social work more generally in addressing migration-related concerns.

The role of social work in addressing migration-related concerns

Healy (2001, p. 115) sees the global movement of people as 'undoubtedly the most dramatic social indicator of global interdependence', which she argues is of paramount concern to social workers given their primary focus on people and their relationships. She suggests that working with international populations or 'internationally related cases' is becoming increasingly common in social workers' everyday practice. Activities such as refugee resettlement work, international adoptions, practice and policy work at the supranational level and social work in border zones all constitute different types of practice at the international-domestic interface (Healy, 2001, p. 7).

If we accept that the cross-border movement of people is indeed indicative of a significant level of global interdependence, then it is important that we adopt such a perspective in trying to understand migration-related concerns. This is particularly important in the case of asylum seekers and refugees. Ife (2008, p. 87) argues that if social workers continue to 'localize' the refugee crisis, their attempts to assist these groups will be ineffective:

> Even with refugees and asylum seekers, an issue so obviously global and internationally linked, which cries out for a strong global analysis, the response by activists is depressingly confined within national perspectives, seen as 'Canada's refugee problem' or 'Australia's treatment of illegal immigrants', or 'the need for Sudan to be made safe again'.

Historically, social workers have played a key role in working with refugees, particularly in the wake of Second World War when many people who had experienced war-induced displacement found themselves on the move (Cox and Pawar, 2006). Later, refugee work became a focus in developing countries, and more recently, social workers from the developed world have also found themselves working with substantial numbers of refugees and asylum seekers, prompting some writers to claim that this represents a new field of practice (Nash, Wong and Trlin, 2006). The mandate and work of the UN is particularly important in this regard. The UNHCR, for example, has a global mandate to provide protection and material aid to refugees on a non-political basis as well as assisting in their resettlement. In addition, it monitors individual government's compliance with international refugee law. The 1951 UN Convention Relating to the Status of Refugees, while not legally enforceable, states that each nation should recognize basic human rights regardless of a person's legal or illegal status in that country. However, it is individual governments who actually determine the status and rights of a person in accordance with their own legal systems, and this inability to enforce international law underlines the limitations of the UN in this regard. For example, while Australia has at times been the focus of international criticism for being in breach of its responsibilities towards refugees, the UNHCR does not have the power to make the government modify its policies or revoke its determinations on a person's status.

The implications for social workers in this regard relate to the need to be cognizant of government policies and local programmes that have been set up to deal with the resettlement and repatriation of refugees. Along with offering counselling and practical assistance in terms of settlement work with refugees (e.g. housing, income, health), social workers can equally take on a more political role in their work with this population. In particular, they can attempt to influence immigration policies that work against the interests of refugees by taking on an advocacy role (Healy, 2001). This type of policy activism is especially important in an age when receiving countries are less receptive to taking in refugees and commonly deny them their citizenship rights.

In addition, practitioners can work within their existing professional groups on a national, regional and international level to make effective representation on behalf of refugees and asylum seekers in a broader political context. For example, in 2002 the IFSW petitioned the Australian government about the compulsory detention of all asylum seekers, highlighting the poor conditions in these holding centres and pointing out that the government's policies and practices contravened Australia's obligation to uphold these people's human rights. More recently in the United Kingdom, the British Association of Social Workers (BASW) publicly pledged its support to practitioners who refused on ethical grounds to cooperate with immigration workers planning to remove unaccompanied child asylum seekers from care placements (Ahmed, 2007). Alternatively, the IFSW (1998) suggest that social workers can forge strategic links with non-government organizations (NGOs) such as Amnesty International and the World Council of Churches in order to lobby for more humane policies and programmes to address the concerns of refugees. Clearly, the active involvement of refugees themselves is integral to the success of such campaigns, especially in terms of coming up with appropriate, needs-driven and sustainable solutions.

While refugees and some migrants commonly face significant hardship and psychological trauma, it is important that social workers do not construct these groups as 'helpless' individuals who are totally dependent on outside assistance. Rutter (2006, pp. 131–2) contends that welfare professionals have a tendency to equate refugees and asylum seekers with trauma, or alternatively, portray them as 'heroic victims'. Her argument against such simplistic portrayals is that they do not assist social workers dealing with clients who do not fit these stereotypes. As Mupedziswa (1997) points out, refugees have exhibited amazing resiliency and creativity in their attempts to re-establish themselves in new societies. They have done this not only through forming political organizations to represent their interests but also through public campaigns and using strategies of passive resistance to bring their concerns to the attention of the broader public. For example, asylum seekers detained in detention centres in Australia have used hunger strikes and on occasion have even sewn up their lips to publicize their plight, which in turn has attracted the attention of the international media (Evans, 2003).

Similarly, Augustin (2007) is critical of social workers who are part of a moral crusade to 'rescue' women who they believe are caught up in sex trafficking. As mentioned earlier, women and girls may be targets of violence or sexual exploitation through trafficking and sex tourism. However, it is important that social workers recognize the diversity in this group and do not see these women solely as passive victims whose primary need is for protection, especially if the right to protection is made conditional on their leaving the sex trade (Moosa-Mitha, 2007). For some of these women, being constructed as sexually vulnerable and open to exploitation denies their agency and reflects a moralizing agenda about 'correct' sexual relations that has evolved in the West (Augustin, 2007).

At a preventative level, it is important to look into what compels people to flee their homelands in the first place and seek refuge in other countries often via highly dangerous modes of travel. One line of argument goes that if we address the social, political, economic and/or environmental conditions that fuel internal instability and displacement, then asylum-seeking behaviour will abate. However, Mupedziswa (1997) warns social workers against being overly ambitious in this regard, given the complex dimensions and global scale of the refugee crisis. Existing research has failed to conclusively demonstrate that promoting development via aid and trade has any significant impact on dampening people's desire to emigrate; the paradox here is that social and economic development may actually promote migration (De Haas, 2007). Moreover, working towards ending migration carries the implication that it is a problem in need of a solution and reinforces prevalent Western fears that migrants are a burden or a threat (De Haas, 2007). Accordingly, Mupedziswa (1997) argues that social workers are better off using the skills and knowledge they already have – especially in relation to community organizing, group work, counselling, advocacy and developmental work – in assisting refugee and migrant populations rather than working at a preventative level.

Social workers can, for example, advocate for migrant workers who may be at risk of exploitation in the workplace or who may be denied their rights and entitlements because of a lack of familiarity with local laws and the avenues of complaint open to them. Similarly, practitioners have recognized the need to implement support programmes for new migrants and refugees who are socially isolated or who may be affected by loss and trauma (e.g. see Whelan et al., 2002). Another area of practice that is attracting increasing attention is 'transnational caregiving' (Baldassar, Vellekoop Baldock and Wild, 2007). Increasingly, those who migrate to another country are finding themselves faced with the challenge of providing emotional, financial and practical support to family members – particularly older parents – across borders. The capacity to care in this context is very much shaped by factors such as immigration regulations and visa restrictions, access to new communications technologies, employment, and economic considerations (Baldassar et al., 2007). Given the centrality of care to social work, we suggest that caring across borders is a ripe area for further research and investigation in social work.

There is a tendency when thinking about migration to focus on that population who have relocated to another country. However, as pointed out earlier, this in fact is a small minority of the global population. For the bulk of the world's population who do not emigrate, migration still impacts their welfare via remittances, reconfigured social relations, changes in the labour market and heightened competition – perceived and real – over services, jobs and housing (Seglow, 2005, p. 317). Hence, we suggest that social workers need to think about migration not just in the sense of the issues faced by new immigrants engaged in the settlement process but also about how people movement potentially impacts the social fabric, cultural make-up, critical infrastructure and economic conditions of all communities. Community work and social planning are other areas of practice that are important in this regard.

Lastly, it is timely to remember that *all* non-indigenous populations are immigrants and that many of us have histories that are linked to colonization and the development of settler societies. Hence, given current attempts to contain the cross-border movement of people, we equally need to reflect on our own origins. In particular, this requires us to critically examine our relations with indigenous populations who constitute First Nations people. At the same time, the phenomenon of global migration requires us to rethink the continued viability of the constructed nation state, the relevance of political borders and the validity of national identity in an interdependent world.

Summary

In this chapter we have examined some historical and contemporary trends in migration, and the role of immigration policy in regulating and containing the movement of people, particularly in terms of migration flows from the global South to the global North. Consideration was given to how migration has become a racialized practice, and the issue of border control was explored in relation to how state-centric notions of justice and citizenship are often inadequate for protecting the rights of migrants. It was suggested that social workers need to develop an understanding of the politics of immigration in order to more fully understand how anti-immigration sentiment may impact the lives of immigrants and exacerbate transitional stress. Lastly, the role of social work in working with migration-related concerns on both a practical and political level was discussed. It was suggested that because migration affects the community at large – socially, culturally and economically – it is at this level that social workers also need to direct their energies.

Discussion points

1. In your state or country, how do current immigration laws and policies impact the lives of migrants who do not have citizenship status? Do they have the same access to services and employment as those with citizenship?
2. How does adopting an understanding of global citizenship change the way we view immigration, and what might this mean for social workers in practice who work with groups at risk of exclusion such as refugees and asylum seekers?
3. In what ways can anti-immigrant sentiment impact the lives of immigrants and exacerbate transitional stress? How might you support and advocate for people in such situations?
4. Can you identify any ways of working to address anti-immigrant sentiment at the community level?
5. What might be some of the challenges entailed in providing support and care to family members across borders? How might you as a social worker support caregivers in such situations?

Chapter 5

Rethinking Women's Lives and Concerns at the Global-Local Interface

Introduction

In this chapter, we explore the ways in which globalization is believed to have impacted women and gender relations with reference to a number of contemporary social issues. These issues include but are not limited to the increase in women's migration, including labour migration, the global care chain and the feminization of poverty. Along with the general wealth of literature that has emerged on globalization, a number of writers – including those drawing from feminist perspectives – have put forward the thesis that globalization has radically altered the lives of women and women's work and transformed gender relations. In this sense, these writers have proposed that it is appropriate to talk about gendered globalization or alternatively posit a strong link between globalization and processes of feminization (Gunewardena and Kingsolver, 2007; Hawkesworth, 2006). The evolution of an international women's movement has similarly been linked with globalization, and over the past few decades we have witnessed a number of global campaigns on women's issues that have been spearheaded by official world bodies such as the United Nations – UN (Berkovitch, 2004). Hence, globalization has not just led to new understandings of women's lives and concerns but has also enhanced opportunities for forging transnational networks and alliances to promote gender equality and women's rights.

Around the world, and even within the same region, the impact of globalization on women has been uneven and its effects have been mixed. While we do not propose that a direct causal relationship exists between globalization and women's current social situation, we do support the view that the two are related in terms of 'their multiple and complex interconnections' (Jones and Chandler, 2001, p. 174). It is important to recognize that a multitude of factors impact women's social position and circumstances and that the process of globalization is just one such factor. At the same time, it is equally important to acknowledge that women are not a homogenous group and that factors such as location, class, race, ethnicity, religion, caste, disability and age intertwine in a complex fashion to shape women's experiences

68

of the global. Moreover, specific local histories – including experiences of colonization – along with sociocultural norms and economic practices construct the day-to-day lives of women.

In the first part of this chapter we examine the idea of gender and the impact of globalization on women before moving on to examine women's place in the global economy and the relationship between gender inequality and poverty. Next, we focus on violence against women and girls, which has been identified as an issue of grave concern by the UN because it has flow-on effects in terms of women's health and employment. Following on from this, we look at women and the cross-border flow of labour with particular reference to 'care' work. In the latter part of this chapter we explore the potential for women to mobilize locally and globally to promote their common concerns. Lastly, we examine the role of social work in addressing women's issues at the global-local level.

Gendered relations in a global world

Although gender constitutes a pivotal social division in virtually every culture, it is important to acknowledge at the outset that ideas about gender have arisen in the social domain. This means that the meanings attached to 'male' and 'female' are socially constructed rather than representing the natural order of things (Janes, 2002). Categorizing people in terms of perceived differences paves the way for the establishment of hierarchical social relations based on what is presumed to be the norm and what is seen to be different (or sometimes inferior). For example, we see men and women performing different jobs based on gender divisions. This means that ideas about masculinity and femininity tend to restrict the range of roles open to men and women (Kabeer, 2008).

The concept of gender has been employed by social theorists to demonstrate how certain understandings of sex differences are culturally based rather than biological 'givens'. The assumption that all women are 'natural born mothers' and, therefore, suited to care work has been one prominent 'gendered' belief questioned by social theorists. Other writers have used gender to analyse the social organization of relationships between men and women and to analyse the distribution of burdens and benefits in society (Wharton, 2005). Feminist analyses of many global social institutions such as the family, the market, education and government have exposed systematic differences in the experiences and treatment of men and women. Even programmes that do not have an overt gender focus such as economic policy, trade, health services and education exhibit different patterns of access for men and women while producing different outcomes (Jaggar, 2001). Although gender also interacts with race, social position, ethnicity and a range of other factors that are similarly implicated in men's oppression, generally speaking, women receive fewer benefits from these programmes and face more barriers to participation.

While many women have enjoyed newfound freedoms in a more interconnected world that allows greater access to information, travel and work opportunities, other women have been subjected to heightened levels of repression and surveillance under ideologically conservative governments who are keen to keep outside influences at bay. For example, Healy (2001, pp. 189–90) points out that when the Taliban ruled Afghanistan, women were denied education and could not work outside the home. For the Taliban, this was an assertion of traditional Islamic values in the face of a perceived threat of the global dominance of American culture. Hence, globalizing forces are experienced differently by women depending on cultural context, history and location.

Nonetheless, despite these different impacts, some global institutions argue that it is still appropriate to consider the gendered effects of social change and to consider how many global social problems and issues disproportionately affect women (e.g. see International Poverty Centre, 2008; UN Population Fund [UNFPA], 2008). In what follows, some of the more prominent social problems and health issues affecting women are briefly summarized:

- Women and girls make up two-thirds of the illiterate population of the world, with this pattern of illiteracy being particularly pronounced in South Asia, sub-Saharan Africa and the Middle East (UNFPA, 2008).
- In the area of reproductive health, more than half a million women die every year as a result of pregnancy or childbirth coupled with limited or no access to appropriate maternal care and family-planning services (UNFPA, 2008).
- Sex-selected abortion and infanticide are practised in a number of countries that favour boy over girl children, leading to a significant gender imbalance in countries such as China and India. In India, for example, half a million abortions are conducted each year on female foetuses (Ramesh, 2008a).
- Each year, millions of girls are subjected to genital mutilation, and while this practice has traditionally been confined to African countries and the Middle East, it has more recently spread to other countries such as the United Kingdom and France through migration (Guiné and Fuentes, 2007).
- Over the course of their lifetime, one in three women are likely to be victims of physical, sexual or other forms of violence or abuse (UNFPA, 2005).

Many of the aforementioned social problems and health issues disproportionately affect women in low-income and emerging economies. Nonetheless, even though Western women have made considerable progress in equalizing gender relations, around the world women are still predominantly the primary carers of children and responsible for most domestic duties. In addition, sociocultural norms that devalue women, normalize male power over women and sustain the belief that women are the property of men continue to perpetuate gender-based violence in most countries of the world. Hence, while key differences do exist among women and the legitimacy of the social category of 'women' has even been called into question, a common bond between women is their social position in relation to men (Raju, 2002).

Women, work and economic globalization

Women's place in the world economy and their access to paid employment have been ongoing concerns for many development agencies. In some regions of the world, namely, the Middle East, North Africa, Asia and the Pacific, women face exclusion from the labour market and constitute nearly 80 per cent of the unemployed population (International Labour Organization [ILO], 2008). Midgley (1997, p. 14) points out that although women actively contribute to economic development through an array of activities, they often do not enjoy their fair share of the benefits:

> Their labor is critical to the rural economy, the urban informal sector and, increasingly, to the industrial and service sectors, but their incomes are lower than those of men, their status is inferior, and many live in conditions of deprivation and dependency.

More recently, a thesis has been put forward that neoliberal globalization has had a more detrimental effect on women than men and that its benefits and burdens 'are systematically, unfairly distributed not only among nations but also between genders' (Kang, 2008, p. 361). In particular, women living in the global South are seen to be disadvantaged by processes associated with globalization such as the integration of domestic economies into a global market, the promotion of free trade and the loss of protection of domestic markets. Poor and uneducated women constitute one of the most marginalized groups under these contemporary economic and social arrangements (Kang, 2008).

A concomitant trend has been worldwide cuts in social security and public health programmes; women with family responsibilities who have traditionally relied on such programmes have been especially hard hit by these cutbacks (Jaggar, 2001). Women may also face considerable challenges in actually getting remunerated for their labour because of enduring social values and cultural norms that devalue domestic work. Outside paid employment, women spend approximately 70 per cent of their time caring for family members, but this contribution to the global economy is not recognized (UNFPA, 2008).

For some women, globalization has enabled them to access education, information and employment, which in turn has greatly reduced gender inequalities (George and Wilding, 2002). The labour market, for example, has generally favoured women in the advanced economies who have accounted for 60 per cent of employment growth over the past two decades. But in other regions of the world women have accounted for less than one-third of employment growth, while globally the employment rates of women trail those of men by 25 per cent (ILO, 2008). At the same time, women are over-represented in part-time or temporary employment. Taking on this type of 'non-standard' work has been a conscious choice for some women because it allows for a better balance between work and home life. For others, however, this has come about because employers require the flexibility to respond to rapidly changing and unpredictable supply and demand conditions in a globalized economy. The increase in women's temporary and part-time employment is also related to the fragmentation of the production process that has accompanied globalization and the move by many companies to outsource certain manufacturing tasks (ILO, 2008).

Women's employment in the global South has been subjected to new, gendered divisions of labour as domestic markets are opened up to foreign investment and companies outsource parts of the production process. Globally competitive, labour-intensive industries have sought out women workers in developing countries because their labour is cheap. The feminization of factory work has been particularly noticeable in South East Asia, where certain jobs on the assembly line are deemed to be suitable for women because of their 'feminine' characteristics (Caraway, 2007). Other women find themselves 'at the end of the global supply chains, picking and packing fruit, sewing garments, and cutting flowers' (Kang, 2008, pp. 361–2). Women make up more than 80 per cent of the unskilled workers employed by these export-oriented transnational corporations (Gunewardena and Kingsolver, 2007). Consequently, while more women are in paid employment, they are often poorly paid and work long hours in low-status jobs. At the same time, many of these women still hold primary responsibility for work in the home and the care of children.

In addition to the increasing numbers of women working in export-processing zones, women constitute the vast proportion of the 'shadow economy' or the informal sector, which consists of seasonal work that is poorly paid and insecure (George and Wilding, 2002, pp. 115–16). Alternatively, women have started up micro businesses such as home-based dressmaking or roadside stalls selling food. Other women have chosen sex work as a route to economic independence or have moved overseas to seek employment (Augustin, 2007). On the one hand, these types of income-generating activities are indicative of women's innovative approaches to job creation and their will to survive. On the other hand, however, such employment often does not provide a regular, dependable income and is not included in official labour statistics. Consequently, women who are dependent on the informal employment sector are often unprotected, underpaid and open to exploitation.

The term 'feminization of labour' has been coined to describe these developments, whereby women are increasingly employed in low-paid, precarious forms of employment such as subcontracted assembly work. These forms of employment typically lack the social benefits and protection afforded to workers in more high-status and secure jobs, which in turn increases women's vulnerability to poverty (Heintz, 2008). Consequently, these gendered divisions of labour coupled with the restricted roles available to women in the public arena in some countries diminishes their chances of escaping poverty through employment. Another notable trend is the increasing number of female-headed households in Africa, Asia and Latin America who are the primary breadwinners (Kabeer, 2008). It is these households that constitute the bulk of poor people in the world, and in the following section we follow up this theme in terms of the relationship between gender equality and poverty.

Gender equality and poverty

Global statistics on poverty indicate that it is a problem that overwhelmingly affects more women more than men. Women make up 60 per cent of the world's poorest 1 billion people, and these women are also more prone to malnutrition, maternal death, ill health and injury (UNFPA, 2008). This phenomenon has been described as the feminization of poverty. In part, this is due to women's status in society, a lack of access to health care, women's unpaid work in the home and the fact that women in general receive lower wages than their male counterparts. Women's poverty has also been compounded by the impact of neoliberal globalization on contemporary social and economic arrangements, which has seen the gap between the rich and the poor widen even more (Jaggar, 2001). However, it is important to point out that while globalization appears to have increased the risk of poverty for some women, for other women it has allowed them to get out of the poverty trap.

Recent research suggests that focusing primarily on female-headed households to understand women's experiences of poverty does not allow for a full understanding of poverty as a gendered experience; to gain a more comprehensive picture of this phenomenon, it is also important to understand how poverty impacts differently on women than men in the same household, how women and men respond to poverty and the gendered impacts of programmes and policies aimed at ameliorating poverty (Sen, 2008).

We suggest that these are questions that social workers should also be concerned with, especially since poverty – and ways of alleviating poverty – has been a long-standing concern for the profession. If social workers are to work effectively with poor women, then they need to have a good grasp of the social conditions, power relations and policy responses that frame these women's lives. For example, research suggests that it is increasingly women who are taking responsibility for 'dealing with poverty', and in the process working harder and longer (Chant, 2008, p. 27).

The importance of alleviating women's poverty is recognized in the Millennium Development Goals, and the UN Development Programme (UNDP) posits a link between eliminating gender equalities and reducing general levels of poverty (Costa and Silva, 2008). There is a general consensus among the main global institutions that elevating women's economic status is a precondition for ending global poverty. The education of women and girls is crucial to this goal. While progress has been made towards gender equality in education with increasing numbers of girls being given the opportunity to attend school, women in poorer nations still lag well behind men in terms of participation in the labour force, income levels and ownership of land and property (World Bank, 2008b). Accordingly, the World Bank recognizes the importance of investing in women and providing employment opportunities not only to stimulate economic growth but to also break cycles of intergenerational poverty. Women are more likely to exert control over household budgets, to be more family-focused in their spending and to factor in the needs of their children (Chant, 2008; Kabeer, 2008; UNFPA, 2006, p. 29). For these reasons, the role of women is key to alleviating household poverty.

If women are able to work and are appropriately paid for their labour, then households will be less vulnerable to poverty (Heintz, 2008). Similarly in farming and agriculture, if women were given equitable access to land and resources, then agricultural output would be significantly boosted. Although women produce the bulk of food in developing countries, they often have limited access to community resources and land. It has been estimated, for example, that if women farmers in Burkino Faso had the same access to resources as their male counterparts, then agricultural output would increase by 20 per cent (Kelly, 2008). However, due to their primary responsibility for care work, many women also indicate that they are time-poor, and this lack of time has been identified as a key factor that compromises women's attempts to improve their economic situation:

> Women's responsibilities for care fundamentally affect their ability to participate in social programmes, in labour markets, and to derive benefits from household resources. For poor women, time is often the most valuable resource, and poor

women's time is so much taken up by caring work that they can remain caught
in a vicious cycle of poverty. (Sen, 2008, p. 7)

It is clear from the previous discussion that poverty will not be eliminated
until greater efforts are directed towards ensuring women's equality and
addressing gender discrimination. This includes working with men and
boys to challenge dominant masculinist ideas about responsibilities for
care work and gendered beliefs about women that constrain the roles made
available to them (Sen, 2008). While most initiatives aimed at promoting
gender equality have tended to target women, recruiting men as agents
of cultural change is believed to be crucial to achieving gender equality
(UNFPA, 2008). We return to this theme in the latter part of the chapter
when we discuss social work responses to gender inequality.

Along with the need to promote cultural change, eliminating barriers
to women's participation in the labour market is crucial to reducing poverty (Costa and Silva, 2008). Given that caring for children limits women's
ability to gain paid employment, it is important that child care facilities
are made available to poor women. In order to enhance women's economic
status, it is equally important for women's working conditions to be cham-
pioned by trade unions and for women themselves to participate in such
action. By way of example, women working in the export garment industry
in Bangladesh have been active participants in trade union campaigns to
improve their working conditions, which have brought about substantial
improvements in their employment and wages (Kelly, 2008).

At the same time, it is important to remember that poverty has complex
causes and is multifaceted, and if strategies aimed at reducing gendered disadvantage are to be effective, they need to be targeted to specific contexts.
Microcredit schemes, for example, may work better in some locations than
others. These schemes, which aim to assist women start up profit-generat-
ing businesses, generally operate on the individual level and promote the
idea of self-help rather than structural change (Hawkesworth, 2006). In
some countries such as India, such programmes have been very successful.
However, in other contexts, they have encouraged governments to relin-
quish responsibility for addressing structural inequalities that are linked to
women's income poverty (Hawkesworth, 2006).

In addition, it is recognized that gender-based violence is a key factor
preventing women from realizing their full social, economic and political
rights and is indicative of their low status in the family and the broader society (UNFPA, 2005). Violence against women – including domestic violence
and rape – is a prominent social problem in both developing and developed
countries alike. Moreover, it has significant social, economic and health
costs and has implications for productivity. These issues are explored in the
following section.

Violence against women

Living in a more interconnected world has allowed for a greater recognition of gendered violence as well as providing the impetus for global action on this issue. The UN Development Fund for Women (UNIFEM) has identified violence against women and girls as a 'problem of pandemic proportions' that represents 'the most pervasive human rights violation that we know today' (UNIFEM, 2007). Women are at greatest risk of violence from men who are known to them, and domestic violence in particular appears to be a prevalent form of violence across the world. In every country that has conducted large-scale surveys on women's experiences of violence in the home, between 10 and 69 per cent of women report physical abuse by a partner (UNFPA, 2005). Other forms of violence used against women include sexual assault, genital mutilation, sexual harassment, forced prostitution and trafficking. More recently, the use of rape as a weapon of war has also garnered worldwide attention.

Violence not only has a detrimental impact on women's physical and emotional health but is also implicated in constraining economic development. It entails substantial costs in terms of health care, legal protection and loss of productivity. At the same time, violence is seen to be interlinked with the spread of HIV/AIDS while also being a major contributor to disability and death for women under 44 years of age (UNIFEM, 2007). For some women, economic marginalization and poverty also places them at greater risk of violence (Conwill, 2007). For other women, moving to a new country may increase their vulnerability to physical abuse in the home (UNFPA, 2006).

Cultural and social change is a precondition for ending violence towards women. The interventions that we employ to address gendered violence will only succeed if they are relevant to and supported by the cultural context in which they are implemented. In Latin America, for example, women's organizations working in the area of domestic violence have identified cultural traditions that condone men's violence as one of the main barriers to change (UNFPA, 2008). Women themselves may then internalize this belief, which leads them to accept and at times even justify such treatment. Accordingly, in order to change socially and culturally entrenched beliefs that normalize gendered violence, we need to work 'within cultures' to transform power relations through processes of 'contestation and consensus building' (UNFPA, 2008, p. 30).

Human rights advocates argue that as long as women live in fear of violence, they will not be able to realize their other rights and participate in development or enjoy its benefits. Violence against women has been incorporated into international human rights law. Signatories to the UN

Convention on the Elimination of All Forms of Discrimination against Women (CEDAW) are charged with the responsibility to challenge and address any practices that contravene the rights of women; this includes appealing to culture to rationalize violent acts such as genital mutilation (Kelly, 2008). While violence against women is both a public health issue and a human rights issue, a rights-based approach may be one of the most important means of addressing gender-based violence. We examine this approach in more depth in the final section of this chapter when we consider the utility of a human rights framework for advancing the interests of women.

Women, migration, the cross-border flow of labour and care work

The new global economy has impacted women in ways that also implicate migration and the cross-border flow of labour. In Chapter 4, we identified that women now constitute a sizeable proportion of the international migrant population. In addition, they constitute 80 per cent of the estimated refugee population in the world, many of whom suffer material disadvantage upon arrival in a new country and face difficulties in gaining paid employment (Kelly, 2008). Historically, however, little attention has been given to women's migration patterns, the reasons they choose to relocate and the contributions they make to the global economy via their labour and funds sent back home.

More recently, we have witnessed the movement of millions of women from developing and emerging economies to high-income nations, propelled by demographic pressures, economic and political forces and the quest for work. These women make a significant contribution to remittances sent to their home countries and typically send a higher proportion of their income home than their male counterparts (UNFPA, 2006). The UNFPA (2006) claims that these funds are important to poverty reduction and development and that many of the women's home countries also benefit through 'social remittances' such as knowledge and attitudes that promote the status and rights of women.

Overseas demand for domestic labour is a significant driver of international female labour migration. Sex workers and those working in the entertainment and hospitality industry are also moving across borders to seek better conditions and wages in the developed world, although some of these women are victims of human trafficking and bonded prostitution (UNFPA, 2006). 'Care work' in particular has assumed greater importance for women and immigrant workers as the manufacturing industry has gone into decline. Below, Fine (2007, p. 209) describes the links between global-ization, migration and the growth of care work:

> By supplementing the supply of locally born women seeking work in the field of care, the international patterns of migration and labour exchange that underlie globalization have supported the growth of care services based on the econom-ics of low-paid front-line work.

Women from developing countries, such as the Philippines, Indonesia and Nepal are taking up positions in more prosperous regions such as North America, Western Europe, the Middle East and East Asia to take over the domestic and childcare duties of working women (UNFPA, 2006). Ehrenreich and Hochschild (2003) talk about this phenomenon in terms of a mass importation of women from poorer countries who end up work-ing for professional women for minimal wages. These women make up an invisible and non-unionized labour force. They often move to countries like Spain, the United States and Lebanon in order to send money home to their own families. Instead of bringing up their own children, they end up bringing up the children of their employers, while their own children are at greater risk of neglect and abandonment. This phenomenon has been termed 'the global care chain', whereby 'domestic workers wind up running two households, their employers' as well as their own, from afar' (UNFPA, 2006, p. 25).

While countries such as the Philippines have become economically dependent on the remittances these domestic workers send home, their employment is tenuous. Ehrenreich (2003) blames this problem on unregu-lated capitalism, which has created a work culture that expects employees to be flexible and to put in long hours. In such a work culture, women cannot successfully compete and still be mothers and homemakers. The unequal division of labour in the home between men and women is, therefore, cited as one of the reasons for the emergence of this trend of employing domes-tic workers from poorer countries. Accordingly, the global care chain has impacted the economic arrangements and social relations between women themselves, creating new hierarchies in the process and fuelling other social problems such as child neglect.

The notion of care is central to social work and the human services. In a globalized world which has seen the rise of the service economy in post-industrial societies, professional workers in the social services such as social workers enjoy a relatively privileged status and are often involved in the coordination of people's care. In contrast, those who provide direct care – mainly women who are often from an immigrant or ethnic minority background – are accorded little recognition and receive lower rates of pay while also being prone to job insecurity (Fine, 2007). These care workers provide 'cheap, affordable and replaceable care labour, available at short-term notice, wherever, and for however long assistance is required' (Fine, 2007, p. 209). Arguably then, globalization has seen a further lowering of the status of care work.

Recent reports suggest that a growing number of Asian domestic workers who work overseas experience ongoing and routine human rights abuses such as physical or sexual violence, excessive work hours, unpaid wages and forced confinement (Black, 2008). In Lebanon, foreign domestic workers from countries such as Sri Lanka, Ethiopia and the Philippines account for 1 in 16 of the country's population. These women have no legal protection and increasing numbers of reports of abuse or exploitation are being reported to embassy social workers (Torrès, 2007). Similarly in Saudi Arabia, Human Rights Watch has documented hundreds of cases of abuse of Asian domestic workers, some of which they equated with virtual slavery (Black, 2008).

Clearly, these are issues of concern for social workers and other helping professionals working in locations where domestic and care work is in high demand. Equally, however, the global care chain has implications for practitioners in countries that export foreign domestic workers, especially in terms of the consequences for families and children left behind. On a broader level, we suggest that the global care chain is also a political issue that social workers need to be cognizant of because of its potential to devalue care work. In addition, it highlights the failure of many governments to introduce family-friendly work policies and the critical shortage of child care facilities and respite care.

The possibilities for women to act globally

While globalization has produced new challenges for women, it has also provided opportunities to connect more readily with each other, to share information and to engage in coordinated social action across borders. Globalization has opened up new arenas for women to forge alliances based not only on their similarities but also their differences. It has led to the recognition that the disadvantaged position of some women in certain regions is linked with happenings in other parts of the world (Berkovitch, 2004). One example of this type of alliance is a campaign to mobilize mothers in the United Kingdom to act in solidarity with poorer women in other parts of the world who are at significant risk of dying in childbirth due to their lack of access to appropriate health care (Bunting, 2008). Clearly, these women's experiences of childbirth will be very different, but the common bond here is motherhood.

In this sense, globalization has brought about positive outcomes for women because it has provided an opportunity for grass-roots activism to go global and forge an international women's movement (Jaggar, 2001). However, at times tensions have emerged between women from the global South and women from the global North as a result of 'imperial' forms of feminism, whereby Western feminists have adopted a 'civilizing mission' in their attempts to assist 'poor' and 'uneducated' women from colonized countries (Hawkesworth, 2006). Feminists from the global South have actively challenged such attitudes, while organizing autonomously to promote women's rights. Nonetheless, women are still working across borders to pursue issues of common interest, and the UN Conferences on Women have been instrumental in this regard.

The UN Decade for Women (1976–85) saw the recognition of the critical link between the status of women and economic and social development in individual countries (Berkovitch, 2004). The marrying of the discourse of women's rights with the principle of development was also about ensuring that women were able to play a part in development via access to economic resources, land, training and markets. Consequently, many governments around the world established official state agencies to promote and oversee the progress of women's affairs (Berkovitch, 2004).

The UN Conferences on Women have been significant forums for networking, sharing information, debating strategies to improve women's situation in the world and planning social action. The Beijing Conference in 1995 attracted delegates from 181 nations as well as representatives from a diverse range of non-government organizations (NGOs). Since that time, several more global women's forums have been held to monitor the progress of the original recommendations emanating from the Beijing Conference. The Platform for Action that emerged from this conference identified a diverse agenda of issues that need to be addressed for women to enjoy full human rights. They included alleviating women's poverty, enhancing women's economic options, ensuring fair access to education and training, combating negative stereotypes of women through the media, improving access to health services and putting in place strategies to end violence against women (UN, 1996).

While progress on these issues has been variable among countries, what is clear is that the work carried out by both international humanitarian and development organizations and transnational social movements is crucial to bringing about improvements in women's social and economic status. UNIFEM is one such organization that plays a primary role in drawing attention to women's issues and concerns. For example, UNIFEM played a key role in drawing attention to the links between human rights and women's vulnerability to contracting HIV/AIDS. As well as being more biologically, culturally, socially and economically vulnerable to HIV infection, women and adolescent girls are often the primary carers for family members and friends who are sick from AIDS-related illnesses (UNIFEM, 2003).

Accordingly, the work of UNIFEM demonstrated how HIV/AIDS is not just a health issue but also implicates gender relations and women's social position. Thus, organizations such as UNIFEM recognize the importance of developing a gender perspective on a range of social issues and raising community awareness of these issues.

Apart from agencies affiliated with the UN, a diverse range of international and regional networks has evolved to respond to women's issues and concerns. This has been described as 'globalization from below', and advances in Information and Communication Technologies (ICT) have played a large part in the transformation of the women's movement into a dynamic worldwide network that targets gender inequities:

> This allowed the global transmission of images that changed the consciousness of both women and men. Seeing women in new roles such as police officers, pilots, astronauts and doctors, or seeing women standing up to men in popular 'soaps', questioned conventional stereotypes and gendered divisions of labour. (Cohen and Kennedy, 2000, pp. 17–18)

Healy (2001) identifies several global women's networks that social workers have been involved with since their inception, including the Women's International League for Peace and Freedom and the International Congress of Women. She suggests that through working with such international organizations, much can be achieved that is not possible for social workers who confine their activities to the local level. However, we suggest that much can also be gained from working with women at a local grass-roots level. It is at this level that a communicative space can be easily created to hear women's concerns, and an added bonus is that such forums are not constrained by bureaucratic structures (Hawkesworth, 2006). In the following section, some other social work responses to women's issues at the global-local interface are considered.

Social work responses to women's issues at the global-local interface

If social workers wish to gain a comprehensive understanding of women's lives and issues, then they need to focus on linking 'the personal' to the economic and social dimensions of globalization and examine the situation of different women at the global-local interface. This framework is in fact consistent with the person-in-environment perspective commonly used in social work practice (Jones and Chandler, 2001). At a practice level, the benefits of interfacing the global with the local is that it enhances our understanding of women's situations and allows us to consider alternative options for action. Adopting a global perspective may help us understand why increasing numbers of women from poor countries are moving to countries such as Australia, the United Kingdom and the United States to work in the sex industry or take on poorly paid and unprotected domestic work. Additionally, it offers us a broader lens to examine issues such as the feminization of poverty and how global initiatives can be deployed in combating violence against women.

A global perspective allows us to explore how initiatives and strategies devised to address women's issues and problems in one part of the world may be effectively employed or modified to suit local conditions in other locations. For example, the idea of micro credit for women, originally implemented in Bangladesh through the Grameen Bank, has spread to some 52 countries (Lyons, 1999, pp. 98–9). This scheme allows women to take out small loans to finance initiatives to improve their economic position and living circumstances, which in turn has a positive flow-on effect to their families.

Similarly, the 'Women in Black' campaign, based on the philosophy of non-violence, was initially organized by Israeli and Palestinian women in 1988 to draw attention to Israel's occupation of the West Bank and Gaza. This form of 'silent protest' has since been adopted by women from all around the world to demonstrate solidarity, promote peace and draw attention to the multiple forms of violence suffered by women (Hawkesworth, 2006). In countries such as Australia, Argentina and Bosnia, social workers and others working in the areas of domestic violence, sexual assault and women's services have also taken up this form of symbolic action, with one notable campaign being 'Thursdays in Black'. In this instance, the wearing of black on Thursdays became symbolic of women's suffering through rape, sexual harassment and other forms of violence. This form of activism can be adapted to local circumstances while also promoting transnational alliances among women (Hawkesworth, 2006).

However, social workers also need to think beyond symbolic activism if, rather than just drawing attention to women's issues, they want to bring about real improvements in women's lives. In addition, if gender equality is to become a reality, then men must also be factored into the equation. Previously in this chapter, reference was made to the importance of promoting behavioural change in men. Around the world, a number of innovative programmes, including gender transformation workshops and media campaigns, have been introduced to change men's sexist, risk-taking and abusive behaviour. Such behaviours have negative ramifications for the health and welfare of women and in turn compromise their productivity. These programmes have been particularly successful in the areas of sexual and reproductive health, and to a lesser extent, reducing violence towards women (World Health Organization [WHO], 2007a). Some social workers are already actively involved in this form of transformational work with men and boys, and given the priority it is being given by global agencies such as the UN and WHO, potentially it is an area of practice that will assume greater importance in social work.

On a broader development level, Estes (1992) highlights the importance of adopting a gender analysis in social development. He points out that in the past, social and economic development programmes in developing countries have been primarily targeted at men and failed to consider a gender perspective. In other words, development initiatives impact men and women differently. Estes (1992), therefore, contends that social workers need to be cognizant of the gendered nature of development when engaging in this type of practice. For example, violence against women has been conceptualized as a 'development issue' because it undermines economic growth and social justice, limits women's participation and thwarts developmental goals and the realization of their human rights (Burton, Duvvury and Varia, 2000).

Another option open to social workers is to work through their existing professional associations to promote the advancement of women (Healy, 2001). For example, under the auspice of the International Association of Schools of Social Work (IASSW), social workers conducted a symposium on violence at the NGO forum that coincided with the 1995 UN Conference on Women in Beijing. Through the IASSW's official consultative status with the UN, the participants then put forward a range of recommendations for responding to violence against women and promoting women's economic and social development. It is noteworthy that 27 different countries were involved in this venture and that the social workers involved were able to strategically use the status of an international professional organization to put forward their proposals for ending violence against women (Healy, 2001, pp. 12–13).

Several writers in international social work promote the value of a human rights perspective in social work practice with women (Healy, 2001; Ife, 2008; Lyons, 1999). The task for social worker practitioners working within a rights framework is to expose and challenge human rights violations and other forms of systematic discrimination perpetrated against women. An equally important task is to assist women re-conceptualize human rights in accordance with local conditions and in their own language (Ife, 2008). Nonetheless, the concept of human rights has been subjected to critique on the basis that it represents a masculine construction of rights, while giving primacy to political and civil rights rather than economic and social rights (Hawkesworth, 2006). Alternatively, others see the imposition of a universal set of rights, which predominantly reflect Western values, as a form of cultural imperialism. Some Third World feminists also question the relevance of human rights when inadequate legal mechanisms are available for women to seek redress when their rights are violated, such as in the case of culturally endorsed violence (Jaggar, 2001).

Notwithstanding these criticisms, however, Jaggar (2001) points to the power that the slogan 'Women's rights are human rights' carries in the global arena. She also describes how feminists who are part of a broader transnational movement have rewritten and expanded the notion of human rights to reflect the reality of women's lives and living conditions around the world. Hence, the usefulness of employing a human rights discourse as a political tool to advance the interests of women should not be underestimated. In particular, Jaggar (2001, p. 213) claims that 'the movement for women's human rights reveals how women's equality is inseparable from other aspects of social progress' and constitutes a form of 'globalization from below'. The political utility of employing a human rights framework in social work is explored further in Chapter 9.

Lastly, we suggest that it is important for social workers to develop an awareness of representational practices that construct women in a negative light, especially when those representational practices deny women's agency, negate the creative ways that women make changes in their lives or over-emphasize their 'victim' status. Mohanty (1988, p. 22) points out how 'Third World' women in particular are often portrayed as religious, family oriented, domesticated and ignorant of their rights. She suggests that these sorts of caricatures of women are a continuation of the 'colonial gaze' and reinforce the notion that they are passive and dependent, while setting up a hierarchical relationship between 'Western' and 'non-Western' women. Social workers can be active in challenging such images or promoting more realistic portrayals of women that attest to their diversity, their agency and their potential.

Summary

In this chapter, we have demonstrated that while women's experiences of globalization have been diverse, there are commonalities among women, such as their social position, in relation to men and the greater level of responsibility they hold for domestic and care work. In addition, poor women tend to assume the most responsibility for coping with household poverty, and if poverty is to be eradicated then gender inequalities in the labour market need to be addressed. In order to improve women's economic status, the education of women and girls must remain a priority. Ending discrimination and working towards improving women's economic position, including bringing women into the paid-labour market, are key to alleviating global poverty. At the same time, addressing sociocultural beliefs that constrain the roles available to women is a prerequisite to women fully realizing their human rights and achieving gender equality. Countering negative images of women with more positive portrayals of their agency and potential is equally important in bringing about cultural change.

Supplementing the person-in-environment perspective with a global lens will assist social workers to gain a more comprehensive understanding of women's lives and concerns at the local level. Globally, violence against women, poverty and 'care work' have been long-standing concerns in social work. We suggest that along with the practical and support work that social workers routinely carry out with women affected by these issues, they can also be active as agents of cultural change. In particular, they can work with men and boys to promote positive behavioural change and assist men to take on more responsibility for care work. Working with local and global women's networks to bring about better conditions for women is a further option open to social workers.

Discussion points

1. How do you understand the feminization of poverty? Why do you think it is the case that it is often poor women who assume most responsibility for household poverty?
2. What are some practical ways that social workers can work with men and boys to promote positive behavioural change in relation to violence against women?
3. Globalization is believed to have enhanced opportunities for transnational activism to promote gender equality and women's rights. What opportunities exist at your local level for engaging in this type of practice?
4. Why does the 'global care chain' have the potential to lower the status of 'care work'? What do you think are some of the implications of this for social work?
5. How might you orchestrate a campaign to promote more positive images of women and girls that do not just signify their 'victim status'?

Chapter 6

Mental Health – an Emerging Global Health Issue

Introduction

Globalization has not only profoundly influenced the way we think about issues such as economics, poverty and migration but has also provided us with a new lens to look at contemporary health concerns. In this chapter we examine mental health in the context of globalization. Despite the fact that globalization and related processes such as migration, relocation and workforce restructuring have significant implications for people's mental health, this aspect of health has been a neglected topic within broader discussions and debates on global health. Mental health receives far less attention in both the international and national public health arenas than physical health, and this is especially the case in developing countries. Most of the world's health resources are directed at combating the high rates of morbidity and mortality arising from communicable and infectious diseases (Saxena et al., 2007). Yet rates of neuropsychiatric disorders are similarly high and mental health is inextricably linked with a range of other issues such as poverty and disability.

In the first section of this chapter we examine the nature and incidence of mental health disorders at a global level before examining how broader processes associated with globalization impact mental health. Next, we examine some particular issues facing low- and middle-income countries in responding to mental health problems because they have to contend with most of the global burden of mental illness. Following this discussion we highlight the emergence of the global mental health movement, which has arisen to challenge major inequities that exist between developed and developing countries in the provision of mental health services. In the final section, we examine some potential challenges and issues for social work that arise in relation to reconceptualizing mental health at the global-local interface and make some suggestions for how the profession may respond to these concerns.

The nature and incidence of mental health

Although an individualistic and biomedical model has traditionally dominated the field of mental health, global institutions such as the World Health

Organization (WHO) have long argued for a broader understanding of mental health that encompasses the notion of well-being. In this sense, mental health is integrally connected with how people realize their abilities, how they cope with day-to-day stresses, how they can lead productive and satisfying work lives and how they can contribute to their communities. Moreover, mental health cannot be separated out from physical health, while poverty, low levels of education and inequality are risk factors for mental health problems (WHO, 2008a). This broader conceptualization is in accord with social workers' understanding of mental health, which incorporates the 'biological, physical, psychological, material, social and structural' factors that shape people's lives (Heinonen and Metteri, 2005, p. 1). Such a holistic approach takes into account the social, cultural, political and economic factors that impact people's sense of physical and mental well-being.

How individuals themselves conceptualize mental health may depend on a variety of factors, including their cultural background, class, gender, material status, ethnicity, age, social location and relationship with the state (Swartz, 2008). In this sense, mental health is a dynamic concept. Furthermore, discourses surrounding mental illness are subjected to ongoing contestation and revision. This is, for example, reflected in the way that diagnoses are periodically updated in the American Psychiatric Association's *Diagnostic and Statistical Manual of Mental Disorders* (DSM), with new disorders appearing from time to time, some being revised and others being abandoned.

It has been suggested that the use of standardized Western classification systems such as the *DSM* have the potential to over-estimate the extent of mental illness, assigning people with diagnoses that have questionable application in some contexts. For example, over the past decade, mental health researchers have reported an increasing incidence of eating disorders such as anorexia nervosa and bulimia nervosa in countries as diverse as Iran, Egypt, South Korea, South Africa, Turkey and China (Edquist, 2008). This is despite the fact that these disorders were previously seen as culture-bound syndromes. Edquist (2008) argues that the spread of eating disorders has come about as a direct consequence of globalization and the introduction of a transnational mental disorder diagnostic code. In what follows, she describes how a range of actors are implicated in the increased diagnosis of eating disorders around the globe, especially in developing countries where the purported aim is to improve mental health:

Research scientists, states, nonstate advocates and pharmaceutical corporations, among others, in an increasingly broad array of world regions, find it medically, politically, and economically expedient or necessary to engage in the diagnosis and treatment of eating disorders as defined by that diagnostic code.

As a result, eating disorders currently are being diagnosed where once they were not. (Edquist, 2008, p. 376)

Regardless of the truth or otherwise of this statement, it is generally accepted that the incidence of mental illness is significant and under-reported in many countries. It is estimated that, globally, 450 million people experience mental health, neurological and substance abuse disorders, and these disorders account for 14 per cent of the world's total disease burden (Disease Control Priorities Project, 2006). Mental illness in turn is implicated in high rates of long-term disability. The five main neuropsychiatric illnesses associated with long-term disability are unipolar disorder, alcohol-use disorder, schizophrenia, bipolar disorder and dementia (Prince et al., 2007).

Contrary to the common perception that mental health problems are more prevalent in high-income countries, the majority of people with a mental illness live in poor countries. In low- to middle-income countries, the total burden of disease attributable to mental illness is 10 per cent (Pincock, 2007, p. 821). Apart from the personal suffering involved, mental illness has the potential to significantly compromise people's social and economic opportunities, and carers may equally face barriers in this respect. Yet over 75 per cent of people living with mental illness in developing countries receive no treatment or social care (WHO, 2008a).

Although it is difficult to obtain reliable data, WHO (2008a) estimates that one suicide-related death occurs every 40 minutes. Those most at risk come from low- to middle-income countries, and more than half of this population is aged 15 to 44 years. However, in regions such as South India, mental health researchers believe that the number of suicides per year is ten times higher than the official figures (Prince et al., 2007, pp. 859–60).

While the foregoing figures suggest that the numbers of people affected by mental illness are exceedingly high, a cautionary note is needed here as statistics on the incidence of mental illness are contested, and similarly the nature of mental illness itself has been called into question. How mental illness is depicted not only mirrors the political context and social conditions of the time but also reflects historically located psychiatric constructs and views of human suffering (Herman, 1992). WHO relies on standardized international classifications of neuropsychiatric disorders such as the International Classification of Diseases (ICD) and the *DSM*. There are a number of criticisms of these classificatory systems that predominantly relate to the narrow view of mental health adopted in these instruments and their purported universal applicability. Feminist researchers have also identified a gender bias in the *DSM*, claiming that some diagnoses pathologize what are otherwise normal reactions in many women (Astbury, 1996).

The transcultural psychiatry movement has attempted to address some of the perceived limitations of these classificatory systems by seeking to demonstrate how understandings of mental illness are context dependent. Those who subscribe to this frame of reference have sought to map different cultural understandings of mental illness across the world. Nonetheless, Swartz (2008, p. 307) proclaims that the traditional 'spatial metaphor' of 'one world, many cultures' is no longer applicable in a world where boundaries are constantly changing and identities are mutable rather than fixed. Moreover, she suggests that a comprehensive understanding of mental health must incorporate an understanding of how issues such as inequality, poverty and migration intersect with culture. For example, Swartz (2008, p. 305) describes how in South Africa, schizophrenia, a formerly stigmatizing label, has become 'a local asset' in some local contexts because it allows poor people to claim disability benefits which may then be used to support a whole family. Swartz (2008) claims that globalization has significantly challenged our understanding of the relationship between culture and mental illness. In the following section we outline some of the ways in which globalizing forces have reconfigured the contours of mental health.

Globalization and the socio-economic determinants of mental health

There is increasing interest in the socio-economic determinants of mental health and, more recently, recognition has been given to how processes associated with globalization are deeply implicated in the incidence and nature of mental health disorders (Dewe and Kompier, 2008; Manning and Patel, 2008). In 2005, WHO set up the Commission on the Social Determinants of Health, and it is noteworthy that this commission highlighted the impact of globalization on people's health, with particular reference to neoliberal economic policies, global trade, the migration of health professionals and the commodification of health care. Manning and Patel (2008, p. 299) further note that:

> Social processes associated with globalization, such as employment pressures, migration (including migration of health human resources), poverty, culture, and social change can be risk or protective factors for disorders such as suicide, substance abuse, antisocial behaviour, anxiety and depression.

While we do not assert a direct causal link between processes of globalization and mental illness, there is evidence to suggest that the stressors mentioned earlier impact significantly the mental health and well-being of people. In addition, globalization has direct implications for the provision of health and support services for people with mental health problems (Manning and Patel, 2008). As discussed in earlier chapters, neoliberal economic policies pursued by both national governments and supranational institutions such as the World Bank have seriously undermined the provision of public services in many countries, including health care. This lack of provision of adequate health care is particularly pronounced in developing countries. Some of these countries are also forced to spend a considerable amount of their GDP on repaying loans to wealthier nations or organizations such as the World Bank and, subsequently, have less money available for essential services such as health.

In Western countries that pursued neoliberal economic policy agendas during the 1980s and 1990s, government provision of social services and health was rationalized and funding was reduced for some health services. These policies had a severe impact on the quality of services available for those with mental health problems, as they closely followed on from the move to 'deinstitutionalize' people with chronic mental illness who had been previously accommodated in institutional settings. While policies aimed at community provision were put in place, the actual funding provided for community care was inadequate in many cases (Blakemore, 2003, pp. 204–21).

In Chapter 4, attention was focused on changing patterns of internal and external migration associated with economic globalization, and these too have implications for people's mental health. Many people are moving to cities from rural areas in search of work or migrating to new countries to take up employment opportunities. Psychosocial stressors associated with migration are well documented. They include social isolation, loss of family and community support structures, adjusting to a new culture and contending with settlement issues (McKenzie, 2008, p. 360). Although there is very little research on the mental health problems associated with internal migration in developing countries, increased levels of alienation, social isolation and substance abuse have been cited as key problems faced by migrating workers within many Asian countries. In China, for example, it is estimated that the incidence of mental illness among its 100-million internal migrants is twice as high as that of the rest of the Chinese population (Beech, 2003).

Along with migration, the rapid rate of urbanization in many developing countries, especially those exposed to increased industrialization, has been recognized as a risk factor for mental illness. Various studies report higher rates of mental illness such as psychotic disorders and substance abuse in urban areas, especially in densely populated and poorly serviced areas (see McKenzie, 2008). Rapid urbanization has led to major changes in the composition and density of populations in cities and rural areas, and these changes have occurred over a relatively short time frame. Poverty, substandard housing, insecure tenure, escalating crime, lack of social support and high rates of violence and accidents have also been linked to depression (McKenzie, 2008).

It is anticipated that expanding urbanization will be accompanied by an increase in mental illness due to numerous social and economic pressures, as well as factors arising from the physical environment such as crowding and competition for scarce resources. In many countries, existing social infrastructure and services will not be able to meet population demand and the growth of urban slums and shanty towns will place new strains on families and communities (UN Population Fund [UNFPA], 2007). Although it is difficult to predict the nature or extent of mental disorders associated with such changes, what is clear is that urbanization is likely to bring more people into contact with a range of risk factors for mental illness (McKenzie, 2008).

Globalization, employment, trade and mental health

The globalized economy has differential impacts on workers. As mentioned earlier in Chapter 2, though there has been an increase in work opportunities for people in a number of developing countries, there have also been significant restructuring and job losses in some developed countries. However, globally, many workers are experiencing stress related to job insecurity, changes to work conditions and benefits, the increasing casualization of labour, the shift to the informal sector and longer working hours (Corrigall et al., 2008; Dewe and Kompier, 2008). The International Labour Organization reports increasing rates of work-related stress among workers in all countries, and there are reports of a growing epidemic of work stress that has been partly fuelled by the threats posed by global trade to job security and work standards (Corrigall et al., 2008).

Existing research demonstrates clear links between employment, the work environment and mental health. Mental health problems associated with occupational stress include depression, chronic fatigue and alcohol abuse (Corrigall et al., 2008, p. 344.). In the United Kingdom, for example, workforce changes and employer demands for people to work longer hours have been linked with higher levels of absenteeism due to stress and mental health problems (Dewe and Kompier, 2008).

Changing work conditions have impacted women's mental health. In some regions of the world, increased rates of mental illness have been linked with working long hours, toxic work environments and engaging in low-skilled, repetitive labour. Such working conditions are particularly common in the informal sector, where many women are employed (Corrigall et al., 2008). Workers are aware that transnational companies will move to keep their production costs down, so they are more likely to put up with poor work conditions which have adverse effects on their mental and physical health. Over the past decade, we have also witnessed an increase in offshore outsourcing of service work and an expansion in the call centre sector. While the mental health implications of these developments are currently not well understood, some workers in call centres have reported sleep disturbances and heightened levels of stress (Rani, 2003).

In developed countries, research conducted on behalf of the Organization for Economic Cooperation and Development (OECD, 2006) reveals a high level of permanent unemployment arising from disability, which encompasses mental health disorders. Once people are put on disability pensions, significant structural and attitudinal barriers reduce their opportunities to re-enter the workforce. This has serious economic and social costs for individuals, their families and national economies. In the meantime, more Western welfare states have introduced compulsory welfare-to-work regimes for people with disabilities, which are designed to force people back into the workforce. People with a mental illness who have been out of the workforce often find it difficult to negotiate complex income maintenance systems, let alone those based on new compulsory employment conditions. In the United Kingdom, it has been claimed that mental health disorders are a greater burden on the national economy than poverty, and it has been estimated that one in six people will spend some of their working life on a disability pension (Layard, 2004). Consequently, increasing numbers of people with mental health problems are at risk of poverty, homelessness and social exclusion.

Another phenomenon associated with economic globalization has been the mass migration of mental health professionals, including psychiatrists, nurses and social workers, from developing countries to high-income countries. Many of these workers have been attracted by better wages and conditions in richer countries. However, this has created a crisis in human resources in poorer countries that are unable to train sufficient personnel for their own understaffed health services. This problem is particularly pronounced in sub-Saharan Africa and some Asian countries (WHO, 2006a). Arguably, there is a need for recruiting countries to develop recruitment policies that balance the right of health workers to relocate with the need to mitigate the drain of human capital from developing countries (OECD, 2007).

The contemporary global economic downturn has led to stagnation and slowing of growth in many national economies, with forecasts of massive job losses across the world. Several Western countries have experienced high rates of mortgage foreclosures and rapid growth in unemployment, and some commentators have predicted a greater demand for mental health services fuelled by job losses, home repossessions and debt (Corry, 2008). In newly industrializing countries, some of the groups who have been lifted out of poverty through employment will be displaced by a global economic recession. An economic downturn will increase food scarcity, poor nutrition and poverty, all factors that exacerbate mental health conditions (Corrigall et al., 2008). As countries use public funds to shore up their failing economies, they are likely to cut back on funds to public mental health services. Similarly, it is anticipated that private donors and Western governments will reduce levels of international aid. This will have serious consequences for developing countries, which rely heavily on local and international non-government organizations (NGOs) to provide mental health services.

Another important factor influencing mental health is global trade. We have argued previously in Chapter 3 that contemporary global trade relations, characterized by unbalanced 'free trade' arrangements, disadvantage many developing countries. In particular, farmers in poorer countries have been unable to benefit from the global trade system because of unfair tariffs and trade agreements. Small-scale farmers are under pressure to produce export crops instead of food, but cannot compete with heavily subsidized farmers and agribusinesses in the global North. Along with a lack of access to credit, this has led to hunger and famine in many regions, and countries such as India and China have seen a sharp rise in rates of suicide and depression among farmers (Corrigall et al., 2008). In Australia as well, farmers are reporting higher rates of depression which have been linked to a prolonged drought and market deregulation accompanying globalization (Alston, 2007).

Aggressive trade liberalization may also erode national governments' power to control the importation of substances that are hazardous to mental health, and the trade in alcohol is a case in point. There has been a rise in alcohol consumption in many emerging economies, and multinational companies have targeted the markets of developing countries for future growth and expansion, especially because many of these countries have large populations of young people (Corrigall et al., 2008). These companies have taken advantage of lax restrictions on alcohol promotion and control in developing countries, as well as limited public education about the effects of excessive drinking. This is of some concern given that developing countries have the highest rates of harmful drinking practices. The World Trade Organization (WTO) has ruled that domestic taxes on high alcohol products, designed to promote public health, must be removed if they 'harm' trade between countries. Accordingly, the individual concerns of nation states about levels of alcohol consumption and abuse are not permitted to outweigh the economic benefits of trade (Corrigall et al., 2008, pp. 342–4).

Globalization, conflict and mental health

There has been increasing awareness of the intersections between globalization, conflict and mental health. Piachaud (2008, p. 317) asserts that violent conflict was an integral part of colonization and, similarly, that 'violent conflict has played a central role in the emergence of globalization.' The borders of countries have become more permeable, and this has resulted in challenges to national sovereignty with ensuring conflicts within and between countries. Along with a spate of civil conflicts, more recently we have witnessed 'humanitarian' interventionist strategies initiated by international bodies such as the United Nations (UN), in conjunction with richer and more powerful countries, to resolve regional conflicts. Alternatively, some of these missions have focused on intervening in 'failing' states, which are justified on the grounds of the violation of human rights or a government's inability to protect its citizens in civil conflicts (Jaeger, 2007, pp. 264–5).

Violent conflict and war have long been associated with mental health problems, and mental health professionals have highlighted the needs of soldiers, displaced civilians, workers in NGOs and refugees when dealing with post-conflict situations and transitions to peace. There is growing awareness of the social and psychological needs of different groups in post-conflict situations, and the need to provide culturally appropriate psychosocial interventions that also promote community cohesion, peace building and justice (Piachaud, 2008).

In addition to conflict and war, terrorism may promote psychological and social distress in whole communities that are both directly and indirectly affected by such indiscriminate violence. For example, an international student from India made the following observation about the terrorist attacks on Mumbai in 2008:

> I have been deeply affected by the recent terrorist attacks in India. There is now a constant sense of insecurity and fear. I could see the difference in my parents and especially my younger sister this time. The day they were flying back there was high alert in New Delhi again. It makes me angry to see that 'it has become a way of life' and the attitude that 'life goes on'. People don't have a choice; that is why they go on. Whether it is Hindus or Muslims, the people who lose their loved ones are brothers, sisters, mothers, fathers etc. and those relationships hold similar meaning across cultures. ... The only thing that the government can do is to increase security ... but that makes me wonder whether that is the life people should be accustomed to ... constantly living under threat ... constant security checks. (Personal email correspondence from Aastha Malhotra, 19 January 2009)

The ongoing threat of terrorism poses new challenges for mental health professionals, including social workers, in terms of how to work not only with individuals but also with whole communities who may be affected by such events and who may fear further attacks. The impact of the threat of violence on people's mental health is difficult to determine, but some research carried out in Northern Ireland suggests that the key factor here is a person's perception of the risk of violence (Piachaud, 2008).

Given escalating civil conflicts, wars and natural disasters in many parts of the world, much discussion has been devoted to the impact of trauma on the people subjected to these events. In particular, post-traumatic stress disorder (PTSD) has become a prominent diagnosis linked to precipitating events such as war, torture, physical assault and sexual violence. For example, it has been estimated that 75 per cent of adults in Cambodia who survived the Khmer Rouge regime suffer from post-traumatic stress reactions (Beech, 2003). Nonetheless, the literature on psychological trauma has been subjected to criticism because it places too little emphasis on social, cultural, spiritual and environmental factors that contribute to variations in people's responses. As a diagnosis, PTSD has been further criticized for decontextualizing reactions to traumatic events and individualizing modes of intervention (Bracken, Giller and Summerfield, 1995).

Ideas about the resolution of trauma and recovery are culturally constructed, and individualized approaches to treatment are common in Western contexts. However, in other contexts the privatization and separation of trauma symptoms from their socio-political origins is thought to exacerbate trauma (Becker et al., 1990). Further, Becker and his associates stress the importance of social reparation for the victim, not only in terms of clarifying responsibility for what has happened but also in terms of providing a wider social endorsement of the victim's truth:

> ...traumatization is not a private affair, but a social reality. The victim knows that individual therapeutic intervention is not enough. They need to know that their society as a whole acknowledges what has happened to them. (Becker et al., 1990, p. 147)

In other words, the impact of the wider social environment is a key factor in recovery and, in some sociocultural contexts, the notion of individual recovery may be inappropriate when social reparation, collective responses or broader political solutions are called for. For some traumas affecting large populations such as war and community disasters, political responses are just as necessary as individual aid in terms of resolution of suffering. Moreover, there is greater recognition of the idea of collective trauma and how the cultural context of the precipitating event may in itself be an obstacle to recovery. As Quarantelli (1985) argues, it is the response of the environment rather than the actual event that determines the resolution of trauma. For instance, if relief efforts after a community disaster are poorly organized and involve an inequitable distribution of aid, a secondary disaster may be produced (Quarantelli, 1985, p. 196).

Communities with strong social ties may deal with trauma on a social and political level rather than an individual level (Bracken et al., 1995).

For example, Bracken and his associates refer to the experiences of women who were subjected to sexual violence in Uganda, where the sociocultural and political context determined the most appropriate interventions. For these women, organizing themselves into meeting groups that focused on developmental projects and the mending of social relations was more beneficial than specifically talking about their responses to being raped (Bracken et al., 1995, p. 1079). Accordingly, it is important to consider the importance of social institutions and cultural institutions in the resolution of trauma.

The 'treatment gap' and the emergence of the global mental health movement

In many low-income and middle-income countries, mental health services are characterized by severe shortages of health care workers and funds, inequitable access to services and inefficient use of available resources (Saxena et al., 2007). Effectively, this means that the majority of people suffering from mental illness in developing countries receive minimal or no treatment. This is commonly referred to as the 'treatment gap', and WHO (2008a) has more recently called on governments and donors to increase funding for basic mental health services to close this gap.

Globally, there are huge disparities in the availability and distribution of resources and health care staff for mental health care. While there is a worldwide shortage of mental health workers, this problem is particularly marked in South East Asia, Africa, East Mediterranean and Western Pacific regions. A shortfall in professional staff including psychiatrists, nurses and social workers is one of the primary barriers to providing treatment and care for people with mental illnesses in low- and middle-income countries (Saxena et al., 2007). For example, the median number of psychiatrists per 100,000 people in low-income countries is 0.05, compared to 10.5 in high-income countries. These disparities are also evident in social work, where the respective figures are 0.4 and 15.7 (WHO, 2005a, pp. 33, 39).

Whereas funding for mental health services in high-income countries tends to come from public taxation and social or voluntary insurance, more than 30% of low-income countries tend to rely on out-of-pocket payments as their chief source of funding for mental health services. Moreover, nearly a third of countries do not have a designated mental health budget, while in Africa and South East Asia the majority of countries allocate less than 1 per cent of their health budgets to mental health (Saxena et al., 2007). As a consequence, mental health services in many developing countries are struggling to meet existing needs, let alone cope with the projected social and economic 'fallout' arising from globalization.

Lack of access to affordable and effective medicine is another factor that constrains the treatment of mental illness in developing countries. The use of Trade-Related Aspects of Intellectual Property Rights (TRIPS) by pharmaceutical companies has restricted the production and sale of psychotropic medicine to those suffering from mental illness (Corrigall et al., 2008). It is estimated that 25 per cent of low-income countries have no access even to basic antidepressive medicines (Saxena et al., 2007). Drug companies have used regional and bilateral trade rules to prevent licensing of cheaper versions of new psychotropic drugs (Corrigall et al., 2008). If drugs are the treatment of choice for alleviating the suffering and unpleasant symptoms of mental illness, there are obvious human rights concerns when people cannot afford them. Some have suggested that a similar campaign to that mounted by HIV/AIDS activists is needed so that people in poor countries, especially those with severe psychiatric disorders, can access inexpensive medicines.

In recent years, a new movement for global mental health comprising researchers, practitioners, civil society and global health organizations has begun to challenge the low profile and lack of resources allocated to mental health, especially in developing countries. Research on the prevalence of mental illness has helped to dispel the myth that mental illness is predominantly a Western phenomenon. Vikram Patel, an Indian-born British-trained psychiatrist, has written about his misconceptions of mental illness when he went to practise in Zimbabwe. In what follows, he relates how he came to appreciate that mental illnesses such as depression – caused predominantly by social factors – were a significant problem in developing countries:

> I went in there highly sceptical that mental illnesses like depression were valid diagnostic categories of suffering in a place like Zimbabwe. ... I set out to prove myself, but left convinced I had been wrong. (Pincock, 2007, p. 821)

Patel observed that while people may present with different symptoms and use their own concepts to describe their experiences, their conditions were in fact similar to those reported in developed countries. He has since become a leading proponent of the new global mental health movement, which aims to raise awareness of the prevalence of mental illness in developing countries and its links to poverty and social disadvantage, along with the treatment gap in mental health service provision. He is a strong advocate of local treatment programmes that rely on lay health workers and are not dependent on specialist clinical services like those that exist in the West. In resource-poor countries, involving community health care workers in mental health service provision has proven to be both effective and affordable (Patel, 2008).

The stigma associated with mental illness is a major barrier to the adequate provision of resources to mental health services around the world. As Sartorius (2007, p. 810) points out, 'Stigma makes community and health decision-makers see people with mental illness with low regard, resulting in reluctance to invest resources into mental health care.' At the same time, stigma promotes discrimination in service delivery and is implicated in the under-diagnosis of many mental illnesses. Its effects are perhaps more pronounced in low- and middle-income countries because of the limited amounts of funding available to meet health care needs. The bulk of countries in Africa and Southeast Asia allocate less than 1 per cent of their health budgets for mental health, and a third of countries around the world make no provision for mental health services (Saxena et al., 2007, p. 881).

In China, for example, while mental illness accounts for 20 per cent of the country's burden of illness, only 2 per cent of the health budget is set aside for mental heath services (Beech, 2003). Consequently, treatment options are limited, and this problem is compounded by a lack of free public health facilities, the high cost of medication and limited knowledge of mental illness among many health professionals, especially in rural areas. In addition, the government views mental health as predominantly a law and order issue rather than a health issue, and this view is mirrored in other parts of East Asia (Beech, 2003).

A major priority of the global mental health movement is to tackle the stigma and discrimination associated with mental illness, as this acts as a strong disincentive to people seeking help and treatment. For example, a survey conducted in South Africa demonstrated that many people associate mental illness with stress or a lack of will power rather than medical causation (Saxena et al., 2007). In China and India, studies have revealed that many families were ashamed of members with schizophrenia and hid the condition for fear of losing face in the community (Saxena et al., 2007). Nonetheless, even when individuals or families do seek help, treatment options may be inappropriate. Evidence suggests that a mix of both community-based and hospital-based services provide the best outcomes for people with a mental illness (Saxena et al., 2007). However, Beech (2003) notes that in some poorer Asian countries such as Pakistan and Indonesia, limited therapeutic or drug treatment is available and many people are locked up in hospitals no better than prisons. Such institutions are often overcrowded and function mainly as places of confinement, where patients may be subjected to a wide range of human rights abuses (WHO, 2005b).

WHO (2004) predicts that mental illness will be the leading cause of disability by 2020, pointing to an urgent need to invest resources and develop specific policies on mental health in those countries that currently afford it a low priority. It is estimated that 40 per cent of countries have no policies specifically dedicated to mental health (WHO, 2005b). Consequently, there are no minimum standards of treatment or institutional mechanisms to monitor or seek redress for human rights abuses experienced by people with a mental illness. Even though many Western countries have established mental health policies in addition to public health campaigns and strong consumer advocate movements, human rights abuses still occur in these countries. Indigenous and minority groups are particularly at risk of such abuses, and discrimination against ethnic, religious and linguistic minorities is a salient factor in the poor mental health status of these groups (WHO, 2007b).

The preceding discussion has highlighted the politics of mental health service provision both locally and globally, and in particular how the treatment gap has resulted in many people in low- and middle-income countries being unable to access appropriate mental health services. This poses significant challenges for health professionals, including social workers, and it has been suggested that there is both a 'moral and ethical case for redressing the imbalance in provision for people with mental disorders' (Prince et al., 2007, p. 871). It is also clear that mental health problems affect not only the individuals involved but also their families and carers, as well as having implications for people's employment, income and housing. In the following section, we explore some of these challenges in the context of social work.

Emerging issues for social workers in a context of global mental health

In some countries, mental health has evolved into a specialist field of social work practice where workers need to complete additional training to practise in mental health services. However, it is likely that most if not all social workers work with people with mental health problems and substance abuse issues in a broad range of settings. This is especially the case in those countries where community care is a key feature of mental health service provision. In addition, mental health intersects with a range of broader health and welfare issues such as child protection, domestic violence, housing and income security (Bland and Renouf, 2006).

On one level, social workers are well equipped to work with mental health issues at the global-local interface because of their capacity for thinking beyond narrow biomedical models of illness and incorporating understandings of how material, structural and social factors are implicated in mental illness. Social workers recognize that poverty and related stressors such as unemployment and social exclusion can promote mental illness and are equally aware of the barriers faced by people with mental health problems in gaining productive employment. This situation arises not only because people who are unwell find it difficult to work but also because of the societal stigma surrounding mental illness that pervades many workplaces.

On a broader political level, tackling global health inequalities has been identified as a challenge for social workers, and to this end a Social Work and Health Inequalities Network was formed in 2004 (Bywaters, 2009). The International Federation of Social Workers (IFSW) is similarly a strong advocate of health equality, and their policy statement on health makes explicit reference to the equal right of all people 'to enjoy basic conditions which underpin health' and 'to access resources and services that promote health and address illness, injury and impairment, including social services' (IFSW, 2008b). In this sense, the IFSW sees health as interlinked with human rights and social justice, while also acknowledging the broader context of globalization in which health inequalities arise, with explicit reference to neoliberal economics, privatization of health services, unfair trade practices, environmental destruction and violent conflict:

> International political and financial institutions and corporations impact on the standards of living of billions of people. Current patterns of economic growth are affecting the climate, the quality and availability of food, water and clean air, and the safety of people's homes and livelihoods throughout the world. Warfare and political conflict spirals out across national boundaries. Globalisation also directly affects the experience of living with illness. International companies control pharmaceutical treatments, medical equipment, hospitals and care facilities. Governments trade expenditure on their population's health care against competing priorities. (IFSW, 2008b)

WHO have popularized the slogan that there is 'no health without mental health', and on that level we suggest the opportunity exists for social workers to join with the new mental health movement that is working towards greater global distributive justice for people with a mental illness. In particular, there is a need to support initiatives that seek to address the stigma surrounding mental illness, raise the profile of mental health, improve access to good-quality treatment and care and strengthen the mental health workforce. The latter issue is of considerable concern given that WHO (2006a) has estimated a global shortage of over 4 million health workers, with poorer countries in Asia and Africa contending with severely depleted workforces. Many Western countries have actively recruited mental health professionals – including social workers – from these countries to meet the shortfall in their own workforces. At a national level, there is a need for both professional and government bodies to work on addressing their workforce and human capital needs, which has been an area prioritized by the new mental health movement.

The treatment gap for mental health service provision is not only evident in resource-poor countries in the global South, but also in many Western nations, albeit in a different form. In many of these countries, deinstitutionalization has seen policies aimed at community provision put in place, where the costs of care traditionally borne by the government have been transferred to the community. In some locations these policies have actually increased homelessness and the social exclusion of people with a mental illness (Prior, 2007). While at a practical level social workers may provide support and coordinate care for people with a mental illness living in the community, on a broader level they also need to challenge the policies and priorities of governments with respect to the resources available to this group.

Ideas about the treatment and nature of mental illness have changed considerably over the past 30 years. Critical traditions within psychiatry and feminism that have revealed material and social status inequalities between different groups have informed social work knowledge and practice interventions, in turn making them more culturally and gender appropriate. These traditions have encouraged social workers to recognize the social context of and social causes underlying mental illness where 'disadvantage and despair can go hand in hand' (Sheppard, 2002, p. 794). In addition, there has been greater recognition given to the resilience of people living with a mental illness, the opportunity for recovery and the importance of involving families and carers in treatment plans (Bland and Renouf, 2006).

In order to understand people's experiences of mental illness and determine appropriate interventions, it is important to afford the social, political and cultural realities of people's lives a central place in the conceptualization of mental health. Across Europe, North America, Australia and New Zealand, a robust mental health consumer advocacy movement and service user groups have been successful in raising concerns about treatment options and promoting positive images of people with a mental illness. Social workers have worked closely with service user and advocacy groups in promoting their views about appropriate service provision, and their perspectives have also informed research agendas and social work education (Bland and Renouf, 2006). These initiatives have been equally important in reducing the stigma associated with mental illness, and it is important that such partnerships continue to be given priority in social work.

The preceding discussion has demonstrated how people with mental health problems may be marginalized within the global economy. Mental health has concrete links with poverty, and rather than just focusing on ameliorating the psychosocial stress associated with material poverty, social workers need to be proactive in community and economic development initiatives which are equally important in safeguarding and restoring people's mental health. In this regard, WHO (2008a, p. 6) has similarly highlighted the importance of introducing community initiatives that aim to promote economic independence, raise literacy and educational standards and improve the status of women.

Social workers need to be cognizant of the changing nature of work and its impacts on people's mental health. As highlighted earlier in this chapter, there has been an increase in work-related occupational stress, anxiety and depression. Predictably, the contemporary global economic downturn will result in many more people seeking assistance from government and community agencies as people come to terms with the sudden loss of employment, income and housing. Some have predicted an increase in mental health problems and substance abuse among this population. While it is important for social workers to respond to the practical and support needs of this group, it is equally important to consider what contribution social work can make to broader policy debates about nation states' policy responses to this crisis.

In an era of changing patterns of migration and the displacement of people through war and environmental disasters, innovative forms of mental health practice are emerging. Transcultural mental health services have been established in some countries to assist new migrants access culturally appropriate services. In some instances, there may be a need to supplement therapeutic modes of intervention with community work when working with displaced populations (Whelan et al., 2002). This may include assisting these groups to build new support networks and learn new life skills. In other contexts, it may be appropriate to use Western models of psychiatric care in conjunction with indigenous forms of care that also recognize people's spiritual beliefs (WHO, 2007b).

Finally, we suggest that it is important that social workers work within a framework of human rights to ensure equitable access to services and medications for people with mental illness. Social workers can also work in coalition with human rights bodies and professional organizations to highlight violations of human rights in mental health systems. It is still, unfortunately, the case that such abuses occur on a routine basis in most countries (Saxena et al., 2007). Human rights discourses equally offer powerful moral arguments for addressing the treatment gap in mental health service provision and, in that sense, can serve as tools for political action.

Summary

In this chapter we have examined the nature and incidence of mental illness and highlighted how, compared to physical health, mental health is a marginalized issue in broader discussions and debates on global health. Globalization has significant implications for people's mental health, while also offering us a new lens to examine the treatment gap in mental health service provision and related concerns regarding distributive justice. This treatment gap, characterized by a lack of health care personnel, inequitable access to services and inefficient use of existing resources, is particularly pronounced in low- and middle-income countries. The low priority given to mental health by these countries is largely due to the stigma attached to mental illness, and in recognition of this a new global mental health movement has been formed to raise the profile of mental health and close the treatment gap.

Mental health is a well-established area of social work practice, and the personal, social and economic costs of mental illness to individuals, families and communities are well recognized. Social workers have incorporated progressive modes of intervention based on concepts such as resilience and recovery into their practice, as well as working with service user groups to improve service delivery and education. The opportunity also exists for social workers to join with the new global health movement to promote and protect the rights of people with mental illness.

Discussion points

1. What social processes associated with globalization are believed to impact people's well-being and mental health?
2. Do you agree with the proposition that mental illness is culturally specific? What might be some of the potential problems and issues associated with a lack of recognition of a mental illness such as depression?
3. In what situations may 'collective trauma' arise? What methods of practice might be important in working with people who are affected by this form of trauma?
4. Why is the stigma attached to mental health such an important issue in both developed and developing countries in terms of accessing treatment? What role can social workers play in combating the stigma and discrimination associated with mental illness?
5. What is meant by the term the 'treatment gap' in mental health? How can social workers play a role in raising the profile of mental health and addressing this treatment gap?

Chapter 7

Information and Communication Technologies and Social Work in a Global World

Introduction

In this chapter, we foreground some recent trends in the proliferation of information and communication technologies (ICTs) that have greatly enhanced the global flow of information, ideas and imagery. These technologies have radically compressed time and space. They have allowed us not only to learn more about what is happening in the world at large but also to link up with a range of individuals, groups and organizations around the globe. Hence, the global human network occupies a much smaller space and it is argued that we now live in 'a connected age'. Essentially, these developments have made instantaneous communication possible between all parts of the globe. Giddens (2002b) calls this the communications revolution, a term which is suggestive of its power to transform people's lives in radical ways and change the course of history. These new forms of technology – characterized by high-speed data transfer and multimedia capabilities – such as the Internet, wireless laptops and mobile phones have similarly had diverse impacts on the social life and work environment of social workers.

For others, however, access to these new forms of technology has been more limited, and considerable debate has ensued on the relevance and benefits of ICTs for social development in poorer countries. While there is a high penetration of ICTs in Europe and North America along with some Asian and Latin American countries, the spread in Africa is limited. As a result, much of the literature about ICT – including that written by social workers – has been generated in the West. Accordingly, the following discussion reflects a noticeable Western bias. Nonetheless, there is an emerging body of literature on innovative forms of practice using ICT in sub-Saharan Africa, India and South America, which we selectively draw on in this chapter.

In the first part of the chapter, we explore the nature and uses of ICTs in people's everyday lives, before moving on to examine their unequal global distribution. Following on from this discussion, we examine how ICTs have been employed in social work. For some social workers, ICTs present new and exciting opportunities for developing innovative forms of practice. For others, however, these technologies are perceived as serious threats to the autonomy of the profession. In particular, there are concerns that ICTs are being appropriated for managerial and organizational imperatives rather than for the benefit of practitioners and their clients. In recognition of these concerns, we present some of the major critiques of the use of ICTs in social work. In the last part of the chapter, we examine the potential of these new technologies to promote social change and social justice at local and global levels before briefly considering issues concerning representational practices and identity construction on the Internet. It is suggested that these issues are relevant to social work because, as a discipline, social work has a long-standing interest in identity construction and the portrayal of difference.

ICT and everyday life

For those of us who live in the 'connected' world, ICT has been implicated in shaping the political, cultural, work and social realms of our everyday lives. New forms of ICT, such as the Internet, have allowed us to communicate instantaneously around the world, altered our sense of time and space and contributed to a heightened sense of global connectedness. Castells (2004) uses the term 'networked society' to describe the new social structure that has emerged with these technologies. Over the past 20 years, the Internet, mobile phones and satellite technology have become commonplace in business (e-commerce), education, defence, travel, security, entertainment and leisure. In our personal, social and work lives, many of us have become accustomed to downloading music and videos, doing Internet banking, joining online discussion forums, watching live video streaming, using electronic databases and surfing the Web. These practices have become increasingly embedded in our everyday lives. They have also brought about dramatic changes in the workplace, including the human services, and in some parts of the world have radically changed the nature of service delivery in social work. Moreover, these new technologies are constantly evolving and throwing up new challenges for the social work profession.

More recently, the Internet has moved into a significantly different phase of development characterized by a set of highly interactive tools. Some of the features of Web 2.0 technologies – such as podcasts, wikis, blogging, online multi-player games and social e-networks – are becoming common applications for those using the Internet. They are attractive to a new generation of social workers who see the potential to incorporate them into practice (Schembri, 2008). In contrast to the linear functionality of the early World Wide Web (Web 1.0), Web 2.0 is deemed to be a 'people-centric Web' that 'encourages a more human approach to interactivity on the Web, better supports group interaction and fosters a greater sense of community in a potentially "cold" social environment' (Boulos and Wheeler, 2007, p. 3).

The emergence of these new technologies means that we need to broaden our understanding of ICT. Many existing definitions are narrow and over-emphasize their technological features. For example, the European Commission writes that ICT is 'currently used to denote a wide range of *services, applications* and *technologies,* using various types of *equipment* and *software,* often running over telecom [landline] *networks*' (European Commission, 2001, p. 3). However, this definition does not take into account the ways in which human beings interact with technology. We argue that technology is inherently 'social'. In other words, the way people interact with ICT helps to shape it. A good example here is an experiment conducted with illiterate children living in slums and rural villages across India who, prior to the study, had not used a computer. The children were given access to a computer via a 'hole in the wall', and a webcam was placed above it so that the children's reactions could be monitored. Without any assistance, over the course of the next few days the children learnt to surf the Internet, download games and use the drawing program. In addition, they learnt how to copy text and save it as a file. Perhaps even more remarkably, the children established their own rules around turn taking and developed their own social etiquette for using the computer. The hole-in-the-wall project has since spread to South Africa, Venezuela and Cambodia (Veldhoen, 2007).

The study mentioned earlier clearly demonstrates how social interaction is a key factor in the use of ICT. People construct identities in cyberspace, live second lives on the Web and relate to virtual communities. Other new interactive technologies such as biometrics allow for the automatic recognition of people via techniques such as digital fingerprinting or iris scanning. These technologies have bodily consequences in that they produce subjects who can be easily monitored by the state (Kruger, Magnet and Van Loon, 2008). In the United States, for example, welfare claimants must now agree to be biometrically fingerprinted as a condition of receiving benefits and consequently have been 'moved out of the hands of social workers and into the scientized practices of biometric identification' (Kruger, Magnet and Van Loon, 2008, p. 114). In a similar vein, new genetic engineering technologies converge with ICTs because they are 'able to reprogram the communication networks of living human matter' (Castells, 2004, p. 7). These examples reflect the intricate ways in which ICTs have infiltrated every aspect of human life, which has implications for social work practice not only in existing domains but also in new arenas such as health and bioethics.

It is important to remember that computers and the Internet are only one aspect of the modern communications revolution. According to Giddens (2001), one of the most important features of modern communication has been the rapid expansion of the mass media, and television in particular. The mass media has played a major role in the globalization of ideas, cinema, the music industry and popular culture, with global media events such as concerts and sport generating huge audiences. Ahmadi (2003, p. 17) suggests that advances in ICT have been a significant factor in promoting a 'globalization of consciousness' whereby the Internet, television and overseas travel have radically altered people's consciousness of lifestyles and events in other parts of the world. As a result, people are more acutely aware of lifestyles attainable in other parts of the world, as well as the huge economic inequalities that exist both within and between countries.

While ICT is seen to be a driving force behind social change, not everyone has benefited from the digital revolution. Indeed, major inequalities exist in access to ICTs at the global level, and concerns have been expressed that we now live in a world made up of the 'connected' and those who remain outside the loop and fail to reap the benefits of this connectivity. This is commonly referred to as the digital divide, and one of the main concerns expressed about digital inequality is that it will exacerbate and reproduce existing socio-economic disparities on both a global and local level. In the following section we examine this phenomenon in more detail.

ICT and the digital divide

The International Telecommunications Union (ITU) estimates that in 2007 there were over 1.3 billion Internet users in the world (ITU, 2007a). However, with several exceptions, the majority of these users come from high-income countries. The top ten countries in Internet usage are China, the United States, Japan, India, Germany, Brazil, the United Kingdom, France, South Korea and Italy (Miniwatts Marketing Group, 2008). In 2005, one in every two people residing in G8 nations used the Internet. In stark contrast, in the same year, only 4 per cent of people living in Africa were able to log on. Nonetheless, these disparities do not only apply to the Internet. It has been estimated that worldwide, 30 per cent of all villages have no access to a telephone (ITU, 2007b).

The United Nations (UN) has conducted a number of world summits on global social problems that are seen to require urgent attention, and in 2003 and 2005 two world summits were devoted to the digital divide. Uneven access to digital technology has only been framed as a social problem, first, due to the advent of this technology, and second, due to the attribution of a particular meaning to this technology whereby 'ICT is conceived as a means for both progress and justice' (Drori, 2007, p. 311). Apart from the risks associated with being left behind by the information society, lack of access to ICTs has major social and economic consequences for developing countries. Overcoming these access problems is seen to be a necessary step to achieving the Millennium Development Goals (ITU, 2008).

Good communications infrastructure, including a reliable and extensive telephone system, facilitates economic growth by reducing the cost of financial transactions, expanding markets and dramatically increasing information flows. Historically, countries and regions without fixed-line infrastructure have been highly disadvantaged in the global market place, and this problem has been particularly pronounced in Africa (ITU, 2008). However, newer mobile technologies may be about to change all this. Until recently, Internet access was totally dependent on fixed telephone land lines. Now, this is starting to change with advances in wireless technology and the increasing uptake of mobile phones. Wireless technology provides cheap, accessible and user-friendly technology, and the use of mobile phones in Africa is growing at twice the global rate (ITU, 2008). Moreover, some writers argue that these new wireless technologies will promote major foreign investment and economic growth in developing countries (Arthur, 2008; Sinha, 2005; Steinmueller, 2001).

Mobile phones provide a cheap and convenient means of banking and transferring money in many developing countries (Arthur, 2008). The potential of 'm-commerce' is continually expanding in these countries, enabling new forms of social enterprise and transforming the way business is conducted. Fisherman, farmers and small business operators are using mobiles to check the prices of goods and find out information about markets. They are able to locate new markets directly, bypassing intermediaries, which potentially allow them to expand their profits. In some remote areas, mobile phones are also being used to access health care and emergency services (Dholakia and Kshetri, 2001; Wray and Mayet, 2007). While on their own these technologies will not solve deep social and economic inequalities, they do play a part in enhancing the communicative power and economic literacy of very poor and disadvantaged communities.

Digital inequality does not lend itself to simplistic dichotomous representations where the developed world is equated with connectivity and the developing world with no or limited access to ICT. Various forms of digital inequality exist in developed nations and impact different groups. Lack of access to ICTs is not just a problem that affects minorities or disadvantaged groups. Instead, it is a problem that 'transcends all cultural boundaries to include everyone with limited access or command of technology' and includes 'rich people, poor people, older people, illiterate people, physically challenged people, educated people, and people without access to computers or bandwidth' (Pariso, 2005).

Consequently, the digital divide needs to be understood as a multidimensional issue rather than simply a lack of access to digital resources and technology (Norris, 2001). Regardless of socio-economic status, age, gender, culture or disability, a range of different factors impact the usage of computer technology. These include limited or no access to computers, a lack of digital skills or experience and a lack of significant usage opportunities (Van Dijk, 1999 – cited in Van Dijk and Hacker, 2003, pp. 315–16). Clearly then, the digital divide needs to be conceptualized in terms of its social and political dimensions, rather than just being understood as a technological problem requiring improved access to digital communication technologies.

Being excluded from the world of information technology and telecommunications is a critical issue for those living in locations where these technologies are deeply embedded in the culture, work practices, health systems, education and business transactions of everyday life. Information inclusion is increasingly being seen as a human right and a prerequisite for effective citizenship (McIver, 2004) In this regard, some writers suggest that social workers need to act as 'information intermediaries', to help people gain access to the Internet and assist them to negotiate electronic service delivery (Geoghegan, Lever and McGimpsey, 2004). While this is one example of how the role of social workers has been envisaged in the digital age, there is a growing body of literature emanating from Europe, North America and the Asia-Pacific region that points to many points of intersection between social work practice and ICT. In the following section, we chart this emerging terrain.

ICT and social work practice

Over the past two decades there has been increased interest in how technology may be used to enhance social work education and practice. In a European context, the adoption of ICT in social work has been conceptualized in terms of three distinct technological waves. The first wave focused on the administrative functions of ICT, such as word processing and developing data bases of client records. The second wave saw the development of practice interventions using the Internet, along with the use of sophisticated information and data management systems and email communication (Cwikel and Cnann, 1991). The third wave focused on the use of ICT in education, research and advocacy and also saw the evolution of practice interventions such as online therapy and support groups for clients (McCleary, 2007).

In line with our previous discussion, we suggest that we have now entered a fourth wave of ICT in social work, where new technologies are so deeply embedded in our social life and workplaces that we can no longer avoid using them. Moreover, the opportunity is now available to social workers to take advantage of the new interactive forms of technology mentioned earlier in this chapter to promote participation, mutual support and social activism (Schembri, 2008). A cursory review of the literature would suggest that in addition to well-established modes of technologically assisted service delivery, such as telephone counselling, social workers are also using email, videoconferencing, online counselling, chat facilities, social e-networks and websites to reach vulnerable or isolated client groups.

In this digital age, it is clearly desirable for all social workers to be computer literate. In some countries, social work graduates are now required to develop computer literacy skills as part of their professional training. In contemporary social work education, a range of e-learning and teaching tools such as Blackboard, WebCT, videoconferencing, podcasting and bulletin boards are now used to facilitate student learning. Practitioners, researchers and policy makers make extensive use of the Internet to access information and network with colleagues around the world. It is increasingly common for social workers (and social work students) to set up websites, which encourage professional exchange and social networking, as well as posting information about employment opportunities. In addition, both national and international professional social work bodies maintain websites and use ICT for ongoing professional educational development and training.

Like many other professionals, social workers use the Internet for social research. The Internet enables researchers to publish their research findings quickly and reach a broader audience. Social work researchers use a range of tools and methods to collect primary data, including online surveys, password-protected websites, chat forums and email interviews. Some researchers also use existing data from interactive sites such as multi-user domains or listservs to mine secondary data for research. There are particular ethical issues and challenges associated with online research, which are different to those experienced in face-to-face situations, and extensive guidelines have been developed to guide ethical practice in conducting online research (Melville, 2007a). On the other hand, there are a number of advantages of conducting research online. It is possible to access groups that are less likely to participate in conventional forms of research that involve face-to-face contact, such as people living with mental illness, young people, those with limited mobility and carers. Online research is similarly advantageous for recruiting participants living in rural and remote areas.

Similarly in counselling, some people prefer the anonymity, privacy and ease of access of e-therapy. In particular, young people appear to feel more at ease in an online counselling environment, and research indicates that this group appears to appreciate the lack of face-to-face contact that this medium affords them (King et al., 2006). One innovative, online, interactive service developed for children and young people in the United Kingdom by the National Society for the Prevention of Cruelty to Children (NSPCC) is called There4Me. This service provides text-based information, a message board and an 'Agony Aunt' real-time chat resource and is staffed by social workers and social work trainees (Waldman and Rafferty, 2006). Other practitioners are experimenting with games, 3D simulations and dedicated websites to create alternative counselling contexts.

While group work is a well-established medium used by social workers and human service workers, more recently a wide range of online support groups have been established for people experiencing health-related or emotional problems. While some of these online groups operate as self-help groups, others have been initiated by health professionals and those working in the human services. One example of such a group is an online support chat group developed for single mothers in Canada, which proved to be successful for two reasons: first, it offered anonymity to the women in the group, and second, it gave them an opportunity to connect with others in similar circumstances. The participants were also provided with computers, Internet access and technical support, which addressed potential access issues faced by these women (Miller, 2006).

A range of government and non-government organizations (NGOs) also provide dedicated websites and free phone numbers for people to call and talk to a counsellor online. Many of these websites are interactive and people can now access services and not simply information. In the United Kingdom, a new initiative, CareZone, has been developed in consultation with children who have been subjected to numerous moves in the public care system to provide them with secure online space to digitally store personal mementos such as letters and photos (Parrott and Madoc-Jones, 2008). Other writers have urged social workers to further explore how the communicative potential of new technologies may be employed in the interests of clients, such as making Web-based records available to service users (Tregeagle and Darcy, 2008).

Most forms of online practice intervention supplement rather than replace face to face. As more social workers use new technologies, professional bodies in a range of countries have worked towards defining ethical guidelines for social workers using the Internet for practice interventions. At the same time, some social work educators have suggested that the growing popularity of e-provision means that we need to 'rethink the way communication skills are taught to students' (Waldman and Rafferty, 2006, p. 127). Other writers have floated the possibility of the development of a social work informatics specialty, similar to that which exists in nursing to support practice and inform decision making (Parker-Oliver and Demiris, 2006).

The potential of ICTs for assisting with disaster relief and recovery has also been a prominent theme in the literature. In 2005, the Asia-Pacific branch of the International Federation of Social Workers (IFSW) in conjunction with the Commonwealth Organization for Social Work (COSW) set up a project called Families and Survivors of Tsunami (FAST) to support recovery efforts in the aftermath of the Indian Ocean tsunami disaster. Part of their work included setting up a website to raise awareness of the project, share ideas and enlist support for their relief work (Tan, Rowlands and Hall, 2007). In this sense, the potential of ICTs for facilitating community development is also evident.

The previous discussion suggests that many social workers have an optimistic view of the potential of ICTs to serve the interests of both clients and practitioners. However, others are less keen to tap into this potential, claiming that face-to-face work constitutes the heart of social work and that using technologically assisted interventions are not in the best interests of clients. Dunlop (2006), however, wryly notes that most resistance to using ICTs in practice might in fact come from social workers rather than clients, and in the next section we examine this resistance.

A critical view of ICT and social work practice

Many social workers appear to have adopted an ambivalent and sceptical attitude towards the use of ICT in their work. Finn and Holden (2000, p. 1) suggest that such ambivalence stems from concerns regarding 'loss of personal contact, use of unproven services, erosion of personal privacy, potentially negative outcomes for both children and adults, channelling of limited funds for technology, and lack of access for already disenfranchised consumer groups'. In the following discussion, we consider this resistance to using technology-based practice in social work in terms of broader discourses surrounding technology per se, as these discourses frame the way ICTs are viewed and in turn used in social work. We then examine more specific criticisms of the use of ICTs in social work.

Two major schools of thought have emerged to explain the history and role of technology in society. They are commonly referred to as the *technological determinism* and *social shaping of technology* (SST) approaches. There are variations within each school, so our discussion is limited to their main points of difference. Put simply, the 'technological determinism view holds that technology is autonomous with respect to society; it shapes society, but it is not reciprocally shaped by society' (Mackay and Gillespie, 1992, p. 686). On the other hand, the social shaping approach emphasizes the role played by social, political and economic factors in determining what technology is designed in the first instance and how humans use it (Mackay and Gillespie, 1992, p. 686). According to this perspective, people determine the shape, priority and use of technology.

We can see a similar dichotomy in viewpoints held about the use of ICT. Cyber utopians, or cyber optimists, tend to emphasize the utopian or liberating role of technology to enhance social networking and promote social change, democracy, economic growth and equality (Bellamy and Taylor, 1998; Norris, 2001). On the other hand, the cyber dystopians tend to focus on the social control aspects of ICTs, such as surveillance, data mining and privacy violations, along with the digital divide and the limitations of technology (Bellamy and Taylor, 1998). Writers in social work and social policy have similarly drawn attention to the negative potential of ICTs, such as their powers of surveillance over workers and clients, how they are used to serve managerial interests and how they promote technical rather than professional practice (Coleman and Harris, 2008; Henman and Marston, 2008; Sapey, 1997).

In many Western countries, various political, economic and managerial imperatives have pushed ICT onto the agenda of public sector workplaces and transformed practices in agencies where social workers are employed. Over the past 30 years sweeping managerial public sector reforms and restructuring of welfare state services has been accompanied by calls for increased efficiency and effectiveness of public and NGOs (Dominelli, 1997). These reforms have been closely interlinked with the rapid expansion of ICT in the delivery of welfare services in government and NGOs and have had a direct impact on social work practice. During the 1980s, social workers in the United States expressed concerns about privacy and confidentiality issues following the introduction of large-scale standardized data management information systems, which were ushered in during a period of massive welfare-state budget cuts (Mutschler and Hasenfeld, 1986). A decade later, related concerns were raised by social workers in the United Kingdom. Sapey (1997), for example, argued that increased use of ICT was less about efficiency and effectiveness and more about the monitoring and standardized control of practitioners' work.

Apart from public sector reform processes associated with new public management, Western governments have been pursuing a wider reform agenda known as the *e-government project*, which is accompanied by a management philosophy of 'joined-up government' or seamless provision of government services (Gil-Garcia and Martinez-Moyano, 2007). In both the United Kingdom and Australia, for example, the provision of online services became a central plank of the e-government agendas pursued by the respective governments of these countries in the late 1990s. The underlying assumption here is that the use of increasingly sophisticated databases and interlinked government services will improve efficiency and provide a better quality of service to citizens. It involves a major push to put government services and information online, including a wide range of public services, in fields as diverse as health, social and personal services; income security; child protection; and housing (Melville, 2007b).

One issue arising from these developments for social workers is a lack of control over the development of various standardized intake and assessment tools used in fields such as child protection and health (Parton, 2008; Webb, 2003b). A related issue is the impact of this on the nature of the social worker–client relationship. In child protection services, workers are concerned that they are spending an inordinate amount of time filling in computer-generated risk-assessment intake forms and spending too little time working with clients on their needs and issues. Parton (2008) suggests that one major challenge now facing social workers in these services is the loss of autonomy in professional practice and an inability to use discretion to accommodate individual needs and circumstances. A second challenge is that service users' stories are not seen as an important part of the information system. This privileging of the 'informational' over the 'social' is in turn altering the knowledge base of social work practice (Parton, 2008).

On a related note, social workers have expressed concerns that they are being subjected to increased electronic surveillance. As Harris (1998) notes, ICT can be used to check on the productivity of social workers by monitoring client loads and outputs. Data information systems can be used to track the work of an individual and relate this to the overall productivity of the agency. Workers may then be subjected to pressure from management if they do not meet some pre-specified quota of interviews or placements per month. As a result, workers may find it more difficult to spend time with clients whose situations are very complex or whose circumstances are particularly problematic. Research indicates that the introduction of computerized record keeping and data collection in social security systems has similarly increased the surveillance of clients, while potentially disadvantaging clients who do not possess good digital skills (Henman and Adler, 2003). Such systems tend to serve the interests of management rather than workers and clients.

As governments provide more electronic services on the Internet, concerns are increasingly being expressed about the privacy and confidentiality of citizens' data accumulated in large networked public and private organizations. In some countries, data collection for health and welfare agencies has been outsourced to private companies under competitive tendering arrangements (Hudson, 2002). Such changes herald a set of complex dilemmas concerning privacy, security and the changing relationship that citizens have with the state. In an attempt to counter some of these concerns, many countries have implemented public and private data protection and privacy legislation or measures. Some of these involve mandatory compliance, whereas others rely on voluntary compliance. Another way of addressing these concerns is to develop a set of cyber digital rights – or virtual rights – to supplement existing social, political and civil rights (Fitzpatrick, 2003, pp. 131–3).

Given the range of concerns expressed about the negative capabilities of ICTs, social workers need to be critically reflexive about both the potential and limitations of these technologies in social work practice. On a more practical level, we suggest that practitioners need to develop strategies to have greater influence over the ways in which ICTs are used in the work-place, although we also recognize the constraints in doing so. As Parrott and Madoc-Jones (2008, p. 186) point out, 'as long as social work disregards its potential to mould its environment then inevitably a reification of the power of technology occurs.' In a similar vein, we suggest that social workers can shape the connective possibilities of ICTs for their own interests and purposes. More specifically, we suggest that ICTs have significant potential for promoting social change, and in the following discussion we examine the capacity of these technologies for enhancing the work of social movements and social justice activism.

ICT and social change

Giddens (2001, pp. 441–2) claims that information technology and social movements have been two of the most influential developments in late modernity and that combined they constitute a powerful force for change. For social activists, information technology provides the means for a new form of global citizenship to evolve that moves beyond traditional loyalties to the nation state. Along with the Internet, Giddens (2001) sees mobile phones, facsimile machines and satellite broadcasting as other vital technological developments that have allowed social movements to propagate and influence public opinion around the world. In particular, it is social activists' ability to gain access to the global stage that he suggests is most alarming to governments, for their sphere of influence is seen as a formidable threat to existing power arrangements under the state:

> From global protests in favour of cancelling Third World debt to the international campaign to ban landmines ... the internet has proved its ability to unite campaigners across national and cultural borders. Some observers argue that the information age is witnessing a 'migration' of power away from the nation-states into new non-governmental alliances. (Giddens, 2001, p. 441)

The potential of the Internet as a tool of social justice activism relates to its capacity to increase access to a greater number of resources, enable global coverage at a very low cost and at great speed and enhance networking between individuals and social movements (Eagleton-Pierce, 2001). The Internet is seen as having democratic possibilities in terms of its accessibility to a wide range of disparate social movements and individuals with diverse political agendas. In this sense, despite the digital divide, the Internet has considerable potential for groups and individuals to voice their concerns to a widespread audience and to forge alliances (Kidd, 2001).

Information technology offers NGOs and humanitarian groups the possibility of coordinating their efforts on both an international and regional level to address issues of social concern. Working within such broad-based networks allows for not only the identification of common social problems but also the sharing of expertise and the development of creative solutions (Eagleton-Pierce, 2001). The growth in both number and size of social action groups and NGOs over the past three decades signals the emergence of the globally networked social movement. Not only have we seen the birth of the 'anti-globalization' movement but we have also witnessed organizations such as Oxfam and Greenpeace going global. This has only been possible through technological advances such as networked communications satellites and the development of new information technologies that allow for increased social interaction and the rapid sharing of information on a global scale (Giddens, 2002b). Accordingly, opportunities are open to social workers to join with existing social movements, or alternatively, seed new ones.

The attraction of the Internet for social activists lies in its potential for linking up people around the world, as well as providing an expedient means of global information distribution and exchange. In this sense, its communication capacity is its chief asset, and cyberspace is now the place where social movements are often born, allowing participation and activism at local, regional and international levels. Social campaigners who have reaped the benefits of having access to cyberspace include anti-globalization activists, indigenous movements such as the Zapatistas in Mexico, labour unions, feminists and environmental groups (Kidd, 2001, p. 327).

One example of a global activist organization is the World Social Forum (WSF), which is a worldwide network opposed to the dominant model of neoliberal globalization. The WSF sees itself as providing an open platform for sharing information, debating ideas, forging links with other like-minded bodies and devising strategies to resist and subvert global capitalism (WSF, 2008). The first WSF was held in 2001 in Brazil and grew out of the anti-capitalist movement of the late 1990s. Its main aim is to develop alternative ways of living that favour participatory democracy, the redistribution of wealth, the reduction of poverty, non-violence and the elimination of corruption. The WSF is heavily reliant on cyberspace as its primary means of organizing and strategizing. Rather than representing itself as a global institution, the WSF describes itself as 'an open meeting place' and a 'permanent world process' that favours decentralized processes and networking (WSF, 2008).

Accordingly, we can see that computerized communications have significant potential to unsettle existing power relations and social arrangements through facilitating rapid connections between people, places, information and finance. A number of writers in social work have similarly recognized this potential, advocating the use of electronic advocacy and lobbying, blogging, online networking and information exchange as vehicles to promote social and economic justice both locally and globally (Healy, 2001; Hick and McNutt, 2002; Ife, 2008; Queiro-Tajalli, Campbell and McNutt, 2003). Electronic lobbying, for instance, can be used to supplement more traditional means of lobbying such as letter writing and media campaigns to influence social policy and promote social concerns. Similarly, email and dedicated websites can be used for a variety of purposes including sharing information, circulating petitions, educating the public and lobbying policy makers (Healy, 2001, p. 226). The IFSW, for example, uses its website to publicize its position statements on social issues and human rights to a potentially global audience.

More recently, we have also witnessed what has been termed 'hacktivist' social activism, whereby hackers with a social conscience use their computer skills to promote social justice on the Web using strategies such as parody, sabotage and satire (Eagleton-Pierce, 2001). Of course the effectiveness of such political statement making is open to debate and equally invites critical reflection on the ethics of this form of social campaigning. Nonetheless, despite these dilemmas and uncertainties, it is clear that cyberspace offers possibilities for innovative and creative forms of social action that potentially have global reach.

However, while these possibilities exist, commentators have questioned whether the Internet and other forms of ICT have actually been instrumental in widening civic participation and enabling political mobilization. In those countries where there is a high penetration of ICTs, some research suggests that it is those individuals and groups who are already politically engaged who are using the Internet as an additional medium in their work (Vromen, 2007). It is, therefore, questionable whether the Internet has mobilized new groups of people to social action or just reinforced existing patterns of participation.

On a related note, Ife (2008) cautions us to be circumspect about the democratic potential of the Internet given the uneven global access to this form of technology. As he points out, the Internet is still only readily available to a minority of people who not only have access to computers but who also have the skills and ambition to exploit its potential. In summary then, these new forms of communication provide people in different regions and countries with varying opportunities for increased political engagement and the pursuit of social change at the local and global levels.

ICT and representational practices

The preceding discussion has highlighted how the Internet provides social movements with the capacity to politicize, educate, network, share information, organize and mobilize. Along with these practices, we suggest that social workers can also harness the potential of ICTs to promote positive images of marginalized populations and challenge those representational practices that denigrate or objectify such groups. Given the significance of mass media in people's lives, we further suggest that there is value in incorporating insights from studies on popular culture into social work to enhance our understanding of the media's role in constructing and propagating negative images of these populations.

Debates about the representation of minority and indigenous groups have been of major concern to feminist and postcolonial scholars. In Chapter 2, we highlighted how, historically, subordinated populations were constructed within the confines of colonial discourses, which in turn negated these groups' agency. Similarly, the Internet is similarly a site where identities are constructed and complex relationships between dominant and less powerful groups are played out. It can mirror the dominant power relationships of the 'real world'. For some postcolonial writers, the Internet is viewed with a sense of ambivalence because of its potential to promote the ongoing misrepresentation of indigenous and minority groups (Oguibe, 2002). This occurs because of the appropriation of their identities by dominant groups enabled by the open and accessible nature of Internet technology. Consequently, these groups might be misrepresented for two reasons: first, such groups are not in a position to control these subjective representations, and second, they are transformed into the objects of those who speak on their behalf (Oguibe, 2002). These representational practices may in turn further disenfranchise already marginalized groups who do not have access to the Internet to counter or challenge such images.

Social activists have equally been accused of appropriating images of vulnerable groups for their own purposes. Oguibe (2002, pp. 175–6) describes such activists as 'representatives of the absent' who, perhaps despite their good intentions, have failed to critically reflect on their own motivations for engaging in such political work:

> They include lone campaigners and makeshift pressure groups, organizations of concerned friends and self-appointed revolutionaries, messianic figures coming to the rescue of the helpless, anarchists in search of preoccupation and activists

left over from failed courses eager to find new ones that might assuage their passion to serve.

Accordingly, Oguibe (2002, pp. 179–80) argues that we need to foster a new form of Internet activism, one that 'aims to engender a culture of sensitivity and responsibility within the Net' and includes 'awareness of a conscionable relationship with those who are on the outside'. In conclusion, we suggest that social workers equally need to critically reflect on their own representational practices, especially in terms of the implications of these practices for those who remain 'unconnected' and on the other side of the digital divide.

Summary

Over the past decade there has been a proliferation of interest in ICT in social work, especially in the fields of education, information exchange, management and developing innovative forms of practice. In this chapter we have examined the embedded nature of digital communication technologies in many people's everyday lives and in doing so have highlighted the social and interactive nature of these technologies. At the same time, we have cautioned against viewing ICTs simply in terms of technological solutions for complex social, political and economic problems, while also highlighting how the digital divide has disadvantaged some populations in their quest for social and economic development.

ICTs have significant potential to enhance social work practice and offer new opportunities for social activism, but equally they pose significant threats, especially when they are deployed in the primary interests of efficiency, surveillance or profitability. However, rather than rejecting these technologies, we suggest that it is important for social workers to assume greater control over the use of ICTs in their everyday practice and to develop strategies to deal more effectively with their disempowering features.

Discussion points

1. Which groups are socially excluded from the use of ICTs on a local and global level?
2. How does the 'digital divide' compromise the social and economic development of some localities?
3. How 'democratic' do you think the Internet actually is, and how might it inadvertently perpetuate new or existing inequalities?

4. What are some of the challenges associated with utilizing ICTs in social work practice? What strategies can social workers employ to have greater influence on how ICTs are used in the workplace?
5. What do you see as the advantages of global communication systems such as the Internet for broad-based participation and social activism?

Chapter 8

The Environment, Sustainable Development and Social Work

Introduction

Social work has long endorsed a holistic approach to practice that emphasizes people's interactions and interdependent relationships with their environments. Traditionally, the environment has been conceptualized in a rather narrow sense in social work, reflecting a preoccupation with a person's social circle and community rather than the actual physical environment. More recently, however, social workers have been urged to turn their attention to the state of the physical environment and to embrace the concept of 'sustainable development' (Hoff, 1997). This is particularly important in an age where environmental decline is affecting people's quality of life and promoting disease, poverty, stress, pollution and toxic exposure from chemicals. Global warming, in particular, has been implicated in this environmental decline, which according to the United Nations Intergovernmental Panel on Climate Change (IPCC) is affecting every continent on earth (Rosenzweig et al., 2008). In other words, this is a truly global problem.

In the first part of this chapter, we consider why the welfare of the environment is a critical concern for the global community and explore the idea that obligations of environmental justice extend beyond state borders. Following on from this discussion, we examine the implications of environmental change for social work practice. Assisting people to cope with and adapt to change has traditionally been a major focus for social workers, and global warming is likely to have significant physical and economic effects, as well as social consequences. Moreover, government policies and initiatives to combat climate change are likely to have long-term implications which could see the restructuring of our economy, employment and social systems. Predictably, there will be uneven 'fallout' from these changes, and it is likely that social workers will encounter people in practice who are struggling to cope with these new arrangements. In the final part of the chapter, we explore the idea of sustainable development and examine ways that social workers can actively play a part in raising environmental awareness and promoting sustainable development.

The current state of the environment and its impact on health and welfare

Social workers have traditionally been concerned about environmental impacts on people's health and welfare, but have perhaps tended to pay more attention to the social, economic and political domains of people's lives rather than their physical environments. However, given that media reports are now saturated with news about environmental issues, societal awareness of these issues is now much greater. Almost daily, we are presented with bleak reports in the media about global warming, rising sea levels, water shortages, the destruction of forests, threats to endangered species and catastrophic weather patterns. Moreover, now that people are starting to experience the effects of climate change and environmental degradation, there is a greater collective awareness of the importance of addressing these issues in order to ensure the survival of the planet and humankind.

The IPCC has concluded that greenhouse gas emissions have altered the climate, and the available evidence would suggest that regardless of efforts to reduce emissions, further changes are inevitable in the future. These projected changes include rising temperatures and sea levels, more frequent and severe droughts and increased storm activity, which in turn will affect natural ecosystems, biodiversity and human settlements (Rosenzweig et al., 2008). Nonetheless, the IPCC (2007) claims that the risks associated with climate change can be reduced or even avoided if appropriate investment is made in mitigation efforts over the next few decades. Of critical importance is the need to reverse the trend in rising greenhouse gas emissions.

It has been estimated that human activity is responsible for at least 90 per cent of environmental damage, which suggests that it is human behaviour that is the problem here (Rosenzweig et al., 2008). Our reliance on fossil fuels, such as oil, coal and natural gas, for cheap energy has contributed significantly to global warming. Burning fossil fuels releases carbon dioxide – a primary greenhouse gas – into the atmosphere, and this process in conjunction with land use change is believed to have contributed to an increase in global average temperatures (IPCC, 2007, p. 5). In particular, environmental theorists link the consumption patterns of affluent societies to global warming and environmental degradation, although more recently there has been a notable expansion of consumption in some developing countries as well. Along with the United States and Europe, Brazil, India and China are responsible for 60 per cent of global greenhouse gas emissions (Worldwatch Institute, 2008).

Those of us living in the industrialized world are implicated in appropriating a good share of the earth's natural resources, generating waste and releasing huge amounts of greenhouse gases into the atmosphere in order to maintain our cars, housing, agriculture, technology and industry. Even the seemingly innocuous act of buying a hamburger from a fast-food outlet has implications for the environment. In what follows, Gomes (2002, pp. 248–9) identifies a number of interconnected practices associated with the industrial production and consumption of hamburgers that can lead to environmental degradation on a global level. These include the following:

- The continual clearing of forest habitats and their transformation into pasture lands for cattle raising;
- The resultant increase in greenhouse gases from deforestation, which in turn contributes to global warming;
- The destruction of vegetation and crops resulting from rising sea levels caused by global warming and the melting of ice caps;
- The depletion of the ozone layer caused in part by increased methane emissions from cattle and the use of chloro-fluorocarbons (CFCs) to refrigerate the beef in transit and make the disposable foam packaging for hamburgers; and
- The dumping of huge amounts of plastics and foam packaging which take years to break down.

This is a clear example of how one simple act can have multiple consequences for the environment and adversely impact people's health and welfare. It also represents a production process that binds both producers and consumers in different locations across the globe via commodity chains (McMichael, 2008). Below, Gomes (2002, p. 254) sums up the links between the promotion of economic growth as a 'global good' and industrialization, consumerism and environmental degradation:

> ... industrial and industrialising nations have promoted the maximization of output to meet increasing market demands, spurred on by growing consumerism. It is a chain reaction with dire environmental consequences, as more and more resources (fossil fuels, minerals, timber) are tapped and transformed into commodities. Since most transformation processes create waste, industrialism causes increasing atmospheric and water pollution, leading subsequently to ecological problems such as global warming, acid rain, the ozone hole, radioactive radiation, deforestation, soil degradation, and desertification.

Like all other global processes, climate change is experienced locally and, depending on ones location, its effects will be experienced differently. For example, while more prolonged droughts and water shortages have become a reality for Australia, for other countries such as the South Pacific island nation of Tuvalu, rising sea levels threaten to 'sink' the islands and displace its residents. The situation has become so severe that New Zealand has entered an agreement to take a quota of residents from Tuvalu each year (Adger, 2007). In Chapter 1, mention was made of how the negative effects of climate change on some developing countries have produced a new type of environmental refugee. These displaced groups are in turn predicted to significantly increase migratory pressures on Europe and North America.

In other regions, food production is under threat as climate change and variable weather patterns are already altering agriculture. The current global food crisis has been exacerbated by extreme weather conditions such as flooding and droughts in major grain-producing regions such as West Africa, Australia and China (Borger, 2008b). This in turn has resulted in food shortages and rising commodity prices, exacerbating malnutrition, poverty and hunger in many parts of the world. The drive to develop alternative sources of energies in the face of dwindling oil supplies has further contributed to food shortages as agricultural land and food crops are diverted to the production of biofuels. The groups who will be hardest hit by the global food crisis are women and children, along with other marginalized groups such as slum dwellers and temporary farm workers residing in Africa, Asia, the Middle East and Latin America (Oxfam, 2008a). Clearly, this is an issue of some relevance for social workers, who have traditionally been concerned with marginalized populations.

Climate change is recognized as not just having environmental consequences but is also believed to pose a security threat as groups compete for diminishing resources such as energy and arable land and whole communities are displaced. The UN Security Council has similarly acknowledged this threat by putting climatic security on its agenda (European Commission, 2008). The conflict in Darfur is perhaps a point in case, with some suggesting that the prolonged drought and heightened competition for basic resources was the impetus for a war that displaced hundreds of thousands of people and destabilized the region (McMichael, 2008).

The importance of the physical environment to people's health and welfare is illustrated by the stark statistic that globally, environmental risk factors are responsible for 24 per cent of diseases and 23 per cent of all deaths (World Health Organization [WHO], 2006b). While much environment-related disease is preventable, governments and many aid agencies alike have been slow to act on issues such as unsafe water supplies and sanitation. It is estimated that more than 1 billion people throughout the world lack access to clean water, while a further 2.5 million people are deemed to be at risk of diseases such as diarrhoea because of bad sanitation (WHO, 2008b). Disease and illness associated with unclean water, poor sanitation and hygiene disproportionately affects poor people. Poor sanitation kills more children than HIV/AIDS while malaria is responsible for twice as many deaths as HIV/AIDS (WHO, 2006b). While one of the UN's Millennium Development Goals is to halve the number of people without access to basic sanitation by 2015, progress in this area has been slow. In sub-Saharan Africa, for example, the number of people who lack access to sanitation has actually increased rather than decreased (Vidal, 2008a).

Regrettably, governments and many aid agencies alike have failed to recognize the fundamental importance of water to people's lives, despite the fact that water can be considered to be a basic human right.

Currently, the survival of the planet is believed to be under threat from a range of environmental factors. These include a lack of accessible fresh water, the extensive destruction of forest and crop land, global warming, overuse of natural resources, a rising population, decreased biodiversity and a loss of species. These environmental factors are at many levels interconnected. What they all have in common is that they implicate human behaviour as a key threat to the survival of the planet. In other words, rather than being inconsequential, what we do (and choose not to do) has a significant impact not only on the local environment but also on the global community at large (Gomes, 2002).

Concerns about environmental degradation are now widely diffused across the globe, and environmental activism appears to be on the increase. However, a worrying trend is that people's concerns about the environment are not necessarily translated into appropriate environmental action or behaviour beyond green consumerism or buying 'environmentally friendly' products. For example, if we look at common activities like using the Internet, the amount of carbon emissions produced by worldwide Internet usage is now on a par with that produced by the global airline industry (Connolly, 2008). Yet for a good number of people in the global North the Internet is now just part and parcel of their everyday lives that they do not question.

Efforts to address climate change tend to be tempered by local social, political and economic concerns, such as an unwillingness to reduce material production and consumption and a desire to preserve affluence. Such desires are not just unique to richer countries but are also becoming increasingly apparent in emerging economies such as China and India where there is a growing middle class who aspire to a consumer lifestyle (Hasan, 2006). However, now that the effects of climate change and associated erratic weather patterns are starting to be felt, the tide is starting to turn, particularly given that environmental problems such as water scarcity represent a threat to the livelihood of some richer countries.

At the same time, there is greater recognition that the scale of consumption of these richer countries is not sustainable, especially when they are dependent on importing other countries' scarce resources. The United Kingdom, for example, imports 62 per cent of its water from water-stressed countries such as Spain, Egypt, Morocco and South Africa; this includes 'virtual water' which is used in the production of imported food and textiles (Lawrence, 2008). Arguably, the large 'water footprint' of the United Kingdom is exacerbating water shortages in other countries and demonstrates not only the interlinked nature of environmental concerns but also the potential for conflict over access to scarce natural resources. In the following section, we explore the links between global inequality and the differential impacts of climate change, with particular reference to the idea of environmental justice.

Global inequality and environmental justice

In order to fully appreciate the nature of the current global environmental crisis, we need to understand the historical, political and economic conditions that have promoted environmental degradation and global warming. The earth is our one common natural resource base. However, there is a serious imbalance in the way in which this natural resource base has been and continues to be managed, which tends to advantage an 'industrialized minority' living in the West (Lohmann, 2006, p. 31). During the colonial era, the extraction of natural resources from the global South played a key part in the industrialization of the global North. It is this process of industrialization that has largely contributed to the growth of greenhouse gas concentrations in the atmosphere, in turn promoting climate change. In the contemporary post-colonial era, natural resources continue to be exploited by self-interested industrialized nations, often to the detriment of poorer people in developing countries (Lohmann, 2006). Some of these developing countries are even used as dumping grounds by industrialized nations. For example, the United States and some Western European countries 'export' their e-waste and pollution to West Africa, which in turn has created toxic dumps and compromised the health of whole communities in this region (Wray, 2008).

In addition to these practices, the development of a global marketplace has promoted unsustainable production and consumption practices, whereby the environment is being rapidly transformed into resources for consumption (McMichael, 2008). This in turn has a negative ecological impact and threatens the livelihood of vulnerable groups, particularly those residing in the global South who are dependent on their natural habitats for survival. In what follows, McMichael (2008, pp. 13–14) cites the example of increased demand for meat and fish consumption as an example of this process.

> When we consume shrimp, or chicken, or pork, or beef, chances are that we are simultaneously consuming mangrove swamps (habitat for people who fish and shrimp for a living) or biologically rich rainforests (habitat for indigenous peoples), which are being flattened for fields of soy for expanding feedlot operations around the world.

Until recently, there was a misconceived link between environmental degradation and poverty. Gomes (2002) nominates the World Bank, in particular, as one influential institution that propagated this idea. While 'the poor' were often blamed for problems such as the population explosion that has placed increased demands on the environment, in reality poor people often live more frugally in subsistence-based economies (Gomes, 2002, p. 253). As a result, they utilize fewer environmental resources than their more affluent counterparts in developed countries. Rich people consume more than poor people, and it is the 'West's excesses' in this regard that is believed to have exacerbated global warming (Khaleque, 2007). Highly industrialized nations such as the United Kingdom, Australia, Canada and the United States have contributed to these problems because of their high per capita consumption of fossil fuel energy, which in turn produces increased amounts of greenhouse gas emissions. For example, the average UK citizen is responsible for the same amount of carbon emissions in eight days as that produced by the average person in Zambia in one year (World Development Movement, 2007, p. 8).

Yet it is poorer countries that suffer environmental problems disproportionately. Bangladesh, one of the poorest countries in the world, is particularly at risk because climate change is promoting more extreme flooding, which in turn reduces crop productivity and creates the conditions for spreading waterborne diseases (Khaleque, 2007). Unstable weather conditions, hotter summers, droughts, flooding of lowlands in the Asian-Pacific region and crop failures have all been linked to global warming and left some regions poverty stricken (Worldwatch Institute, 2003). Similarly, the World Bank (2005) points to evidence that implicates climate change and its associated impacts, such as more frequent and severe droughts and floods, in promoting disease in many developing countries. For example, nearly 20 per cent of disease in developing countries is directly related to environmental risks such as unsafe water and poor sanitation.

Poverty eradication programmes that seek to 'modernize' traditional agrarian-based economies have also been implicated in exacerbating environmental decline. These 'modernization' projects, which include encouraging poor farmers to switch from subsistence farming to growing cash crops for export, lead to over-exploitation of the environment and a reliance on the whims of the global market for survival (Gomes, 2002). Such programmes have shown little regard for the moral significance of the environment, which has only been seen as something to be exploited for human benefit and advancement. In other words, the environment is not seen to have intrinsic value in itself but is just viewed as a means to an end.

For colonized groups such as Aboriginal and Torres Strait Islander peoples in Australia, their grievances do not just relate to the appropriation of their land by European settlers but also extend to the blatant disregard demonstrated by Europeans for their traditional spiritual beliefs about the land. Rather than viewing land as property (a capitalist mindset), many

Indigenous Australians believed and continue to believe that people belong to the earth. Such an environmental ethic extends to the view that the earth must be preserved for future generations and that its current inhabitants are custodians of rather than owners of the land.

Indigenous groups, in particular, are at heightened risk of the adverse effects associated with climate change and environmental destruction. For many of these groups, land and water are key to their livelihood and survival. In more extreme cases, whole communities have been displaced and have had to be evacuated. For other groups residing in tropical areas, global warming and associated temperature rises has made these communities more susceptible to mosquito-borne diseases such as malaria and dengue fever (IPCC, 2008). Environmental degradation has resulted in not only the breakdown of fragile ecological systems in many of these poorer countries but also the breakdown of their economic, social and cultural systems. In response to these pressures, many people are migrating from rural to urban areas, placing additional stress on urban facilities and services. Environmental degradation has similarly increased migratory pressure on richer countries (Traynor, 2008).

Clearly, North–South relations are a pertinent issue in the current environmental crisis. Indeed, some argue that because richer countries in the global North carry historical responsibility for increased carbon emissions, then it is these countries that should shoulder most of the responsibility for curbing carbon emissions and mitigating the effects of climate change. However, while it is apparent that the consumerism of developed countries has contributed significantly to climate change, as mentioned earlier this consumer ethic is becoming more pronounced in some emerging economies in the global South. Accordingly, it is important not to view environmental issues solely in terms of a North–South dualism, although it is still the case that the people most likely to be adversely affected by climate change live in poorer regions such as South Asia and Africa (McMichael, 2008). On this basis, it is argued that highly industrialized countries in the global North owe an ecological debt to poorer countries in the global South. In other words, they have obligations of environmental justice to poorer countries.

At the same time, these richer countries are imploring developing countries to curb their own consumerism and conserve natural resources such as forests in order to 'save the environment' and assist in reducing global carbon emissions. For some, this represents a new form of colonization or what could be called eco-colonialism (Vidal, 2008b). In contrast to traditional forms of colonization whereby the colonizers controlled other countries for the purposes of exploiting their natural resources, eco-colonialism refers to the colonization of developing countries by conservationists who purport to be acting in the environmental interests of the global community. According to the Forest Peoples Programme, conservation has compromised the livelihood of many indigenous groups throughout Africa and India via forced expulsions, human rights violations and the buying-up of land for national parks (Vidal, 2008b). The ramifications of some of these conservation projects for poorer countries are described as follows:

> Tens of thousands of people have been evicted to establish wildlife parks and other protected areas throughout the developing world. Many people have been forbidden to hunt, cut trees, quarry stone, introduce plants or in any way threaten the local remains or the ecosystem. The land they have lived on for centuries is suddenly recast as an idyllic wildlife sanctuary, with no regard for the realities of the lives of those who live there. (Vidal, 2008b, p. 26)

Environmental justice operates on the premise that the benefits and burdens of resource use are neither evenly distributed across the globe nor across generations, as it is future generations who are likely to bear the brunt of the cost of resource mismanagement (Sachs, 2004). This is a position similarly endorsed by the International Federation of Social Workers (IFSW, 2005a), who, in their policy statement on globalization and the environment, affirm the importance of sharing the earth's resources in a fair and sustainable manner. A related concern is that mitigation efforts to address environmental problems and climate change will have disproportionately costly and detrimental effects on poor people, which in turn could exacerbate inequitable income distribution. Yet for many poor people, practising environmentally friendly policies such as recycling and limiting consumption are necessities for survival (Chatterjee, 2008). In this way, it has been suggested that wealthier nations that prioritize mass consumption can learn much from their poorer counterparts.

Despite the recognition that understanding and responding to environmental problems necessitates a global approach, the economic and political interests of individual countries have tended to prevent the development of a coordinated and unified response to tackling this issue. Most governments have tended to rely on local cost-benefit analyses when assessing the viability of major new projects such as dams, roads and power plants that are dependent on the exploitation and conversion of natural resources. However, the question must be asked as to whether such local assessments will continue to be appropriate when it is becoming increasingly clear that such developments can have global implications.

Social workers are, in fact, already working with groups affected by climate change and extreme weather conditions such as communities coping in the aftermath of natural disasters, drought-affected farmers and those experiencing environment-related health problems (Agoramoorthy and Hsu, 2008; Hall and Scheltens, 2005; Mathbor, 2007). In the following section, we examine some of the implications of climate change and environmental decline for social work in more detail. In addition, we consider how attempts to mitigate the effects of climate change are likely to pose new challenges for social workers who work with individuals and groups who may, at least in the short term, be disadvantaged by such policies.

The implications of environmental change for social work

Helping people cope with and adapt to change has been a prominent part of social work, and assisting people adapt to the impacts of climate change and extreme weather events is likely to become a more significant part of practice over the coming decades. As pointed out in the preceding discussion, climate change is predicted to have wide-ranging but variable impacts and will pose different challenges for communities all around the world. Of some concern is the prediction that it could push already vulnerable groups and communities with weak infrastructure further into hardship (IPCC, 2007). While those who are relatively well-off are likely to have the resources to make the necessary adaptations to climate change, it is poorer people who will face the most challenges in insulating themselves from its effects. The IFSW (2005a) has pointed out that those most at risk from climate change and environmental change are people who lack political and social power and have limited economic means. As energy becomes more expensive as a result of dwindling oil supplies, this is likely to compound the problem.

While there is much talk about the future consequences of climate change, it is important to recognize that climate change and environmental degradation are already having catastrophic consequences for many people. Indeed, in 2007 the UN calculated that all but one of its 13 emergency appeals for humanitarian aid were climate related (Borger, 2007). Social workers have traditionally played a key role in disaster management in many Asian countries, a notable example being the Asian tsunami in 2004 which devastated areas of South Asia and East Africa, including Thailand, Sri Lanka, India and Indonesia (Tan et al., 2006). It has been suggested that social workers from other countries can learn much about recovery and rebuilding from these countries' experiences, not only in relation to dealing with issues of trauma and displacement but also in relation to enhancing the adaptive capacity of local communities to adjust to the economic and social consequences of such disasters. In particular, there is a need to foster social capital to buffer distress and enhance community preparedness for coping with future natural disasters (Mathbor, 2007). In other words, there is a need to build resilient communities that are better prepared for such events.

A recent example here is provided by a social work colleague from India, Vikas Gora, who has many years of developmental experience and works with SPHERE India, which coordinates an alliance of humanitarian agencies in India. In what follows, he describes his many and varied roles in coordinating disaster management and humanitarian assistance in the aftermath of the devastating 2008 floods in Bihar:

> Today, I am heading to Bihar again as we fear the second coming of the monsoons which may further displace scores of people. The task of reaching out to 3.2 million displaced and 1 million feared missing or dead has been a challenging one. I am involved in planning, monitoring and evaluation. This includes relief camps management, inter-donor coordination, mapping of NGOs and agencies working in the disaster prone areas, and planning the shift from disaster relief to rehabilitation. Other areas of work include trauma counselling and working with people to chalk out their needs. We are trying to create greater social responsibility for and accountability about quality relief aid and its disbursement, coordinating and networking with nongovernmental organizations, so as to avoid duplication of resources. In addition, we work with the government, NGOs, media and other civil society organizations so that greater awareness is created on how to cope with natural and human made disasters both at the policy level and at the grass-roots level. (Personal communication from Vikas Gora, October, 2008)

Vikas goes on to suggest that just as victims of disasters have the right to receive aid, humanitarian agencies have a responsibility to realize the dignity of recipients when they dispense aid. He, therefore, sees his role as not just overseeing the logistics of aid relief but also ensuring that this is carried out in an ethical manner that is in line with social work's value of respect for the worth and dignity of each person. Moreover, disasters such as the Bihar floods tend to expose existing vulnerabilities in communities such as poverty, inadequate housing, poor physical infrastructure and limited communication systems. Bihar is one of the poorest and least urbanized states in India. The bulk of its population rely on farming to make a living, and the floods have seen substantial losses of grain crops which have severely curtailed agricultural output (Ramesh, 2008b). Many people lived in substandard dwellings that were no match for the floods, and as a result, thousands of people are now homeless, incomeless and stranded in refugee camps. The case of Bihar clearly highlights the importance of addressing pre-existing vulnerabilities in order to foster resilient communities that are better able to cope in the advent of future adverse weather events.

Social workers who are concerned with finding solutions to poverty-related social problems must factor in environmental considerations if their interventions are to be effective. Climate change is exacerbating poverty, especially in developing countries where people are highly dependent on their natural resources for survival. According to Hoff (1997, p. 33), practitioners need to be cognizant of how certain populations are at more risk than others from environmental degradation and attend to 'the social justice dimensions of environmental breakdown'. These populations include members of minority ethnic groups, poor farmers and mining communities in developing countries, and those forced to work in unregulated industries. She nominates a range of social problems faced by these groups which include: conflicts over access to land, water and other natural resources; poverty and unemployment; hunger and malnutrition; escalating levels of violence and wars; and rising rates of urbanization and the development of slums. For many of these groups, a lack of recognition of their human rights compounds the problems discussed previously. Displacement is also a threat faced by these groups and, previously in this chapter, mention was made of how environmental refugees now represent a new and growing class of refugees.

Predictably, social workers will be working with increasing numbers of people affected by droughts, floods, famines and other climate-related disasters and will also be assisting communities adapt to climate change. Clearly, there is a need for social workers to advocate for the rights of these vulnerable groups. One way of doing this is to research and document the plight of groups who are at most risk from climate change and environmental degradation and work with such groups to ensure that their concerns are put on governments' political agendas. Community development and social planning are other domains of practice where social workers can focus efforts in promoting environmental concerns and addressing environmental degradation. As mentioned previously, there is a need to prioritize infrastructure development, including the identification of new sustainable industries for communities residing in stressed environments or vulnerable to the effects of climate change. It will also be important to build resilient communities that can withstand the effects of natural and human-induced environmental hazards. This will include strengthening both physical and mental health care systems, as adapting to changed environmental conditions will test the adaptive capacity of many individuals who are affected by temperature, water, pollution and/or extreme weather-related health impacts.

Human behaviour has contributed significantly to global warming and climate change, and modifying our behaviour is crucial to addressing environmental problems. Accordingly, governments and industry alike are devising new policies and initiatives to combat climate change such as reducing carbon consumption, cutting waste, conserving water and protecting and restoring forests. For example, countries seeking to make the transition to a low-carbon economy are moving away from traditional power generation industries to renewable energy programmes, which in turn have implications for people's employment (Lohmann, 2006). Those who are likely to suffer in this transition process, such as miners, farmers and forestry workers, will require considerable support in this transition period, and it is conceivable that social workers will have a role in supporting these workers and their families.

Many governments are already investing in climate change infrastructures to assist people cope in the advent of extreme weather events. However, the adaptation strategies adopted are likely to differ markedly depending on the region one lives in. This is a process that has been likened to 'adaptation apartheid' (UN Development Programme [UNDP], 2007, p. 13). For example, while some rich countries such as the United Kingdom and the Netherlands are investing in elaborate flood defences and expensive floating homes, people living in the Ganges Delta are building bamboo flood shelters on stilts while women and children in the Mekong Delta are learning how to swim (UNDP, 2007, p. 13). Clearly, these inequalities in adaptive capacity signal the need for international action, especially given the fact that it is the richer industrialized nations that are responsible for most greenhouse emissions. Accordingly, the UN Framework Convention on Climate Change (UNFCC) commits richer countries to assist developing countries in meeting the costs of adapting to climate change.

Adopting a human rights framework, the IFSW (2005a) acknowledges that environmental degradation and climate change can compromise people's ability to achieve their full potential. In this regard, it recognizes the interconnectedness of the social environment and the natural environment and calls on social workers to take an active part in the promotion of a healthier environment. However, rather than working in isolation, the IFSW suggests that social workers need to work collaboratively with other professionals and community groups in advocating for environmental protection.

Arguably, the environment is a concern for all social workers who subscribe to principles of social justice and practice in accordance within the person-in-environment framework. What the preceding discussion has made clear is that the pursuit of social justice is inextricably linked to environmentalism. In the following section, the idea of sustainable development is explored as an environmental approach that is consistent with the person-in-environment framework and ecological justice.

Sustainable development and social work

Sustainable development has been defined as 'development that meets the needs of the present without compromising the ability of future generations to meet their own needs' (World Commission on Environment and

Development, 1987, p. 43). The relationship between economic development and environmental quality is central to sustainable development, along with a commitment to social equity. Sustainable development is concerned with balancing the economic and sociocultural needs of people with the regenerative capacity of the natural environment. In this sense, it represents a philosophy as well as a social movement (Hoff, 1997, p. 35). It implies an ethical responsibility to be 'future orientated' rather than giving priority to one's immediate needs and wants.

Several writers in social work make a case for social workers' active involvement in the movement towards sustainable development because it is consistent with the profession's holistic 'person-in-environment' approach (Coates, 2003; Healy, 2001, pp. 275–6; Hoff, 1997; Marlow and Van Rooyen, 2001). The environment in this case also refers to soil, air and water, and maintaining a healthy environment requires recognizing the importance of the principles of interdependence and biodiversity. Sustainable development equally involves recognizing people's subsistence rights: the right to food, health, housing and a livelihood. In this regard, environmental justice is interconnected with sustainable development. It is the more affluent economies in the global North who carry most responsibility for overtaxing natural ecosystems, which in turn has threatened the ability of poorer people to make a living from their natural spaces. In line with principles of environmental justice, these economies must then curb economic growth and prioritize global subsistence rights over the pursuit of affluence (Sachs, 2004).

Both social and political adaptability are required for sustainable development. Nevertheless, persuading governments and citizens alike to adopt strategies such as reducing their use of fossil fuel energy in the interests of global survival has proved to be a difficult task. A dominant attitude that has prevailed in the global North is that advances in science and technology will solve the current environmental crisis and allow for the development of alternative energy sources. Alternatively, initiatives such as carbon trading have been proposed as strategies for curbing carbon emissions. However, it is questionable whether such strategies will be enough to deal with climate change and its impacts, and it has been suggested that rather than solving the problem, 'the carbon market is getting in the way of solutions to the climate crisis' (Lohmann, 2006, p. 329).

It is questionable whether capitalism as a growth economy – with its need for expansion, finding new markets and promoting consumption – can be reconciled with an environmental ethic and sustainable development. While governments, big business and environmental agencies alike are putting considerable effort into researching and developing alternative energy sources and associated infrastructures, such strategies are still underpinned by a capitalist ethos in that they require considerable investment.

As Leahy (2008, p. 480) suggests, this is really 'all about substituting cheap ways of producing useful energy with more expensive ways of producing the same energy'. The other alternative is a drastic reduction in production and consumption.

Cutting down on the use of such non-renewable resources implies cultural and lifestyle change. It means that we must reduce our consumption of non-essential material goods and start utilizing renewable sustainable energy sources such as wind and solar power. However, for many of us, our 'consumer-centric' lifestyles are firmly based on the use of fossil fuels and revolve around having ready access to cars, air conditioning, domestic and overseas air travel, a wide range of products to choose from in our local supermarket and disposable products. Arguably, the challenges involved in convincing people to change their consumption practices are considerable.

The goals of sustainable development are somewhat inconsistent with those of a global economic system that favours rapid economic growth based on an ethos of profit at all costs. However, this 'growth fetish' is seen to be unsustainable in the long term because it entails the rapid conversion of non-renewable natural resources into wastes and a subsequent disregard for environmental and social consequences. As pointed out earlier, the exploitation of the world's natural resources is creating a chain reaction effect, leading to complex social and environmental problems that have serious implications for a range of populations. Accordingly, advocates of sustainable development are concerned with a variety of social issues that range from women's position in society to workers' rights (Hoff, 1997). The key principles of sustainable development include the following:

- Directing resources to meet essential human needs rather than those demands justified only by consumerism and affluence.
- Conceptualising development goals in terms of people's wellbeing (eg health, literacy, education, human rights) rather than just wealth and material gain.
- Recognising the asset value of cultural diversity and promoting culturally sustainable development as well as sustainable economic systems.
- Challenging inequitable power and wealth distribution, particularly between poor and rich countries.
- Promoting the democratization of the key political bodies in social and economic development (eg the World Bank).
- Balancing ecology and development and conserving natural resources. (Hoff, 1997, pp. 35–7)

These principles underscore a concern with *balanced* development, where social, cultural, economic and environmental needs are integrated. Given that sustainable development is ultimately played out on a local level, it is equally important that decision making and resource allocation occurs as much at possible at this local level. At the same time, the recognition of environmental justice necessitates a global perspective. This in turn will require collaboration and cooperation across a range of local and international government instrumentalities and agencies. While it is unlikely that many social workers will find themselves working at this international level, there are opportunities at the local level for promoting sustainable development and environmental justice.

Traditionally, social workers have not played an active part in the protection of the environment, although the ecological model, which favours a 'person-in-environment' perspective, has been an influential framework in practice (Germain and Gitterman, 1980). According to this model, people constantly interact with their environment and, therefore, impact each other in a reciprocal manner. The social worker's mandate is to intervene not only at the 'personal' level but also at an environmental level in order to enhance a better 'fit' between the two. Healy (2001, p. 275) claims that the concept of 'sustainability' is consistent with the ecological perspective in social work, as it 'requires practice that is sensitive to the interactions among ecosystems, economies, and social and human factors'. Similarly in community work, Ife (2001) stresses the ecological principles of sustainability and diversity.

Given the current threats to the planet's survival, it has been suggested that environmentalism must be incorporated as a new 'ethic' in social work (Berger and Kelly, 1993, p. 524). In accordance with this ethic, several writers in social work have mapped out a range of roles and tasks that are consistent with the idea of sustainable practice. They include broadening existing assessment practices in social work to encompass an analysis of environmental stressors and related social injustices that impact people's lives (Hoff, 1997). On a community level, this could also include investigating the effects of public planning and proposed developments on people's environments through social impact assessments (Carrilio, 2007; Hoff, 1997). An associated task here is developing outcome measures that incorporate financial, social *and* environmental dimensions of people's well-being.

In order to build resilient communities, it will be necessary to foster the development and effective utilization of social capital to strengthen people's social networks and civic associations and forge links both within and between communities (Mathbor, 2007). Social capital – which is essentially about the extent and quality of people' relationships and networks – is seen to be important because it facilitates cooperation both within and between groups. In other words, it promotes collective welfare (Agoramoorthy and Hsu, 2008; Mathbor, 2007).

On a broader political level, the opportunity exists for social workers to link with national and global social movements and non-government organizations (NGOs) that promote environmental protection, human rights and sustainable development (Coates, 2003; Hoff, 1997). Advocacy will also be an important role here, and social workers can advocate for environmental protection by drawing attention to the social and economic dimensions of unbalanced development, such as poverty or population displacement. An equally important task will be to highlight the impact of environmental degradation for future generations, including its potentially negative effects on children's development (Hoff, 1997).

Summary

In this chapter we have argued that the welfare of the environment is a critical issue for the global community and that obligations of environment justice extend beyond the local level. A failure to halt climate change and address environmental decline will result in substantial economic, social and health costs, and it is poorer people who are likely to feel the brunt of these costs. Already, we have witnessed some of the effects of climate change and environmental degradation in terms of the displacement of communities, a heightened incidence of diseases such as malaria and increased food costs that are exacerbating existing levels of poverty. Global warming will have an inevitable impact on people's health and welfare, and initiatives to address climate change are likely to have implications for the economy, employment and social systems. However, as yet it is difficult to comprehensively determine the mental, physical, economic and social effects of climate change and increased extreme weather events such as droughts and floods. What is apparent, however, is that some groups are more vulnerable to dislocation and poverty due to their physical location. The rapid rate of environmental degradation on a global level adds a sense of urgency to the task of promoting an environmental consciousness in social work. It is, therefore, incumbent upon social workers to learn more about the connections between the environment and people's welfare, to challenge unworkable environmental policies and to advocate for sustainable development.

Discussion points

1. What is the relationship between climate change and poverty? Why are poorer people likely to face the most challenges in insulating themselves from the effects of climate change?
2. What role can social workers play in assisting to build resilient communities that can withstand the effects of natural and human-induced environmental hazards?

3. How can social workers actively challenge government policies that promote unbalanced development? How can they promote an agenda of sustainable development?
4. Do you agree with the proposition that our obligations of environmental justice go beyond the local level and extend to other countries? Why? What might be the implications of this for social work?
5. What are the implications of incorporating environmentalism as a new ethic in social work? What might this mean for practice?

Chapter 9

The Value of a Human Rights Perspective in Social Work

Introduction

In this chapter, we examine the place of human rights in contemporary social work. Globalization and the movement for global citizenship have provided a new impetus for examining the role and utility of human rights in social work. The IFSW, along with many national social work bodies, has incorporated human rights principles into its professional statements and ethical codes. Social work's mandate, in this regard, is to assist people to maximize their civil, political, economic, social and cultural rights. However, while human rights 'talk' pervades many social work texts – including this one – it is equally a contested domain. Hence, one of our main purposes in this chapter is to explore the value of a human rights perspective in social work.

It is over 60 years since the United Nations (UN) launched the Universal Declaration of Human Rights (UDHR), which was ratified in 1948. Since then the framework of human rights instruments has expanded to include new groups and issues. At the current juncture, some argue that there is a pressing need for the international community to reassert the value of a human rights discourse. Human rights abuses still occur in every country of the world. For the majority of the world's population, economic globalization, increasing militarization and climate change all pose new threats to realizing the human rights of freedom from want and freedom from fear (Annan, 2005). Although the UDHR proclaims 'human rights as a common standard of achievement for all people and all nations' (UN, 1948), it is patently clear that the international community has not yet managed to make this proclamation a reality.

As a broad-ranging discourse that encompasses ethical, legal, political, cultural and philosophical dimensions, human rights can be viewed from a variety of angles. Given the complexity of this discourse and the range of actors involved, it is perhaps not surprising that the idea of a set of Universal Human Rights is itself subjected to considerable debate. Writers in the fields of globalization, feminism and postcolonialism have added new dimensions to this debate, and in this chapter we also consider some of these critiques and their implications for social work.

In the first part of this chapter we briefly examine the role, structure and main activities of UN. Next, we provide an overview of human rights and identify some of the challenges to their implementation and realization. Following on from this discussion, we canvas some of the more prominent cultural and feminist critiques of human rights and social work's response to these critiques. In the final part of the chapter we explore the relevance and potential of a human rights framework for social work practice.

The United Nations

The UN came into being at the end of the Second World War in 1945. It emerged at a time when many countries were keen to prevent future conflicts of the scale that had occurred in the previous two world wars and a humanitarian ethos was in evidence. Historically, the UN was instrumental in the direction that social work took at that time as it catalysed the profession to engage in international humanitarian efforts and played a part in extending the reach of social work education across the developing world (Healy, 2001). Although this later led to accusations of 'imperialism' on the part of social work educators in the United States, Healy (2001, p. xi) points out that this was not due to 'a determined desire to propagate American casework', but rather a limited understanding of other cultures that mirrored the social conditions of that time.

While the UN initially comprised 51 countries, over a 60-year period its membership has expanded to 192 countries (UN, 2009). At the time of its inception, its stated purpose as outlined in the preamble of its charter was as follows:

- To protect future generations from the devastation of war;
- To restore faith in basic human rights, and the dignity, worth and equality of human beings and nations;
- To put in place the institutions and structures needed for the carriage of international law and justice; and
- To support social progress and promote a better quality of life for all. (UN, 1948)

Clearly, these are laudable and wide-ranging objectives. However, as mentioned earlier, it is apparent that the international community still has a long way to go in terms of achieving these objectives. In the wake of increased levels of civil strife around the world coupled with the growing trend of some countries to take pre-emptive military action to combat terrorism, some might even say that the world has taken a backward step in this regard.

Over the years, the UN has grown into a large interconnected system of global governance. The UN and its affiliated organizations engage in a wide variety of tasks that range from diffusing international crises and humanitarian relief work to promoting environmental protection and expanding food production. In 2000, the UN developed the Millennium Development Goals to address the multiple dimensions of poverty, with the explicit aim of halving the number of people living in extreme poverty, by 2015 (UN, 2008). More recently, we have witnessed the UN playing a somewhat contested and ambivalent role in the so-called war on terror. The UN also operates an International Criminal Court to deal with violations of international humanitarian law, including war crimes and acts of genocide. However, probably what this body is most recognized for is its work on human rights, which have become a more prominent discourse as result of a heightened interest in globalization.

The UN promotes human rights laws and norms and is responsible for monitoring and enforcing them. The main body responsible for this work is the Office of High Commissioner for Human Rights, under whose wing the Human Rights Council (HRC) was set up in 2006. The HRC is an intergovernmental body comprising 47 member states. The primary purpose of this body is to respond to and make recommendations on human rights violations. The HRC has established an Advisory Committee, which serves as a 'think tank' for the council and can seek input from member states, non-government organizations (NGOs) and other intergovernmental bodies. The HRC has also introduced universal periodic reviews, which entails each member state reviewing its human rights record every four years and reporting back to the UN (2009).

The core human rights document, known as the UDHR, was adopted by the United Nations General Assembly in 1948. The document is a fundamental statement about the inherent dignity, respect, rights and freedoms of all people throughout the world and sets out a comprehensive list of 30 human rights. The initial impetus for the UDHR was the massive loss of life and devastation that occurred during the Second World War. In particular, the Nazi Holocaust highlighted how the state can engage in inhumane practices against vulnerable citizens, pointing to the need for a human rights discourse that transcended national sovereignty (Finn and Jacobson, 2003, p. 126).

Human rights are described as universal, indivisible and inalienable (Dominelli, 2007c). They are universal in that every person has the same rights based on their shared humanity, irrespective of race, religion, gender, nationality or other status. Their indivisibility relates to the idea that they all have equal priority and cannot be ranked in terms of importance. This means that neither governments nor individuals can choose to recognize some rights but not others. Human rights are inalienable in the sense that they can never be denied by an outside party, such as the government, or even by the individual concerned (Ife, 2008, p. 16).

In the following section, we provide an overview of some of the historical ideas that have informed contemporary understandings of human rights. We then chart the evolution of the three generation of rights that have been identified by Wronka (1992) and further developed by Ife (2008).

Human rights – an overview

There are competing explanations about the philosophical and political origins of human rights. Some link the evolution of human rights with the ideas of Western liberal philosophers, such as Hobbes, Locke and Kant. Other commentators trace the evolution of ideas about civil and political freedoms back to political struggles in countries such as France, the United States and the United Kingdom. Still others suggest that all ancient civilizations, world religious systems and cultures have beliefs and practices that specifically value human beings, their dignity and right to life (Human Rights and Equal Opportunity Commission [HREOC], 2008). Yet again, Donnelly (2007, p. 287) argues that rather than having 'deep Western cultural roots', ideas about human rights developed in tandem with 'the social, economic and political transformations of modernity' and have applicability to all locations that have undergone such transformations, regardless of the original cultural context.

Ife (2008, pp. 30–4) delineates three generations of human rights that are based on a typology developed by Wronka (1992). The first generation of rights privileged discourses on individual civil and political rights, such as the right to vote, the right to movement, freedom of speech and the right to a fair trail. These ideas emerged during the Enlightenment era in the eighteenth century with the birth of liberalism, which places primacy on individual autonomy. The protection of these fundamental freedoms is seen as a prerequisite for the successful operation of a democratic, civic society. They are classed as 'negative rights' in the sense that priority is given to ensuring that people's basic freedoms are not violated, and they are encoded in the UDHR (Articles 2–21) and the International Covenant on Civil and Political Rights (ICCPR). However, legal mechanisms for ensuring the protection of these formal rights are often insufficient, particularly given the power of the state to make rulings within its own jurisdictional domain (Barkin, 1998).

The second generation of rights identified by Ife (2008) constitutes the economic, social and cultural rights required by people to express their cultural identity and be adequately housed, fed, schooled and employed. They are encoded in Articles 22–27 of the (UDHR), as well as the Covenant on Economic, Social and Cultural Rights (ESCR). They evolved from socialism and are framed as positive rights. They are also referred to as 'effective freedoms', which contrast with the 'formal freedoms' described previously. However, the role of the state in social provision is subjected to ongoing debate and, generally speaking, positive rights are not as well recognized as negative rights. Moreover, legal mechanisms are often ineffective in ensuring that such rights are realized, as they demand positive duties on the part of governments.

Ife (2008) identifies collective rights as the third generation of human rights. These rights are also known as 'solidarity rights'; they are underpinned by the assumption that in order to bring about social justice, we must foster a sense of fraternity where 'every right has a corresponding duty' (Wronka, 2007, p. 54). They are loosely framed in Article 29 of the UDHR, which makes reference to the entitlement to a collective order in which people's rights and freedoms can be realized. In contrast to liberal notions of rights, collective rights reflect a concern with the protection of entire communities, the right to sustainable economic development, the right to a clean environment and so on. Collective rights are of particular concern to developing nations and have become more prominent in the post-colonial era as newer nations seek to control their own destinies. Again, however, legal remedies – enshrined in treaties and conventions – have not been so effective in realizing such rights. Nonetheless, Ife (2008, p. 33) points out that given the relative newness of third generation rights, it is still too early to tell whether such freedoms can be effectively realized in the long term.

Some interpretations of collective or solidarity rights also entail the notion of intergenerational rights. In other words, there is recognition that human rights abuses that have occurred in the past can continue to have resonance for present and future generations (Ife, 2008). This includes recognizing the abuses and wrongs perpetrated against indigenous populations, such as dispossession and the removal of children from their families. Collective rights are particularly relevant to debates about climate change. Some governments in poorer countries have invoked human rights discourses to protect their citizens – and future generations – from the environmental fallout caused by the excessive consumption of richer countries (Oxfam, 2008b). However, in order to encompass intergenerational rights, a radical overhaul of current human rights laws and institutions is needed first (Oxfam, 2008b).

The implementation of human rights

The architects of the UDHR initially envisaged a single code to implement the rights spelt out in this document. However, major political and ideological differences between the United States, Russia and China led to two separate covenants: one on civil and political rights and another on economic, social and political rights (Eide and Rosas, 2001, p. 3). These two covenants – referred to in the previous section – are the ICCPR and the ICESCR. However, the ICESCR is limited to the extent that it contains a caveat that these rights can be recognized progressively, depending on the state's ability to finance them. One of the major consequences of this division is the misconception that there is a hierarchy of human rights, where civil and political rights are seen to be more important than social, economic and cultural rights (Midgley, 2007b). This ideological difference has continued to the present, although there is now greater recognition that the two sets of rights are interdependent. As Annan (2005, p. 5) points out below, the recognition of one without the other does not allow a person to reach his or her full potential:

> Even if he can vote to choose his rulers, a young man with AIDS who cannot read or write and lives on the brink of starvation is not truly free. Equally, even if she can earn enough to live, a woman who lives in the shadow of daily violence and has no say in how her country is run is not truly free.

A number of international NGOs have started to strategically use the provisions of the ICESCR to argue for people's entitlement to 'education, health care, water, food, [and] even the right to development' (Nelson and Dorsey, 2003, p. 2015). Similarly, in Western countries the language of human rights has been used by individuals and groups to argue that the welfare state has an obligation to provide minimum standards of living. For example, the British Institute of Human Rights (BIHR) and Oxfam are exploring the relevance of human rights laws for addressing poverty. Within a human rights framework, poverty is viewed as a structural problem rather than as an individual concern. People living in poverty are robbed of dignity and respect and access to the social and employment services necessary to achieve a fulfilling life (BIHR, 2008, pp. 2–3).

Over the past 60 years, the UN's framework on human rights has expanded from the UDHR to include a range of other instruments. In addition to the ICCPR and the ICESCR, a variety of conventions have evolved that seek to protect the rights of refugees, eliminate discrimination against women, prohibit discrimination in the workplace, prevent torture and protect children. More recently, the rights of indigenous groups have been recognized through the UN Declaration on the rights of Indigenous Peoples (2007), and in 2006, the Convention on the Rights of Persons with Disabilities was adopted. These instruments, along with a number of other treaties, have evolved in response to the recognition of new human rights issues or groups who are not adequately protected by existing frameworks, demonstrating that human rights is an ongoing, emerging discourse (Ife, 2008).

Since the adoption of the UDHR, a number of region- and country-specific conventions and charters on human rights have been developed. These include the European Convention on Human Rights (1950), the American Convention on Human Rights (1978), the African Charter on Human and People's Rights (1981) and the Canadian Charter of Rights and Freedoms (1982). In the United Kingdom, the Human Rights Act (1998) came into force in 2000, in turn making the European Convention on Human Rights part of British Law. This act enables a person to take complaints about human rights directly to British courts. The Act also requires public services – including social services – to adopt a human rights approach to improve service provision and outcomes (Department for Constitutional Affairs [DCA], 2006). Nonetheless, a recent report suggests that public authorities lack an understanding of their legal duties under this legislation (Butler, 2005). Moreover, some argue that the Act does not offer adequate protection for vulnerable and marginalized populations (Harding, 2005). For example, voluntary organizations providing health and welfare services were initially excluded from its purview because they are not legally defined as public authorities. However, following intense lobbying by human rights activists, NGOs which receive government tenders and contracts to provide services are now included under the Act (Equality and Human Rights Commission, 2008). Individuals paying privately for human services provision, however, are still not covered by the Act.

The effectiveness of existing mechanisms for protecting human rights

There are advantages and limitations in locating human rights in a legal framework. Ife (2008, p. 109) identifies one of the major limitations of using legal systems to protect people's rights as the issue of access:

> As long as the law and the legal system are seen as the primary mechanism for protecting an individual's or a group's rights, the question of equality of access to the law becomes a primary human rights question.

Access to the law and representation in court is particularly a problem for poor people. Seeking redress in courts is an expensive and time-consuming process. The adversarial nature of the legal system can be traumatic for vulnerable groups such as asylum seekers and rape victims (Ife, 2001). The onus is on the individual to claim his or her rights and a legal judgement is made about the state's responsibility to protect or promote the human rights of its citizens. Moreover, the enactment of legislation is usually not sufficient in itself to change attitudes and end discrimination that arises through factors such as racism, sexism or ageism. Another problem associated with this framework is that those classified as 'non-citizens', including asylum seekers and guest workers, may have limited legal redress due to their status.

As mentioned earlier, legal mechanisms are often ineffective in ensuring that social rights such as the right to be housed, fed and educated are realized. As Ife (2008, p. 32) points out, it would be difficult to take a government to court for failing to provide an adequate education system. However, on the plus side it also means that individuals can makes rights-based claims on the basis of citizenship entitlements rather than on the basis of need alone. This has the effect of reducing the stigma associated with making such claims, as it 'emphasizes entitlement rather than charity' (Skegg, 2005, p. 671). Formal human rights mechanisms have also been used successfully by Indigenous groups such as Aboriginal Australians to bring to the world's attention discriminatory government policies. These include overt policies of discrimination such as the widespread removal of children by the state on the basis of race.

Nonetheless, while mechanisms are available for placing local human rights concerns on the UN's agenda, there has been sustained criticism of the UN's ability to effectively ensure compliance with human rights laws (Alston and Crawford, 2000). Even when states ratify conventions, the separation between domestic and international law effectively renders the UN impotent unless the state elects to abide by UN law. While member states are obliged to report their activities on a regular basis, UN bodies only have the power to recommend that states comply with their international human rights obligations.

In recognition of these limitations, a parallel system of accountability on human rights issues has evolved outside the UN. Organizations such as Amnesty International and Human Rights Watch have been highly critical of governments that have violated or refused to recognize human rights and periodically provide their own reports to UN monitoring bodies, either in lieu of country reports or in addition to them. These reports carry considerable moral authority by exposing human rights abuses and shaming states within the international community. However, this is still not a satisfactory solution to guaranteeing compliance with human rights treaties.

The UN has to negotiate a balancing act between respecting national sovereignty and acting to prevent human rights abuses, and this balance has been particularly hard to achieve in some post-colonial contexts. On one hand, given the history of colonization and exploitation of developing countries by Western states, the UN is careful to respect these countries' national sovereignty. On the other hand, there are growing demands that the UN become more interventionist to prevent human rights abuses in a number of these countries. Equally, however, the UN has been subjected to criticism because of a perception that its most powerful member states dictates its terms of reference and agendas.

Some have argued that a focus on human rights has become an anachronism in a pluralist and globalized world. However, others have suggested that upholding the basic principles of human rights is paramount to resolving the pressing challenges facing humanity, such as global warming, international security and poverty (Annan, 2005). While the UDHR is an admiral document in its intent, it has also been subjected to considerable debate and critique from a variety of sources. In the following section, we explore some of the more prominent feminist and cultural critiques of human rights.

Feminist and cultural critiques of human rights

Some feminists are wary of the idea of a set of Universal Human Rights that may inadvertently perpetuate existing inequalities between men and women. In particular, they argue that the first generation of human rights, embedded in the liberal tradition of civic and political rights, is gender blind. According to these critics, the existing declaration privileges the public sphere over the private sphere where women have traditionally operated (e.g. see Peterson and Parisi, 1998). Thus, women's work and private spheres of concern are marginalized in human rights discourses. For example, violence directed at women in the home has traditionally been seen to fall outside the scope of human rights. Yet violence against women occurs in every country irrespective of culture, race, ethnicity or religion. More recently, however, issues such as rape and other forms of personal violence have been put on the UN's agenda as a result of feminist campaigns to expand the language of human rights. This has also been facilitated by the UN's adoption of the Convention on the Elimination of All Forms of Discrimination against Women in 1979 and the Declaration on the Elimination of Violence against Women adopted in 1993.

In addition to feminist critiques of human rights, a central debate revolves around the assertion that all humans have the same universal and natural rights arising from their shared humanity. Typically, this debate manifests in an appeal to a universal set of human rights versus the claim that rights are contingent on cultural context (Healy, 2007b). Those espousing cultural relativism argue that there are no universal human rights, as all cultures are different and thus human rights must be viewed from a range of different cultural perspectives. Rather than adopting a uniform approach to human rights, they argue that countries should be allowed to develop human rights in accordance with their particular circumstances.

Some commentators argue that human rights are predominantly a Western invention, based on individualistic values, which are inappropriate in some cultural contexts. A stronger version of this argument is that the UDHR is an extension of the colonial project, used by 'the West' to exert control over poorer Asian nations and undermine their development. This argument has been employed in those countries that have prioritized second-generation rights, such as China, Indonesia, Malaysia and Singapore. According to this argument, the right to eat, receive health care, be educated and housed takes precedence over first-generation rights such as the right to vote and freedom of speech (Suh, 1997). These critics argue that the adoption of Western forms of individual expression and lifestyles would undermine the moral fabric and social cohesion of their countries. 'Asian values', which emphasize the collective over the individual, are seen to be more conducive to promoting economic growth and social cohesion (Magnarella, 2004).

However, not everyone agrees with this view. The Asian Human Rights Commission (1998), a voluntary NGO, argues that 'Asian values' are invoked by governments to justify the suppression of political and civil freedoms, including the development of democracy. Feminists are also critical of how 'Asian values' are used to resist universal norms in human rights, claiming that they perpetuate discrimination on the basis of gender (Amirthalingam, 2005). The reification of these values has had unfortunate consequences for women, especially those working towards local domestic violence reform. Cultural explanations are used to normalize the power differential between men and women and hence minimize men's responsibility in perpetrating violence against women. On the other hand, a gender analysis 'helps to dissipate the cultural relativist arguments by demonstrating that, in many cases, violence against women is a patriarchal interpretation of cultural norms' (Amirthalingam, 2005, p. 707).

Some African and Middle Eastern countries are suspicious of the liberal human rights agenda promoted by Western nations and see human rights as part of a neocolonial project. For example, the United States has been criticized for using human rights as a political tool to legitimize its own economic and political interests in those countries and gain access to their oil and gas resources (Hölscher and Berhane, 2008, p. 318). In a similar vein, Amirthalingam (2005, p. 701) describes how some Asian leaders' resistance to universal norms in human rights was fuelled by the perception that Western governments were strategically employing human rights obligations to curb the competitive edge of economies with low labour costs. However, in this context Goodhart (2003, p. 941) notes an unfortunate tendency to 'conflate human rights, Western values, and neoliberal globalization, and to conceive the proliferation of human rights as a form of cultural hegemony'.

In order to move beyond the impasse presented by cultural relativism and extreme universalism, it is necessary to rethink the meaning of culture, especially as it relates to human rights. Cultures are not static; cultural norms and practices change over time in response to both internal and external pressures. Furthermore, no culture is homogeneous, and there are considerable variations within cultures based on gender, race, class, status, age and religion (UN Population Fund [UNFPA], 2008). In practice, this means that the principles and concepts of the UDHR should be seen as universal, but their implementation must be done within a particular cultural context, without lapsing into moral relativism (UNFPA, 2008).

Huang and Zhang (2008) highlight a tendency by some writers in social work to reify the differences between 'Eastern' and 'Western' cultures, portraying them as monolithic, fixed entities that lack any commonalities. They further argue that strictly adhering to cultural relativism obliges us to turn a blind eye to practices that may be harmful to people. While respect for cultures is seen to be integral to 'good' and 'moral' practice in social work, Healy (2007b, p. 23) warns:

> The ethical dangers in viewing culture as sacrosanct are serious and include trampling on the rights of those who may wish their rights respected; according fewer rights for some than others; and not paying attention to the concept of harm in all its complexities.

In accordance with this view, all social and cultural structures that promote victimization and oppression need to be subjected to critical examination. Moreover, Skegg (2005, p. 670) argues that even if human rights are a Western invention, 'shielding such cultures from exploring Western culture patronizes those cultures by denying them the opportunity to make their own decisions.' By the same token, social workers need to be aware of how the 'difference' argument can be used to perpetuate existing inequalities and human rights abuses.

The UNFPA (2008, p. 22) suggests that in order to engage in culturally sensitive practice, we first need to recognize that while people *across* cultures may understand rights in different ways, even people *within* the same culture will have different understandings and experiences of rights. This then allows for people both within and across cultural contexts to advocate for rights in ways that are relevant for their particular contexts, ensuring that such rights have 'cultural legitimacy'. In this sense, it may be more helpful to talk about the '*relative* universality of human rights, rather than their relative *universality*' (Donnelly, 2007, p. 292; emphasis in original).

Ife (2008, pp. 81–5) suggests that we need to engage in a dialogical process in the construction of what human rights mean in different cultural contexts. The discourse of human rights is a dynamic one and should not consist of top-down, imposed legal or abstract principles. At a crosscultural level, people do not need a sophisticated understanding of the legal or philosophical theory of human rights to appreciate that their basic needs are not being fulfilled or that their physical, mental or psychological sense of self is being violated.

In spite of the critiques and debates discussed previously, the language and norms of human rights have come to be accepted by almost every nation in the world (Donnelly, 2007, p. 288). Similarly, discourses on human rights are strongly infused in the social work literature while also being subjected to considerable debate. On a practice level, social workers deal with human rights issues in many aspects of their work, although they may not always be articulated as such. In the next section, we explore some of these links between social work and human rights.

The place of human rights in social work

In social work, we are witnessing a renewed interest in human rights, which in part has been fuelled by the efforts of the International Federation of Social Workers (IFSW) to make this theme a key focus of its work (Healy, 2001, p. 58). This is evident in a range of documents produced by the IFSW, including its definition of social work, its statement of ethical principles, its policy on human rights and its human rights manuals for practice. The IFSW's 2004 statement of ethical principles accords priority to 'respect for the inherent worth and dignity of all people and the rights that follow on from this' (IFSW, 2005d). Self-determination, empowerment and partici- pation; treating people holistically; and recognizing people's strengths are identified as the key values underpinning this stance. In addition, respon- sibility is placed on social workers to 'uphold and defend each person's physical, psychological, emotional and spiritual integrity and wellbeing' (IFSW, 2005d).

While Banks (2006) points out that codes of ethics in themselves do not safeguard clients' rights, this strong commitment to human rights was recently reaffirmed by the IFSW on the 60th anniversary of the UDHR. In addition, the IFSW has consultative status with the UN and in conjunc- tion with the International Association of Schools of Social Work (IASSW) has established a Human Rights Commission, which advocates for social workers who themselves have suffered violations of their human rights.

Along with the work carried out by the IFSW, many writers have sought to marry human rights discourses with social work theory and practice (Dominelli, 2007c, Ife, 2008; Healy, 2001; Reichert, 2003; Skegg, 2005; Witkin, 1998; Wronka, 2007). Ife and Fiske (2006) further suggest that a human rights framework is consistent with the principles and methods of community work. Indeed, human rights are viewed as being 'insepar- able from social work theory, values, ethics, and practice' (Johannesen, 1997, p. 155 – cited in Healy, 2001, p. 58). Yet while acknowledging the human rights work of individual practitioners and professional bodies it would appear that a good number of social workers experience difficulties in knowing how to translate human rights into practice. In this sense, human rights run the risk of remaining an academic discourse in social work rather than one that that is firmly grounded in practice.

One possible reason for this is the limited amount of attention human rights receives in social work education, which Dominelli (2007c, p. 17) describes as 'death through benign neglect'. Yet human rights do have clear links with social workers' day-to-day practice in terms of helping people gain employment, education, health care and housing; assisting victims of abuse and violence; and advocating for people's rights when they face discrimination. While practitioners may not use the language of human rights to describe this type of work, these are clearly social work roles. As Ife (2008, p. 42) points out, 'While only a minority of social workers would be seen as concerned primarily with first-generation rights, most if not all social workers are concerned with helping people realize second-generation rights.'

However, it is perhaps less common for social workers to use human rights frameworks when conducting assessments and planning interventions. There are, of course, exceptions. For example, some social workers have successfully used the 'positive obligations' of the Human Rights Act in the United Kingdom to secure resources for vulnerable people, as illustrated by the following example:

> A social worker from the domestic violence team at a local authority used human rights arguments to secure new accommodation for a woman and her family at risk of serious harm from a violent ex-partner. She had received training on the 'positive obligations' placed on the local authority to protect the right to life (under Article 2) and the right to be free from inhuman and degrading treatment (under Article 3). (D. C. A. 2006, p. 9)

For other social workers, however, organizational factors may impact their ability to work within a human rights framework. Social workers are employed in statutory or government agencies as well as non-government or voluntary organizations. In statutory agencies, social workers may be constrained by management and organizational prerogatives that focus on risk assessment rather than human rights. Social workers are equally called upon to resolve complex ethical and human rights claims with diminishing resources at their disposal. While practitioners in the voluntary sector may be less constrained by the organizational context in which they operate, they still face challenges in securing resources for disadvantaged people.

On a broader level, engagement with human rights does entail an expectation to be involved in transformative politics, and some writers have urged practitioners to be more proactive and to utilize their advocacy skills to address human rights abuses and promote social justice (Healy, 2001;

Noyoo, 2004; Pollack, 2007). However, moving from embracing rhetoric to political action is a perennial dilemma within the social work profession, and some social workers have not embraced this challenge. Indeed, one cross-country study revealed a predominantly conservative approach to advocacy and overt political activities within the profession (Gray, van Rooyen, Rennie and Gaha, 2002).

In a similar vein, Noyoo (2004, p. 365) argues that there has been a retreat from activism among South African social workers following the demise of the Apartheid regime, where 'social workers have gone back to doing mundane day-to-day issues like getting through caseloads.' Noyoo (2004) goes on to suggest that while structural inequalities still exist and keep people in poverty, these inequalities have become obscured and less obvious now that civil and political rights have been achieved.

Alternatively, social workers may be subjected to the influence of conservative political regimes, which may thwart their ability to 'speak out' or advocate on behalf of clients. In one Australian study, it was found that dependence on government funding helped to silence critics from NGOs (Melville and Perkins, 2003). A study carried out on the professional journal of the Philippine Association of Social Workers during the era of the Marcos dictatorship revealed that some social workers embraced the rhetoric of the Marcos regime in spite of human rights abuses (Yu, 2006). It would appear then, that environmental, political and organizational factors are key influences on social workers' political activities.

It is important to acknowledge the role played by broader social movements and civil society in encouraging the participation of individuals and groups in human rights campaigns. We recognize that individual social workers are actively involved in a range of NGOs and civil society political and advocacy organizations. Perhaps another option available for social workers is to establish a dedicated political organization to coordinate human rights campaigns, similar to Nurses for Human Rights and Physicians for Human Rights. This provides institutional independence and would enable social workers who wish to be more actively involved in politics to do so outside the workplace. For example, Physicians for Human Rights were involved with a successful global campaign to force drug companies to allow the development and sale of generic HIV/AIDS drugs in developing countries (Nelson and Dorsey, 2003).

As noted previously, the social work profession has a made a clear commitment to promote human rights in practice. However, there is still a way to go to build human rights into the education, everyday practice and political activities of social workers. Healy (2001, pp. 269–70) argues that one of the benefits of employing a rights framework in practice is that it assists social workers to move away from a personal pathology model and focus on issues of social justice. Symbolically, human rights provides a useful language for challenging 'wrongs' and furthering justice. In this sense, rights discourses represent political tools available to social work activists in their quest for social change. However, Dominelli (2007c) warns that human rights run the risk of remaining embedded in social work's value base rather than being translated into practice. Accordingly, we suggest that the onus is on social work educators to 'rethink' the way they teach human rights in social work and to increase its visibility in the social work curriculum.

Summary

In this chapter, we have examined the birth of the United Nations and the evolution of ideas about human rights. While the UDHR has been endorsed by most countries, there are considerable challenges to its implementation. Human rights discourses are imbued with tensions and contradictions relating to a diverse set of issues ranging from the autonomy of the nation state to cultural relativity and imperialism. Although human rights discourses feature significantly in the social work literature, there is concern that human rights will remain an academic discourse unless more efforts are directed at translating human rights discourses into practice. In spite of a strong commitment to human rights in social work, the profession still has some way to go before the potential of a human rights perspective can be fully realized in local practice contexts. In order to raise the profile of human rights in social work practice, it will be first necessary to raise its profile in social work education.

Discussion points

1. What do you see as the benefits of adopting a rights-based approach to social work practice? How is using the language of human rights different to using the language of need?
2. What do you think is meant by the phrase the '*relative* universality of human rights'? What are the implications of this for culturally sensitive social work practice?
3. Employing the language of human rights can be an effective tool for social work activists in challenging harmful practices and influencing policy. Why do you think the language of human rights is so influential?
4. What are some of the potential organizational constraints that may prevent social workers from adopting a rights-based framework for practice?
5. How might you go about setting up a dedicated political organization for social workers to coordinate human rights campaigns?

Chapter 10

Conclusion – Ending on an Uncertain Note

Introduction

One of the overarching themes in this book is the idea that happenings in the broader global arena along with history shape our experience of locality and that this is a dynamic process. This in turn has implications for social work practice at the local level. However, in Chapter 1, we stated that we were reluctant to make too many concrete prescriptions or predictions for social work because of the rapidly changing and dynamic global environment in which social work practice occurs. Indeed, over the course of writing this book, we have observed that the global credit crisis we referred to in Chapter 1 has morphed into a global economic meltdown that has sent many countries into recession, resulted in massive job losses and compounded existing food shortages. In 2009, the United Nation's Development Programme (UNDP, 2009) proclaimed that this 'global economic crisis' represents a 'human development crisis' that threatens to compound existing poverty and set back the Millennium Development Goals. Moreover, neither of us predicted that by the time we finished this book we would possibly be entering a new political era marked by the election of the first black president in US history. In this changeable environment, predictions and prescriptions for social work can very quickly become outdated and irrelevant.

In the remainder of this chapter, we briefly track the key themes and ideas that have been covered in this book as a way of reorienting the reader to the content covered. We then return to our central thesis that there is a need to rethink social work in a global, postcolonial world, and in this section, we draw on writings from recent social work graduates to hear their ideas about how the global interacts with the local in practice. In some ways, hearing their accounts assists us to negotiate the perceived theory–practice divide that we referred to in Chapter 1, while also demonstrating how the global is experienced differently, depending on one's local positioning. This is in accord with Appadurai's (1996) ideas about subjective experiences of globalization, which were explored in Chapter 2. In the final part of the chapter we outline what we see as some of the main issues and challenges for social work arising from this discussion and conclude the chapter with some thoughts on the actual process involved in 'rethinking' social work.

Retracing our steps

In Chapters 1 and 2, we set the scene for the book by highlighting a 'global' turn in social work and speculated on why discourses on globalization have become so influential in social work at this point in time. We suggested that one reason why 'the global' may resonate with many writers in social work is because, via the media and a range of other influential institutions, we are constantly reminded of how we live in an interconnected and interdependent world. Issues such as climate change, the economy, trade and migration all need to be placed in a global context in order to fully understand their operations and their effects. Moreover, such factors impact practice at the local level, although their linkages may not be immediately discernible. In this way, the global offers a new analytical lens to examine social problems while also challenging us to rethink notions of social justice in terms of global justice. Placing local issues in a global, spatial and historical context can offer new insights into practice. At the same time, we acknowledged that globalization is a contested term, its effects are sometimes overstated and employing such a discourse runs the risk of conflating causation with association and description with prescription. Nonetheless, an appreciation of globalizing forces does help us to both understand and contextualize the social, economic, political and cultural domains of people's lives.

Locating social work in a global context is not necessarily a new idea, particularly if we think about how colonial expansion has been implicated in the development of the welfare state in many countries. In addition, processes of colonization and decolonization continue to profoundly influence the lives of many people around the world, while new forms of imperialism have emerged via capitalist expansion and political control. Indeed, contemporary patterns of globalization actually build on a long history of colonialism and imperialism. However, postcolonial critics have contested deterministic accounts of colonization and globalization, claiming that colonization was and still is actively resisted and that it is not a straightforward process of conquest and domination. Instead, these critics argue that it is a transformative experience for both the colonizer and the colonized.

In this way, postcolonialism is a useful adjunct to globalization for thinking about the interactions between the local and the global. Moreover, it assists us to unpack representational practices that deny the agency of colonized groups and reproduce the power relations of the colonial era. What is equally important here is to think about how we locate ourselves and how we are positioned in relation to others in a global, postcolonial world. For social workers, this is a very important consideration when working with indigenous populations, especially when trying to understand and address the impact of colonization and dispossession on their lives. On another level, indigenous perspectives have been influential in the development of innovative forms of practice in social work, although it is lamentable that they took so long to be acknowledged by the profession.

In the remaining seven chapters, we focused on some key issues and populations that have particular significance for social work in a global, postcolonial context. In Chapter 3, we examined the role of global capitalism and neoliberal market-driven policies in exacerbating poverty and increasing inequality not just between countries but also within countries. Some commentators suggest that global capital has replaced older styles of imperialism. Globalization has not seen the end of the nation state, but most nation states are now much more attuned to global rather than national markets. For many poorer countries, unfair trade relations have worked against their ability to be competitive in the global market place. Nation states also have to relate to a range of supranational institutions such as the World Bank and the International Monetary Fund (IMF). These institutions have been subjected to criticism for imposing structural adjustment programmes on poorer countries that at times have actually increased rather than reduced poverty. Although poverty is a complex and contested phenomenon, what is clear is that the extent of global poverty is alarming, particularly in developing countries. Social workers have long been concerned with the impact of poverty on people's lives, but practical poverty alleviation strategies are not enough to eradicate poverty. In order to be effective in this regard, it will be necessary to build coalitions with other like-minded groups that share a mandate to end poverty and take on a more activist role in advocating for global redistributive justice.

Chapter 4 focused on the politics of migration and people movement. We suggested that social workers need to have an appreciation of these politics in order to understand their impacts on people's lives, especially in terms of how immigration policies may be used to regulate and at times prevent the movement of people. Such policing practices are particularly evident when people try to move from the global South to the global North. Anti-immigrant sentiment may compound the transitional stress experienced by people when they do move to a new country, and in this context it is an important consideration for practitioners working with migrants who are negotiating the settlement process. It was further suggested that we need to go beyond state-centric notions of justice and citizenship in order to protect the rights of migrants. Migration has an impact on communities in both sending and receiving countries. Remittances represent an important source of income for many people in the world, and migration has the potential to reconfigure people's social and economic relations in both sending and receiving countries, while straining critical infrastructure in some poorer countries. Transnational caregiving is another issue that has gained prominence more recently, and it is likely to be an issue that social workers will increasingly become involved with in the future.

In Chapter 5, we examined the ways in which globalization has transformed gender relations and impacted women with reference to four issues: migration, the global care chain, violence and the feminization of poverty. In addition, we explored how globalization has enhanced opportunities for transnational activism to promote gender equality and women's rights. Although women's experiences of globalization are diverse, there are commonalities among women in terms of their social position in relation to men and their prominent role in domestic and care work. Addressing women's poverty is key to the eradication of poverty, and in order do so, efforts need to be directed at keeping girls in school, improving women's economic position and enabling women to enter the paid-labour market. Challenging entrenched cultural beliefs that restrict the roles available to women and normalize gendered violence is also necessary in order to allow women to fully realize their human rights and achieve gender equality. In this sense, we suggested that social workers can act as agents of cultural change, working not only with women but also with men and boys to promote attitudinal and behavioural change.

In Chapter 6 we focused on mental health as a neglected topic in broader discussions on global health. Mental health is inextricably linked with poverty and disability, and it is low- and middle-income countries that have to contend with most of the global burden of mental illness. Moreover, the migration of health professionals to richer countries has been implicated in severe shortages of professional mental health staff in poorer countries. A global mental health movement has arisen to challenge major inequities that exist between developed and developing countries in the provision of mental health services, which has been referred to as the 'treatment gap'. In this chapter, we suggested that this is an issue that the social work profession equally needs to be concerned with. Given the link between mental health and poverty, it is also important for social workers to recognize the importance of community and economic development to safeguard people's mental health. The global mental health movement has recognized the need to combat the stigma and discrimination associated with mental illness in order to increase the profile of mental health and improve uptake of services. In order to ensure equitable access to services and medications for people with mental health problems, it is also important to locate mental health within a human rights framework for practice.

Information and communication technologies (ICTs) have radically altered many people's work and social lives, and in Chapter 7 we explored these effects along with the unequal global distribution of ICTs. The digital divide has compromised the social and economic development of 'unconnected' populations, and in that sense it is of concern to social work. While some in social work have embraced these technologies, others see them as serious threats to the autonomy of the profession because they are seen to primarily serve managerial and organizational interests rather than the interests of workers and clients. Nonetheless, given the potential of ICTs for linking up people around the world, cyber enthusiasts have pointed to their potential to promote social change at both local and global levels. For these social activists, the communication capacities of ICTs represent the means for a new form of global citizenship to evolve. However, post-colonial critics have also drawn attention to some of the representational practices employed on the Internet that misrepresent or propagate negative images of 'unconnected groups', including indigenous and minority groups. Social workers, therefore, need to be critically reflexive about their own representational practices, especially in terms of their implications for those who remain outside the 'connected' world.

In Chapter 8 we turned to the issue of the environment. It is now well recognized that climate change and its impact on the environment is a crucial issue for the global community and that our obligations of environmental justice go beyond the local level. Climate change has significant implications for poorer people who are likely to shoulder most of the economic, social and health costs associated with environmental degradation. Communities have been displaced, diseases such as malaria are on the increase and food costs have escalated, in turn exacerbating existing poverty. Although it is difficult to predict the full impact of climate change, what is clear is that some populations are more at risk of poverty and dislocation than others because of their physical location. Social workers are likely to be working with increasing numbers of people affected by droughts, floods, famines and other climate-related disasters while assisting communities adapt to climate change. The rapid rate at which these changes are taking place points to the need for an environmental consciousness in social work, whereby workers develop a sound understanding of the links between the physical environment and people's welfare. This may also entail challenging government policies that favour unbalanced development while promoting sustainable development.

Finally, in Chapter 9, we considered the value of a human rights perspective in social work. Globalization, along with the movement for global citizenship, have brought human rights to the fore and provided a timely opportunity to rethink the place of human rights in social work. While a human rights framework for practice has been strongly endorsed in social work at both national and international levels, the universal applicability of the Universal Declaration of Human Rights (UDHR) has been called into question. Moreover, there are significant challenges in translating these rights into practice. Despite these challenges, at a political level, human rights provides a useful language for challenging injustice via a set of common standards that all signatory countries are expected to abide by. However, there is a danger that human rights will remain a predominantly academic discourse in social work unless more efforts are directed at the educational front in assisting practitioners learn how to employ a human rights framework in practice.

While all of the foregoing issues have been examined as discrete themes in separate chapters, on closer examination their interconnections are apparent. For example, Yujuico (2009, p. 63) points out: 'The art of sending remittances overlaps with migration, technological innovation and marketing – three of globalization's driving forces.' Similarly, human rights interconnect with global redistributive justice, improving the status of women, ensuring that migrants and refugees receive fair and equitable treatment, protecting vulnerable populations at risk of environmental degradation, closing the treatment gap in mental health and addressing digital inequality. There are, of course, many other interconnections, but again their relevance is really only meaningful at the local level.

Hearing practitioners' accounts of the global-local interaction

At this juncture, we think it is appropriate to provide some examples of how social workers themselves are factoring in a global perspective into their practice. The following commentaries were written by fourth-year social work students in Brisbane, Australia, who were completing their final placement in a variety of settings, including a hospital, a health centre, a centre for homeless people, an international student service and a migrant support service. These services were located in both metropolitan and rural areas. The students were asked to comment on what importance they attached to a global perspective in social work, and we have reproduced some of their ideas below.

For one student, the impact of the global on the local was in evidence at all levels of her practice, which she illustrates below, with reference to examples:

> I can see globalization in action in all facets of my current placement. For example, the role of my supervisor was created due to the influence of international research and continues to evolve as new findings emerge. In addition, as a Primary Health Care Unit, we rely heavily on the World Health Organization's definition of 'health', the Ottawa Charter and the Universal Declaration of Human Rights as supporting evidence for the need for a holistic approach to health. At a macro level...the influence of neo-liberalism and market forces on State and Federal levels of government have resulted in drastic cuts to our service's resources and to the health sector generally. In contrast, at a micro level, I see the impact that globalization is having on clients of our service – rising fuel costs have resulted in people being unable to travel from

their remote properties to major towns for appointments and the rising cost of food is also affecting many clients. (Frances Cheverton, 10 September 2008)

Similarly, another student highlighted social problems in rural Australia that she attributed to global forces. In addition, she commented on how increasing levels of migration and her contact with diverse communities has resulted in her adopting a new form of reflexivity in her practice that does not rely on a Western framework:

> Locally, I am motivated by the rise in the number of suicides which have occurred in rural Australia. Changes associated with global environmental and economic conditions which have gained greater momentum ... cannot be ignored in this context. Additionally, I am enthused by the opportunities which have been presented to me ... to walk alongside and learn from those in the community who came to this country from culturally and linguistically diverse communities to form new communities. I intend to become more reflexive from a perspective other than that promoted in the Western literature. (Christine Gardiner, 12 September 2008)

A global perspective had alerted one student to innovative forms of social work practice. In addition, he flagged the importance of social workers contributing to broader debates on global issues such as climate change:

> Perhaps a better approach is in using tangible examples of how a global perspective plays an important role for social work practice on several levels. One example is with Family Group Conferencing in Child Protection, a model adopted from Maori knowledge and method that has had success in different settings. Similarly, social work can respond to global issues such as the climate change debate by outlining social issues and costs of inaction, particularly as business appears to be currently dominating debate and shifting focus to the immediate short term financial costs. (Keirnan Fitzpatrick, 12 September 2008)

Another student highlighted the importance of employing a global lens for assessment purposes, along with the value of professional exchange for acquiring knowledge and pursuing global justice agendas:

> A global perspective is needed to critically evaluate the practice implications of such global issues as climate change, oil shocks, population movements, unfair trade, wars, and natural disasters. The effect of the global on the local is illustrated in my placement agency, which supports the settlement of unaccompanied humanitarian minors. These minors have experienced grief and loss, torture and trauma, as well as facing an array of complex settlement issues. Social workers engage with people from many countries and cultures in diverse fields of practice. It is therefore important for social workers to have a global perspective so they can practise in a culturally competent and ethical way. A global

perspective promotes practice competence through professional exchange and the application of knowledge. These exchanges can pre-empt the development of global policies which emphasize social justice and which foster cross-cultural advocacy on behalf of the world's oppressed. (David Meddings, 12 September 2008)

Other students highlighted the impact of war, displacement and immigration on receiving countries. For example, one student suggested that relocating to a new country has implications for both migrants and the receiving country and that in this respect social workers need to adopt a global perspective:

My position on globalization as an emerging social worker has to do with the inter-relatedness and interconnectedness [of] the world. For example, the effect of the civil wars in Africa has had a great change on the social, cultural, economic and political structures of Australia. These people come with social roles, including their race, ethnicity and religion. Sociologically speaking, social roles help people build their identity, community, etc. Moreover, it can pose a challenge for people living in a multicultural nation such as Australia. As an African myself, despite assuming Australian citizenship I will not forget my cultural background. It is at this juncture that social workers in a multicultural nation need to acquire and understand global perspectives. (Lawrence Massaquoi, 12 September 2008)

A variation expressed on this theme was that while migration could be directly linked to globalization, it was still a local issue that required a local response:

Social workers in frontline practice are face-to-face with local conditions, local culture and local diversity. ... The worldwide movement of people ... is a direct result of globalization, and I believe this has the greatest impact for social workers at a national/local level. ... Nevertheless, social workers will remain in the best position to understand and deal with local issues while knowing these issues are influenced or even caused by globalization. (Lorraine O'Reilly, 12 September 2008)

Similarly, another student took a more nuanced view, warning that social workers should not be too ambitious in embracing a global outlook but that they should be equally aware of when a global perspective in practice is needed:

The connection of local practice and global forces in social work is complex. ... Overemphasizing globalization might simplify the function of culture, language and the nation state in effective practice. But ignoring the importance of globalization might oppress exploration of how these processes impact on the social and cultural conditions of contemporary society. Therefore, social workers should be critically conscious of ambitious global expectations in social work, but equally conscious of their capacity to draw attention to global issues that have important consequences for clients, and all of humanity. (Thomas Pritzler, 12 September 2008)

For one student, her own identity and overseas study experiences were salient factors in informing her stance on the importance of a global outlook:

The stance that I adopt reflects my own experiences as both a social work student studying in Australia and an individual with a Japanese background. During my current placement with International Student Services, I have had many opportunities to find social work practice influenced by globalization...even social workers in a non-multicultural nation need to be engaged in local practice with global perspectives. (Kyoko Ishigure, 10 September 2008)

Finally, it was suggested that a global perspective in social work was already a 'given' and that the more pertinent question was what do social work graduates need to know to work effectively in this context:

I have worked in the slums of urban Thailand where wealthy white businessmen create an industry around exploiting young Thai men and women. I have worked in a locally conceived micro finance program in rural Kenya, where international trading practices, colonization and amoral pharmaceutical distribution have created massive intergenerational poverty, and I have worked at the Multicultural Development Association in supporting the settlement of refugees in Australia....My current role at [a] homelessness service centre is also inextricably linked to the international economic-rationalist agenda that has seen the market become the distributing mechanism for resources through the outsourcing of welfare services....It is my contention that globalization has had a massive impact on everyone on the planet. That is a given. The pertinent question is 'How has globalization affected social work practice and what, if anything, do graduating social workers need to know about the process to best meet the needs of our clients?' (Timothy Carroll, 12 September 2008)

Rethinking social work – an ongoing process

The previous commentary by Timothy Carroll alerts us to the importance of social work educators going beyond just pointing to the importance of locating social work in a global context and thinking about what is it that students need to know to practise effectively in this context. However, as stated earlier, we do not believe it is advisable to make too many concrete prescriptions for practice in such an uncertain, changeable environment.

Social work has been identified as a profession that has a robust capacity for coping with uncertainty, and perhaps this is a virtue that we need to reinforce more in social work education with our students. On a more concrete level, however, we do believe that there is value in 'rethinking' the nature of social work assessment processes in order to take account of the broader global environment and how this might impact local practice. Assessment is seen to constitute the essence of social work while denoting a core skill for practice (Milner and O'Byrne, 2002). Its importance lies in its ability to inform our interventions and how we work with people. In addition, the foregoing commentaries suggest that emerging social work practitioners are already beginning to factor in global perspectives into their assessment practices. The challenge then is to think about how to more clearly articulate this process and to also incorporate a human rights framework into such assessment practices.

The previous commentaries also point to the value of learning from others and how this may even promote the ideal of global citizenship. Such learning necessitates intercultural engagement and thinking beyond our own local frames of reference, which in turn expands our interpretive frame of reference for social work. It also entails a 'decentring' of our own perspectives. In Chapter 2, we pointed out that many people have transnational identities and that with practices such as transnational care and international adoption, many social workers are actually forced to think on a broader level about their practice. Indeed, it is rarely the case these days that a person relates to one 'culture' that equates with a particular geographical location, and the advent of the Internet has expanded our notions of social space and allowed us to forge global connections. Moreover, the global economic crisis that emerged in 2008 has served to heighten people's awareness of the interconnectedness of the world, especially in terms of its flow-on effects in individual countries such as rising unemployment.

In Chapter 2 we pointed out that postcolonialism affords us a way of thinking about the present that is informed by the past and that this knowledge can never be fixed because our ideas about the present change in accordance with the passage of history and happenings. These new ways of understanding the present can in turn prompt us to raise new questions about the past. By way of example, contemporary media commentators suggest that the current global economic crisis has caused us to rethink the ongoing viability of a global capitalist market economy, and many people in turn have started to speculate about what will replace this system. At the same time, some writers have begun to interrogate taken-for-granted assumptions about neoliberal economics and have sought to gain an understanding of what historical factors may be implicated in the contemporary economic crisis.

Given that we appear to be at a critical moment in history where the two key crises of the moment – the uncertainty surrounding the global economy and the environment – are ever changing and constantly being 'reassessed', this book ends on a note of uncertainty. Our stated purpose for this book was to rethink social work in a global, world, and we suggest that this is actually a dynamic process where we are constantly 'rethinking' social work in line with contemporary developments and new understandings of the past. In this way, the topics broached in the previous chapters are open to ongoing investigation, debate, refinement and reformulation. In this book, we have guarded against offering a deterministic account of social work and making clear predictions for its future. However, what we are more certain about is that social work needs to be positioned within a broader context of a diverse and changeable global landscape that in turn interacts with the particularities of local contexts.

Bibliography

Abrahamson, P. (2007) 'Free trade and social citizenship: Prospects and possibilities of the Central American Free Trade Agreement (CAFTA-DR)', *Global Social Policy*, vol. 7, no. 3, pp. 339–57.

Adger, N. (2007) 'The shape of things to come?' *The Guardian Weekly*, 5 November, available at: http://www.guardian.co.uk/environment/2007/nov/05/greenlist.comment1 (accessed 10 December 2008, p. 28).

Agoramoorthy, G. and Hsu, M. J. (2008) 'Reviving India's grassroots social work for sustainable development', *International Social Work*, vol. 51, no. 4, pp. 544–55.

Ahluwalia, P. (2006) 'Race', *Theory, Culture & Society*, vol. 23, no. 2–3, pp. 538–45.

Ahmadi, N. (2003) 'Globalisation of consciousness and new challenges for international social work', *International Journal of Social Welfare*, vol. 12, no. 1, pp. 14–23.

Ahmed, M. (2007) 'Social workers should refuse to co-operate with "unethical" removals of asylum-seeking children in care, British Association of Social Workers says,' *Community Care*, 8 May, available at: http://www.communitycare.co.uk/Articles/2007/05/08/104406/social-workers-should-refuse-to-co-operate-with-unethical-removals-of-asylum-seeking-children-in.html (accessed 28 May 2009).

Alston, M. (2007) 'Globalization, rural restructuring and health service delivery in Australia: Policy failure and the role of social work?', *Health and Social Care in the Community*, vol, 15, no. 3, pp. 195–202.

Alston, P. and Crawford, J. (2000) *The Future of UN Human Rights Treaty Monitoring*, Cambridge University Press, Cambridge.

Amirthalingam, K. (2005), 'Women's rights, international norms, and domestic violence: Asian perspectives', *Human Rights Quarterly*, vol. 27, no. 2, pp. 683–708.

Aneesh, A. (2006) *Virtual Migration: The Programming of Globalization*, Duke University Press, Durham.

Annan, K. (2003) 'Opinion' in Trade: An insight into the way the world does business, The Guardian Weekly in association with Traidcraft, *The Guardian Weekly*, 11–17 September, p. 2.

———— (2005) *In Larger Freedom: Towards Development, Security and Human Rights for All, Report of the Secretary-General*, UN General Assembly 59th session, Agenda items 45 & 55, available at: http://www.un.org (accessed 7 January 2009).

Appadurai, A. (1996), *Modernity at Large: Cultural Dimensions of Globalization*, University of Minneapolis Press, Minneapolis.

Arthur, C. (2008) 'Developing nations leapfrog West as mobile phone users explore the limits. Switching on: Connecting the World', *The Guardian Weekly*, 16–22 May, pp. 1–3.

Ashcroft, B., Griffiths, G. and Tiffin, H. (1989) *The Empire Writes Back: Theory and Practice in Postcolonial Literatures*, Routledge, London.

Asian Human Rights Commission (1998) *Our Common Humanity: Asian Human Rights Charter*, available at: http://material.ahrchk.net/charter/pdf/charter-final.pdf (accessed 10 January 2009).

Astbury, J. (1996) *Crazy for You: The Making of Women's Madness*, Oxford University Press, Melbourne.

Augustin, L. (2007) *Sex at the Margins: Migration, Labour Markets and the Rescue Industry*, Zed Books, London.

Australian Human Rights Commission (2006) *A Statistical Overview of Aboriginal and Torres Strait Islander Peoples in Australia*, available at: http://www.humanrights.gov.au/social_justice/statistics/index.html#toc41 (accessed 10 December 2008).

Bagchi, A. (2008) 'Immigrants, morality and neoliberalism', *Development and Change*, vol. 39, no. 2, pp. 197–218.

Bakhtin, M. M. (1981) *The Dialogic Imagination: Four Essays by M. M. Bakhtin*, ed. M. Holquist, University of Texas Press, Austin, pp. 259–422.

Baldassar, L., Vellekoop Baldock, C. and Wild, R. (2007) *Families Caring across Borders: Migration, Ageing and Transnational Caregiving*, Palgrave Macmillan, Basingstoke.

Banks, S. (2006) *Ethics and Values in Social Work*, 3rd edn, Palgrave Macmillan, Basingstoke.

Barkin, J. S. (1998) 'The evolution of the constitution of sovereignty and the emergence of human rights norms', *Millennium: Journal of International Studies*, vol. 27, no. 2, pp. 229–52.

Batalova, J. (2008) *Mexican Immigrants in the United States*, Migration Policy Institute, available at: http://www.migrationinformation.org/USfocus/display.cfm?id=679 (accessed 13 May 2008).

Becker, D., Lira, E., Castillo, M. I., Gomez, E. and Kovalskys, J. (1990) 'Therapy with victims of political repression in Chile: The challenge of social reparation', *Journal of Social Issues*, vol. 46, no. 3, pp. 133–49.

Beech, H. (2003) 'Hidden away', *Time Asia*, 3 November, available at: http://www.time.com/time/printout/0,8816,501031110-536274,00.html# (accessed 10 December 2008).

Behdad, A. (2005) 'On globalization, again' in Loomba, A., Kaul, S., Bunzl, M., Burton, A. and Esty, J. (eds) *Postcolonial Studies and Beyond*, Duke University Press, Durham, pp. 62–79.

Beitz, C. R. (2008) 'Does global inequality matter?' in Brooks, T. (ed.) *The Global Justice Reader*, Blackwell Publishers, London, pp. 145–66.

Bellamy, C. and Taylor, J. A. (1998) *Governing in the Information Age*, Open University Press, Buckingham.

Bello, W. (2008) 'Destroying African agriculture', *Foreign Policy in Focus*, 3 June, available at: http://www.fpif.org/fpiftxt/5271 (accessed 12 January 2009).

Berger, R. and Kelly, J. (1993) 'Social work and the ecological crisis', *Social Work*, vol. 38, no. 5, pp. 521–6.

Berkovitch, N. (2004) 'The emergence and transformation of the international women's movement' in Lechner, F. J. and Boli, J. (eds) *The Globalization Reader*, 2nd edn, Blackwell Publishing, Malden, pp. 251–7.

Bhabha, H. (1994) *The Location of Culture*, Routledge, London.

Bhabha, H. (1995) 'Cultural diversity and cultural differences' in Ashcroft, B., Griffiths, G. and Tiffin, G. (eds) *The Post-Colonial Studies Reader*, Routledge, London, pp. 206–9.

Black, I. (2008) 'Saudis abuse domestic workers, rights group says', *The Guardian Weekly*, 18 August, p. 12.

Blakemore, K. (2003) *Social Policy: An Introduction*, 2nd edn, Open University Press, Buckingham.

Bland, R. and Renouf, N. (2006) 'Mental health' in Wilson, J. and Chui, W. H. (eds), *Social Work and Human Services Best Practice*, Federation Press, Annandale, pp. 83–103.

Borger, J. (2007) 'Climate change disaster is upon us, warns US,' *The Guardian Weekly*, 5 October, available at: http://www.guardian.co.uk/environment/2007/oct/05/climatechange (accessed 17 October 2008).

—— (2008a) 'UN declares it cannot feed the world', *The Guardian Weekly*, 29 February–6 March, p. 27.

—— (2008b) '2025 will see "end of US world dominance,"' *The Guardian Weekly*, 28 November, p. 8.

Boulos, M. N. K and Wheeler, S. (2007) 'The emerging Web 2.0 social software: An enabling suite of sociable technologies in health and health care education,' *Health Information and Libraries Journal*, vol. 24, no. 1, pp. 2–23.

Bracken, P. J., Giller, J. E. and Summerfield, D. (1995) 'Psychological responses to war and atrocity: The limitations of current concepts', *Social Science & Medicine*, vol. 40, no. 8, pp. 1073–82.

Bretton Woods Project Update (2001) 'PRSPs just PR say civil society groups', June/July, available at: http://www.brettonwoodsproject.org/art-15999 (accessed 10 October 2008).

British Institute of Human Rights (2008) *Human Rights and Poverty-Roundtable Pre-Briefing*, available at: http://www.bihr.org.uk (accessed 5 January 2008).

Bunting, M. (2008) 'Pregnancy should not be a death sentence', *The Guardian Weekly*, 4 July, p. 19.

Burton, B., Duvvury, N. and Varia, N. (2000) *Justice, Change, and Human Rights: International Research Responses to Domestic Violence*, International Centre for Research on Women and The Centre for Development and Population Activities, available at: http://www.icrw.org (accessed 4 December 2003).

Butler, F. (2005) *Improving Public Services: Using a Human Rights Approach*, Report for the Department for Constitutional Affairs and IPPR Trading Ltd, June, London: Institute of Public Policy Research (IPPR), available at: http://www.justice.gov.uk (accessed 5 January 2009).

Bywaters, P. (2009) 'Tackling inequalities in health: A global challenge for social work', BJSW Advance Access published on 1 March 2009, DOI 0.1093/bjsw/bcm096, *British Journal of Social Work*, vol. 39, no. 2, pp. 353–67.

Caraway, T. L. (2007) *Assembling Women: The Feminization of Global Manufacturing*, Cornell University Press, New York.

Carey, M. (2008) 'What difference does it make?: Contrasting organization and converging outcomes regarding the privatization of state social work in England and Canada', *International Social Work*, vol. 51, no. 1, pp. 83–94.

Carrilio, T. E. (2007) 'Utilizing a social work perspective to enhance sustainable development efforts in Loreto, Mexico', *International Social Work*, vol. 50, no. 4, pp. 528–38.

Castells, M. (2004) *The Network Society: A Cross-cultural Perspective*, Edward Elgar, Cheltenham.

Chandler, T. (1994) 'Urbanization in medieval and early modern Africa' in J. D. Tarver (ed.) *Urbanization in Africa: A Handbook*, Greenwood, Westport, pp. 15–32.

Chant, S. (2008) 'Beyond incomes: A new take on the "feminisation of poverty"', *Poverty in Focus: Gender Equality*, International Poverty Centre, no. 13, January, pp. 26–7.

Chatterjee, D. P. (2008) 'Oriental disadvantage versus occidental exuberance: Appraising environmental concern in India – A case study in a local context, *International Sociology*, vol. 23, no. 1, pp. 5–33.

Chen, S. and Ravallion, M. (2007) 'Absolute poverty measures for the developing world, 1981–2004', *Proceedings of the National Academy of Sciences*, vol. 104, no. 43, pp. 16757–62.

Christian Aid (2004) *Behind the Mask: The Real Face of Corporate Social Responsibility*, available at: http://baierle.files.wordpress.com/2007/11/behind-mask.pdf (accessed 10 May 2009).

Coates, J. (2003) *Ecology and Social Work: Towards a New Paradigm*, Fernwood Publishing, Halifax.

Cohen, R. and Kennedy, P. (2000) *Global Sociology*, Macmillan Press, Basingstoke.

Coleman, N. and Harris, H. (2008) 'Calling social work', *British Journal of Social Work*, vol. 38, no. 3, pp. 580–99.

Connell, R. (2007) 'The northern theory of globalization', *Sociological Theory*, vol. 25, no. 4, pp. 368–85.

Connolly, K. (2008) 'Planes, trains and laptops?' *The Guardian Weekly*, 4 March, p. 31.

Conwill, W. L. (2007) 'Neoliberal policy as structural violence: Its links to domestic violence in Black communities in the United States' in Gunewardena, N. and Kingsolver, A. (eds) *The Gender of Globalization*, School for Advanced Research Press, Santa Fe, pp. 127–46.

Cook, S. and Kwon, H.-J. (2007) 'Social protection in East Asia', *Global Social Policy*, vol. 7, no. 2, pp. 223–9.

Corrigall, J., Plagerson, S., Lund, C. and Myers, J. (2008) 'Global trade and mental health', *Global Social Policy*, vol, 8, no. 3, pp. 335–58.

Corry, P. (2008) 'Recession depression', *The Guardian Weekly*, 14 October, available at: http://www.guardian.co.uk/commentisfree/2008/oct/14/creditcrunch-mentalhealth/print (accessed 10 December 2008).

Costa, J. and Silva, E. (2008) 'The burden of gender inequalities for society', *Poverty in Focus: Gender Equality*, International Poverty Centre, no. 13, January, pp. 8–9.

Cox, D. and Pawar, D. (2006) *International Social Work: Issues, Strategies, and Programs*, Sage Publications, Thousand Oaks.

Cwikel, J. G. and Cnann, R. A. (1991) 'Ethical dilemmas in applying second-wave information technology to social work practice', *Social Work*, vol. 36, no. 2, pp. 114–20.

Darby, P. (2006) 'Introduction' in Darby, P. (ed.) *Postcolonizing the International: Working to Change the Way We Are*, University of Hawaii Press, Honolulu, pp. 1–10.

Darwin, J. (2007) *After Tamerlane: The Global History of Empire*, Penguin, London.

De Haas, H. (2007) 'Turning the tide? Why development will not stop migration', *Development and Change*, vol. 38, no. 5, pp. 819–41.

Department of Constitutional Affairs (2006) Human rights: Human lives, available at: http://www.justice.gov.uk/docs/hr-handbook-public-authorities.pdf (accessed 10 January 2009).

Dewe, P. and Kompier, M. (2008) *Foresight Mental Capital and Wellbeing Project. Wellbeing and Work: Future challenges*, The Government Office for Science, London.

Dholakia, N. and Kshetri, N. (2001) 'Webbing governance: Global trends across national-level public agencies', *Communications of the ACM*, vol. 44, no. 1, pp. 63–7.

Dicken, P. (2007) 'Economic globalization: Corporations' in Ritzer, G. (ed.) *The Blackwell Companion to Globalization*, Blackwell Publishing, Malden, pp. 291–306.

Dirlik, A. (2005) 'The postcolonial aura: Third world criticism in the age of global capital' in Desai, G. and Nair, S. (eds) *Postcolonialisms: An Anthology of Cultural Theory and Criticism*, Rutgers University Press, New Brunswick.

Disease Control Priorities Project (2006) 'Mental and neurological disorders', *Fact Sheet*, available at: http://dcp2.org/file/60/DCPP–Mental%20Health.pdf (accessed 10 December 2008).

Doel, M. and Penn, J. (2007) 'Technical assistance, neo-colonialism or mutual trade? The experience of an Anglo/Ukrainian/Russian social work practice learning project', *European Journal of Social Work*, vol. 10, no. 3, pp. 367–81.

Dominelli, L. (1997) 'The changing face of social work: Globalisation, privatisation and the technocratisation of professional practice' in Lesnik, B. (ed.) *Change in Social Work: International Perspectives in Social Work*, Arena, Aldershot, pp. 13–25.

—— (2007a) *Revitalising Communities in a Globalising World*, Ashgate, Aldershot.

—— (2007b) 'Globalising communities: Players and non-players' in Dominelli, L. (ed.) *Revitalising Communities in a Globalising World*, Ashgate, Aldershot, pp. 7–15.

—— (2007c) 'Human rights in social work practice: An invisible part of the social work curriculum' in Reichert, E. (ed.) *Challenges in Human Rights: A Social Work Perspective*, Columbia University Press, New York, pp. 16–43.

Donnelly, J. (2007) 'The relative universality of human rights', *Human Rights Quarterly*, vol. 29, no. 2, pp. 281–306.

Doornbos, M. (2006) *Global Forces and State Restructuring: Dynamics of State Formation and Collapse*, Palgrave Macmillan, London.

Doty, L. (2003) Anti-Immigrantism in Western Democracies: Statecraft, Desire and the Politics of Exclusion, Routledge, London.

Drori, G. S. (2007) 'Information society as a global policy agenda: What does it tell us about the age of globalization?' *International Journal of Comparative Sociology*, vol. 48, no. 4, pp. 297–316.

Dunlop, J. (2006) 'Onward and upward: A journey to somewhere' in Dunlop, J. M. and Holosko, M. J. (eds) *Information Technology and Evidence-Based Social Work Practice*, The Hawarth Press, Binghamton, pp. 221–31.

Eagleton-Pierce, M. (2001) 'The internet and the Seattle WTO Protests', *Peace Review*, vol. 3, no. 3, pp. 331–7.

Ehrenreich, B. (2003) 'Maid to order' in Ehrenreich, B. and Hochschild, A. R. (eds) *Global Woman: Nannies, Maids and Sex Workers in the New Economy*, Metropolitan Books/Henry Holt & Co., New York, pp. 85–103.

Ehrenreich, B. and Hochschild, A. R. (2003) 'Introduction' in Ehrenreich, B. and Hochschild, A. R. (eds) *Global Woman: Nannies, Maids and Sex Workers in the New Economy*, Metropolitan Books/Henry Holt & Co., New York, pp. 1–13.

Eide, A. & Rosas, A. (2001), 'Economic, social and cultural rights: A universal challenge' in Eide, A., Krause, C. and Rosas, A. (eds) *Economic, social and cultural rights: A textbook*, 2nd edn, Dordrecht, Boston, pp. 3–7.

Elliott, L. (2003) 'Policy made on the road to perdition', *The Guardian Weekly*, 16–22 October, p. 12.

—— (2007) 'IMF: China biggest contributor to world growth,' *The Guardian Weekly*, 17 October, available at: http://www.guardian.co.uk/business/2007/oct/17/3 (accessed 2 February 2009).

Engelbrecht, L. (2008) 'Economic literacy and the war on poverty: A social work challenge?' *International Journal of Social Welfare*, vol. 17, no. 2, pp. 166–73.

Edquist, K. (2008) 'Globalising pathologies: Mental health assemblage and spreading diagnoses of eating disorders', *International Political Sociology*, vol. 2, no. 4, pp. 375–91.

Equality and Human Rights Commission (2008) *Public Authorities and the Public Sector*, available at: http://www.equalityhumanrights.com (accessed 8 January 2009).

Estes, R. (1992) 'Women and development', *Internationalizing Social Work Education: A Guide to Resources for a New Century*, University of Pennsylvania School of Social Work, Philadelphia.

European Commission (2001) *Communication from the Commission to the Council and the European Parliament: Information and Communication Technologies in Development. The Role of ICTs in EC Development Policy, Brussels 14.12.2001; COM(2001)770 Final*, available at: http://www.ecomaccess.com/iim/pdf/ict_en.pdf (accessed 14 January 2008).

—— (2008) 'Report to the European Council on climate change and international security', *Population and Development Review*, vol. 34, no. 3, pp. 587–93.

Evans, C. (2003) 'Asylum seekers and "Border Panic" in Australia', *Peace Review*, vol. 15, no. 2, pp. 163–70.

Filmer, D. (2008) 'Disability, poverty and schooling in developing countries: Results from 14 household surveys', *The World Bank Economic Review*, vol. 22, no. 1, pp. 141–63.

Fine, M. (2007) *A Caring Society? Care and the Dilemmas of Human Service in the 21st Century*, Palgrave Macmillan, Basingstoke.

Finn, J. and Holden, G. (2000) *Human Services Online: A New Arena for Service Delivery*, Haworth Press, New York.

Finn, J. L. and Jacobson, M. (2003) *Just Practice: A Social Justice Approach to Social Work*, Eddie Bowers Publishing, Peosta, Iowa.

Fishman, J. (2000) 'The new linguistic order' in O'Meara, P., Mehlinger, H. D. and Krain, M. (eds) *Globalization and the Challenges of a New Century: A Reader*, Indiana University Press, Bloomington, pp. 435–42.

Fitzpatrick, T. (2003) 'Introduction: New technologies and social policy', *Critical Social Policy*, vol. 23, no. 2, pp. 131–8.

Fook, J. (2001) *Social Work: Critical Theory and Practice*, Sage Publications, London.

Foreign Policy (2001) 'Measuring Globalisation', January/February, pp. 56–64.

Fraser, N. (2007) 'Reframing justice in a globalizing world' in Held, D. and Kaya, A. (eds) *Global Inequality: Patterns and Explanations*, Polity Press, Cambridge, pp. 252–72.

Geoghegan, L., Lever, J. and McGimpsey, I. (2004) *ICT for Social Welfare: A Toolkit for Managers*, Policy Press, Bristol.

George, V. and Wilding, P. (2002) *Globalization and Human Welfare*, Palgrave, Basingstoke.

Germain, C. B. and Gitterman, A. (1980) *The Life Model of Social Work Practice*, Columbia University Press, New York.

Giddens, A. (1990) *The Consequences of Modernity*, Polity Press, Cambridge.

Giddens, A. (1996) 'On globalization', excerpts from a keynote address. *UNRISD Conference on Globalization and Citizenship*, available at: http://www.unrisd.org.

———— (1999) 'Runaway World', *BBC Reith Lectures 1999*, available at: http://news.bbc.co.uk/hi/english/static/events/reith_99/default.htm (accessed 5 October 2003).

———— (2001) *Sociology*, 4th edn, Polity Press, Cambridge.

———— (2002a) *Runaway World: How Globalisation Is Reshaping Our Lives*, Profile Books, London.

———— (2002b) 'Media and globalisation,' *The Media Report: 19 September, ABC Radio*, available at: http://www.abc.net.au/rn/talks/8.30/mediarpt/stories/s678261.htm (accessed 1 December 2003).

Gilbert, A. (1997) 'Poverty and social policy in Latin America', *Social Policy & Administration*, vol. 31, no. 4, pp. 320–35.

Gilbert, S. (2005) 'Social work with Indigenous Australians' in Alston, M. and McKinnon, J. (eds) *Social Work: Fields of Practice*, Oxford University Press, Melbourne, pp. 62–72.

Gil-Garcia, J. R. and Martinez-Moyano, I. J. (2007) 'Understanding the evolution of e-government: The influence of systems of rules on public sector dynamics', *Government Information Quarterly*, vol. 24, no. 2, pp. 266–90.

Gills, B. K. (2000) *Globalization and the Politics of Resistance*, MacMillan, Basingstoke.

Gomes, A. (2002) 'Environment' in P. Beilharz and T. Hogan (eds) *Social Self, Global Culture*, 2nd edn, Oxford University Press, Melbourne, pp. 247–56.

Goodhart, M. (2003) 'Origins and universality in the human rights debates: Cultural essentialism and the challenges of globalization', *Human Rights Quarterly*, vol. 25, no. 4, pp. 935–64.

Gray, M. (2008) 'Postcards from the West: Mapping the vicissitudes of Western social work', *Australian Social Work*, vol. 61, no. 1, pp. 1–6.

Gray, M., Coates, J. and Yellow Bird, M. (eds) (2008) *Indigenous Social Work around the World*, Ashgate, Williston.

Gray, M., van Rooyen, C., Rennie, G. and Gaha, J. (2002) 'The political participation of social workers: A comparative study', *International Journal of Social Welfare*, vol. 11, no. 2, pp. 99–110.

Guiné, A. and Fuentes, F. J. M. (2007) 'Engendering redistribution, recognition, and representation: The case of female genital mutilation (FGM) in the United Kingdom and France', *Politics & Society*, vol. 35, no. 3, pp. 477–519.

Gunewardena, N. and Kingsolver, A. (2007) 'Introduction' in Gunewardena, N. and Kingsolver, A. (eds) *The Gender of Globalization: Women Navigating Cultural and Economic Marginalities*, School for Advanced Research Press, Santa Fe, pp. 3–21.

Hagen, J. (2003) 'The United Nations at a "fork in the road,"' *UN Chronicle*, vol. 40, no. 4, p. 5.

Hall, A. (2007) 'Social policies in the World Bank: Paradigms and challenges', *Global Social Policy*, vol. 7, no. 2, pp. 151–75.

Hall, G. and Scheltens, M. (2005) 'Beyond the drought: Towards a broader understanding of rural disadvantage', *Rural Society*, vol. 15, no. 3, pp. 348–59, available at: http://search.informit.com.au/documentSummary;dn=193838207212220;res= IELHSS (accessed 10 December 2008).

Harding, T. (2005) *Rights at Risk – Older People and Human Rights*, Help the Aged, London.

Hardt, M. and Negri, A. (2000) *Empire*, Harvard University Press, Cambridge, Massachusetts.

―――― (2004) *Multitude: War and Democracy in the Age of Empire*, Penguin Press, New York.

Harris, J. (1998) 'Scientific management, bureau professionalism, new managerialism, the labour process and state social work', *British Journal of Social Work*, vol. 28, no. 6, pp. 839–62.

Harrison, G. (2006) 'Broadening the conceptual lens on language in social work: Difference, diversity and English as a global language', *British Journal of Social Work* (Special Issue on International Social Work), vol. 36, no. 3, pp. 401–18.

―――― (2007) 'A postcolonial perspective on language and difference in social work: Bilingual practitioners working in the linguistic borderlands', *European Journal of Social Work*, vol. 10, no. 1, pp. 73–88.

Hasan, S. R. (2006) 'China, India lead consumer confidence survey', *Asia Times Online*, 8 February, available at: http://www.atimes.com/atimes/China_Business/ HB08Cb06.html (accessed 10 December 2008).

Haug, E. (2005) 'Critical reflections on the emerging discourse of international social work', *International Social Work*, vol. 48, no. 2, pp. 126–35.

Hawkesworth, M. E. (2006) *Globalization and Feminist Activism*, Rowman & Littlefield, Lanham, Maryland.

Hayes, D. (2005) 'Social work with asylum seekers and others subject to immigration control' in Adams, R., Dominelli, L. and Payne, M. (eds) *Social Work Futures: Crossing Boundaries, Transforming Practice*, Palgrave Macmillan, Basingstoke, pp. 182–94.

Healy, L. (2001) *International Social Work: Professional Action in an Interdependent World*, Oxford University Press, New York.

—— (2007a) 'Retheorising international social work for the global professional community' in Dominelli, L. (ed.) *Revitalising Communities in a Globalising World*, Ashgate, Aldershot, pp. 347–60.

—— (2007b) 'Universalism and cultural relativism in social work ethics', *International Social Work*, vol. 50, no. 1, pp. 11–26.

Heinonen, T. and Metteri, A. (eds) (2005) 'Introduction' in *Social Work in Mental Health*, Canadian Scholars Press, Ontario, pp. 1–5.

Heintz, J. (2008) 'Poverty, employment and globalisation: A gender perspective', *Poverty in Focus: Gender Equality*, International Poverty Centre, no. 13, January, pp. 12–13.

Held, D. and McGrew, A. (2000) 'The great globalization debate: An introduction' in Held, D. and McGrew, A. (eds) *The Global Transformations Reader: An Introduction to the Globalization Debate*, Polity Press, Malden, pp. 1–45.

—— (2007) 'Introduction: Globalization at risk?' in Held, D. and McGrew, A. (eds) *Globalization Theory; Approaches and Controversies*, Polity Press, Cambridge, pp. 1–11.

Henman, P. and Adler, M. (2003) 'Information technology and the governance of Social Security', *Critical Social Policy*, vol. 23, no. 2, pp. 139–63.

Henman, P. and Marston, G. (2008) 'The social division of welfare surveillance', *Journal of Social Policy*, vol. 37, no. 2, pp. 187–205.

Herman, J. (1992) *Trauma and Recovery: The Aftermath of Violence – from Domestic Abuse to Political Terror*, Basic Books, New York.

Hick, S. F. and McNutt, J. G. (eds) (2002) *Advocacy, Activism, and the Internet: Community Organization and Social Policy*, Lyceum Books, Chicago.

Hirst, P. and Thompson, G. (1996) *Globalization in Question: The International Economy and the Possibilities of Governance*, Polity Press, Cambridge, Massachusetts.

Hoff, M. D. (1997) 'Social work, the environment, and sustainable growth' in Hokenstad, M. C. and Midgley, J. (eds) *Issues in International Social Work: Global Challenges for a New Century*, NASW Press, Washington, D.C., pp. 27–44.

Hokenstad, M. C. and Midgley J. (eds) (1997) *Issues in International Social Work: Global Challenges for a New Century*, NASW Press, Washington, D.C.

Holliday, A. (1999) 'Small cultures', *Applied Linguistics*, vol. 20, no. 2, pp. 237–64.

Hölscher, D. and Berhane, S. Y. (2008) 'Reflections on human rights and professional solidarity: A case study of Eritrea', *International Social Work*, vol. 51, no. 3, pp. 311–23.

Hoogvelt, A. (2007) 'Globalisation and imperialism: Wars and humanitarian intervention' in L. Dominelli (ed.) *Revitalising Communities in a Globalising World*, Ashgate, Aldershot, pp. 17–42.

Huang, Y. and Zhang, X. (2008) 'A reflection on the indigenization discourse in social work', *International Social Work*, vol. 51, no. 5, pp. 611–22.

Hudson, J. (2002) 'Digitizing the structures of government: The UK's information age government agenda', *Policy and Politics*, vol. 30, no. 4, pp. 515–31.

Hugo, G. (2003) *Circular Migration: Keeping Development Rolling, Migration Policy Institute*, available at: http://www.migrationinformation.org/Feature/display.cfm?ID=129 (accessed 13 May 2008).

Human Rights and Equal Opportunity Commission (2008), 'Fact Sheet 2–4,' available at: http://www.humanrights.gov.au (accessed 7 January 2009).

Hunter, B. (2001) 'Tackling poverty among Indigenous Australians' in R. Fincher and P. Saunders (eds) *Creating Unequal Futures? Rethinking Poverty, Inequality and Disadvantage*, Allen & Unwin, Sydney, pp. 129–57.

Ife, J. (2001) *Human Rights and Social Work: Towards Rights-Based Practice*, Cambridge University Press, Cambridge.

——— (2008) *Human Rights and Social Work: Towards Rights-Based Practice*, rev. edn, Cambridge University Press, Cambridge.

Ife, J. and Fiske, L. (2006), 'Human rights and community work: Complementary theories and practice', *International Social Work*, vol. 49, no. 3, pp. 297–308.

Intergovernmental Panel on Climate Change (2007) *Climate Change 2007: Synthesis Report. Summary for Policy Makers, an Assessment of the Intergovernmental Panel on Climate Change*, available at: http://www.ipcc.ch/pdf/assessment-report/ar4/syr/ar4_syr_spm.pdf (accessed 4 June 2008).

——— (2008) 'Climate change and water,' *IPCC Technical Paper VI*, available at: http://www.ipcc.ch/ipccreports/tp-climate-change-water.htm (accessed 3 May 2009).

International Federation of Social Workers (1998) *International Policy on Refugees*, available at: http://www.ifsw.org/en/p38000216.html (accessed 2 April 2008).

——— (2003) *Global Qualifying Standards for Social Work Education and Training*, revised version, available at: http://www.ifsw.org/en/p38000255.html (accessed 17 January 2009).

——— (2005a) *International Policy Statement on Globalisation and the Environment*, available at: http://www.ifsw.org/en/p38000222.html (accessed 17 January 2009).

——— (2005b) *IFSW International Policy on Indigenous Peoples*, available at: http://www.ifsw.org/en/p38000138.html (accessed 31 January 2009).

——— (2005c) *International Policy on Migration*, available at: http://www.ifsw.org/en/p38000213.html (accessed 2 April 2008).

——— (2005d) *Ethics in Social Work, Statement of Principles*, available at: http://www.ifsw.org/f38000032.html (accessed 10 December 2009).

——— (2007) *IFSW Statement on the International Day for Eradication of Poverty, 17 October 2007*, available at: http://www.ifsw.org/en/p38001089.html (accessed 12 January 2009).

——— (2008a) *IFSW Statement to the UN Commission for Social Development*, available at: http://www.ifsw.org/en/p38001664.html (accessed 12 January 2009).

——— (2008b) *IFSW Policy Statement on Health*, available at: http://www.ifsw.org/en/p38000081.html?print=true (accessed 10 December 2008).

International Herald Tribune (2008) 'Emerging economies slam new US farm bill at WTO', 3 June, available at: http://www.iht.com/bin/printfriendly.php?id=13423311 (accessed 12 December 2008).

International Labour Organization (2008) *World of Work Report: Income Inequalities in the Age of Financial Globalization*, International Institute for Labour studies, Geneva, available at: http://www.ilo.org/public/english/bureau/inst/download/world08.pdf (accessed 11 December 2008).

International Monetary Fund (2000) *IMF Survey*, vol. 29, no. 20, October, IMF, Washington, D.C.

———— (2007) 'World economic outlook,' *Globalization and Inequality*, available at: http://www.imf.org/external/pubs/ft/weo/2007/02/index.htm (accessed 18 January 2009).

International Poverty Centre (2008) *Poverty in Focus: Gender Equality*, no. 13, January, available at: www.undp-povertycentre.org/pub/IPCPovertyInFocus13.pdf (accessed 7 January 2009).

International Telecommunications Union (2007a) *Key Global Telecom Indicators*, available at: http://www.itu.int/ITU-D/ict/statistics/at_glance/KeyTelecom99.html (accessed 12 January 2009).

———— (2007b) *Facts and Figures*, available at: http://www.itu.int/ITU-D/connect/africa/2007/bgdmaterial/figures.html (accessed 7 January 2009).

———— (2008) *ICTs in Africa: Digital Divide to Digital Opportunity*, available at: http://www.itu.int/newsroom/features/ict_africa.html (accessed 7 January 2009).

Jaeger, H.-M. (2007) ' "Global civil society" and the political depoliticization of global governance', *International Political Sociology*, vol. 1, pp. 257–77.

Jaggar, A. M. (2001) 'Is globalization good for women?' *Comparative Literature*, vol. 53, no. 4, pp. 298–314.

Janes, L. (2002) 'Understanding gender divisions: Feminist perspectives' in Braham, P. and Janes, L. (eds) *Social Divisions and Differences*, Blackwell Publishers, Oxford, pp. 101–57.

Jayasuriya, L. (1998) *Racism, Immigration and the Law: The Australian Experience*, School of Social Work and Social Administration, The University of Western Australia, Nedlands.

Johannesen, T. (1997) 'Social work as an international profession: Opportunities and challenges' in Hokenstad, M. C. and Midgley, J. (eds) *Issues in International Social Work*, NASW Press, Washington, D.C., pp. 146–58.

Johnson, L. (2000) *Placebound: Australian Feminist Geographies*, Oxford University Press, Melbourne.

Jones, J. B. and Chandler, S. (2001) 'Connecting personal biography and social history: Women casino workers and the global economy', *Journal of Sociology & Social Welfare*, vol. 28, no. 4, pp. 173–93.

Jordan, B. (2008) 'Social work and world poverty', *International Social Work*, vol. 51, no. 4, pp. 440–52.

Jordan, B. and Düvell, F. (2002) *Irregular Migration: The Dilemmas of Transnational Mobility*, Edward Elgar, Cheltenham.

Jordan, B., Stråth, B. and Triandafyllidou, A. (2003) 'Contextualising immigration policy implementation in Europe', *Journal of Ethnic and Migration Studies*, vol. 29, no. 2, pp. 195–224.

Kabeer, N. (2002) *Citizenship and the Boundaries of the Acknowledged Community: Identity, Affiliation and Exclusion*, IDS Working Paper 171, Institute of Development Studies, Brighton.

Kabeer, N. (2008) 'Gender, labour, markets and poverty', *Poverty in Focus: Gender Equality*, International Poverty Centre, no. 13, January, pp. 3–5.

Kang, H. (2008) 'Transnational women's collectivities and global justice', *Journal of Social Philosophy*, vol. 39, no. 3, pp. 359–77.

Kelly, A. (2008) 'Battle is joined in the fight for equality', *The Guardian Weekly*, 2 February, p. 7.

Khaleque, V. (2007) 'Cruel price being paid for the West's excess', *The Guardian Weekly*, 19 January, p.31.

Kidd, D. (2001) 'Introduction', *Peace Review*, vol. 13, no. 3, pp. 325–29.

King, R., Bambling, M., Lloyd, C., Gomurra, R., Smith, S. and Reid, W. (2006) 'Online counselling: The motives and experiences of young people who choose the Internet instead of face to face or telephone counselling', *Counselling and Psychotherapy Research*, vol. 6, no. 3, pp. 169–74.

Koser, K. (2007) *International Migration: A Very Short Introduction*, Oxford University Press, Oxford.

Kruger, E., Magnet, S. and Van Loon, J. (2008) 'Biometric revisions of the "body" in airports and US welfare reform', *Body & Society*, vol. 14, no. 2, pp. 99–121.

Krumer-Nevo, M. (2008) 'From noise to voice; How social work can benefit from the knowledge of people living in poverty', *International Social Work*, vol. 51, no. 4, pp. 556–65.

Laird, S. E. (2008) 'Social work practice to support survival strategies in sub-Saharan Africa,' *British Journal of Social Work*, vol. 38, no. 1, pp. 135–51.

Lawrence, F. (2008) 'Britain's water habit leaves others parched', *The Guardian Weekly*, 29 August–4 September, p. 15.

Layard, R. (2004) 'Mental health: Britain's biggest social problem?' Seminar presentation, available at: http://www.cabinetoffice.gov.uk/media/cabinetoffice/strategy/assets/mh_layard.pdf (accessed 10 December 2008).

Leahy, T. (2008) Discussion of 'global warming and sociology,' *Current Sociology*, vol. 56, no. 3, pp. 475–84.

Lemaître, F. (2008) 'A hungry future for the world', *The Guardian Weekly*, available at: http://www.guardianweekly.co.uk/?page=editorial&id=516&catID=17 (accessed 29 January 2009).

Ling, H. K. (2007) *Indigenising Social Work: Research and Practice in Sarawak*, Strategic Information and Research Development Centre, Selangor.

Lohmann, L. (2006) *Carbon Trading: A Critical Conversation on Climate Change, Privatisation and Power*, Development Dialogue, no. 48, September, available at: http://www.thecornerhouse.org.uk/pdf/document/carbonDDlow.pdf (accessed 3 November 2008).

Loomba, A. (1998) *Colonialism/Postcolonialism*, Routledge, London.

Loomba, A., Kaul, S., Bunzl, M., Burton, A. and Esty, J. (2005) 'Beyond what? An Introduction' in Loomba, A. Kaul, S. Bunzl, M. Burton, A. and Esty, J. (eds) *Postcolonial Studies and Beyond*, Duke University Press, Durham, pp. 1–40.

Lorenz (2008) 'Towards a European model of social work,' *Australian Journal of Social Work*, vol. 61, no. 1, pp. 7–24.

Lynn, R. (2001) 'Learning from a "Murri Way,"' *British Journal of Social Work*, vol. 31, no. 1, pp. 903–16.

Lyons, K. (1999) *International Social Work: Themes and Perspectives*, Ashgate Publishing, Aldershot.

Lyons, K., Manion, K. and Carlsen, M. (2006) *International Perspectives on Social Work: Global Conditions and Local Practice*, Palgrave Macmillan, New York.

Mackay, H. and Gillespie, G. (1992) 'Extending the social shaping of technology approach: Ideology and appropriation', *Social Studies of Science*, vol. 22, no. 4, pp. 685–716.

Magnarella, P. J. (2004), 'Communist Chinese and "Asian values": Critiques of universal human rights', *Journal of Third World Studies*, vol. 21, no. 2, pp. 179–92.

Man Ng, S. and Chan, C. L. W. (2005) 'Intervention' in Adams, R., Dominelli, L. and Payne, M. (eds) *Social Work Futures: Crossing Boundaries, Transforming Practice*, Palgrave Macmillan, Basingstoke, pp. 68–82.

Manning, N. and Patel, V. (2008) 'Globalization and mental health: A special issue on global social policy', *Global Social Policy*, vol. 8, no. 3, pp. 299–300.

Marlow, C. and Van Rooyen, C. (2001) 'How green is the environment in social work?,' *International Social Work*, vol. 44, no. 2, pp. 241–54.

Marshall, T. H. and Bottomore, T. (1992) *Citizenship and Social Class*, Pluto Press, London.

Martinez-Brawley, E. and Brawley, E. (1999) 'Diversity in a changing world: Cultural enrichment or social fragmentation?' *Journal of Multicultural Social Work*, vol. 7, no. 1/2, pp. 19–36.

Mathbor, G. M. (2007) 'Enhancement of community preparedness for natural disasters: The role of social work in building social capital for sustainable disaster relief and management', *International Social Work*, vol. 50, no. 3, pp. 357–69.

McCleary, R. (2007) 'Ethical issues in online social work research', *Journal of Social Work Values and Ethics*, vol. 4, no. 1, available at: http://www.socialworker.com/jswve/content/view/46/50/ (accessed 10 July 2008).

McDonald, C. (2006) *Challenging Social Work: The Institutional Context of Practice*, Palgrave McMillan, Basingstoke.

McDonald, C., Harris, J. and Wintersteen, R. (2003) 'Contingent on context? Social work and the state in Australia, Britain, and the USA', *British Journal of Social Work*, vol. 33, no. 2, pp. 191–208.

McIver, W. J. (2004) 'A human rights perspective on the digital divide: A human right to communicate' in Day, P. and Schuler, D. (eds) *Community Practice in the Network Society: Local Action/Global Interaction*, Routledge, London, pp. 155–69.

McKenzie, K. (2008) 'Urbanization, social capital and mental health', *Global Social Policy*, vol. 8, no. 3, pp. 359–77.

McMichael, P. (2007) 'Globalization and the agrarian world' in Ritzer, G. (ed.) *The Blackwell Companion to Globalization*, Blackwell Publishing, Malden, pp. 216–38.

——— (2008) *Development and Social Change: A Global Perspective*, 4th edn, Pine Forge Press, Thousand Oaks.

McVeigh, T. (2008) 'Britain tries to close the door' in 'Migration: A world on the move', *The Guardian Weekly*, 25–31 January, p. 3.

Melville, R. (2007a) 'Ethical dilemmas of online research' in Anttiroiko, A-O. and Malkia, M. (eds) *Encyclopedia of Digital Government*, Ideas Group, Hershey, pp. 734–39.

———— (2007b) 'E-social policy and e-service delivery' in Anttiroiko, A-O. and Malkia, M. (eds) *Encyclopedia of Digital Government*, Ideas Group, Hershey, pp. 734–39.

Melville, R. and Perkins, R. (2003) *Changing Roles of Community Sector Peak Bodies in a Neoliberal Policy Environment in Australia, An ARC Funded Study (2000–2002)*, available at: http://www.uow.edu.au/arts/archives/iscci/publications/peakstudy.pdf (accessed 17 January 2009).

Memmi, A. (1967) *The Colonizer and the Colonized*, Beacon Press, Boston.

Midgley, J. (1981) *Professional Imperialism: Social Work in the Third World*, Heinemann, London.

———— (1990) 'International social work: Learning from the third world', *Social Work*, vol. 35, no. 4, pp. 295–300.

———— (1991) 'Social development and multicultural social work', *Journal of Multicultural Social Work*, vol. 1, no. 1, pp. 85–100.

———— (1994) 'Transnational strategies for social work: Toward effective reciprocal exchanges' in Mienert, R. G., Pardeck, T. J. and Sullivan, W. P. (eds) *Issues in Social Work. A Critical Analysis*, Auburn House, Westport, pp. 165–80.

———— (1997) 'Social work and international social development' in M. C. Hokenstad and J. Midgley (eds) *Issues in International Social Work*, NASW Press, Washington, D.C., pp. 1–11.

———— (2007a) 'Global inequality, power and the unipolar world – Implications for social work,' *International Social Work*, vol. 50, no. 5, pp. 613–26.

———— (2007b) 'Development, social development and human rights' in Reichert, E. (ed.) *Challenges of Human Rights: A Social Work Perspective*, Columbia University Press, New York, pp. 97–121.

———— (2008) 'Microenterprise, global poverty and social development', *International Social Work*, vol. 51, no. 4, pp. 467–79.

Migration News (2007) 'Global: Remittances, aging, aid' *Migration News*, vol. 14, no. 4, October, available at: http://migration.ucdavis.edu/MN/more.php?id=3335_0_5_0 (accessed 30 October 2007).

Miller, P. (2006) 'Benefits of on-line chat for single mothers' in Dunlop, J. M. and Holosko, M. J. (eds) *Information Technology and Evidence-Based Social Work Practice*, The Hawarth Press, New York, pp. 167–81.

Milner, J. and O'Byrne, P. (2002) *Assessment in Social Work*, 2nd edn, Palgrave Macmillan, Basingstoke.

Miniwatts Marketing Group (2008) *Top 20 Countries with the Highest Number of Internet Users*, available at: http://www.internetworldstats.com/top20.htm (accessed 19 January 2009).

Mishra, R. (1999) *Globalisation and the Welfare State*, Edward Elgar Publishing, Cheltenham.

Mohanty, C. (1988) 'Under western eyes: Feminist scholarship and colonial discourses', *Feminist Review*, no. 30, Autumn, pp. 3–8.

Moore, D. C. (2001) 'Is the post- in Postcolonial the post- in post-Soviet? Toward a global postcolonial critique', *PMLA*, vol. 116, no. 1, pp. 111–28.

Moosa-Mitha, M. (2007) 'Citizenship rights in a globalising world: Child trafficking and lessons for a social justice education' in Dominelli, L. (ed.) *Revitalising Communities in a Globalising World*, Ashgate, Aldershot, pp. 315–31.

Morrissey, M. (2003) 'Poverty and Indigenous health', *Health Sociology Review*, vol. 12, no. 1, pp. 17–30.

Moses, J. (2006) *International Migration: Globalization's Last Frontier*, Zed Books, London.

Mubangizi, B. C. (2008) 'Responses to poverty in post-apartheid South Africa: Some reflections', *International Journal of Social Welfare*, vol. 17, no. 2, pp. 174–81.

Münkler, H. (2007) *Empires: The Logic of World Domination from Ancient Rome to the United States*, Polity Press, Cambridge, Massachusetts.

Mupedziswa, R. (1997) 'Social work with refugees' in M. C. Hokenstad and J. Midgely (eds) *Issues in International Social Work: Global Challenges for a New Century*, NASW Press, Washington, D.C., pp. 110–24.

Mutschler, E. and Hasenfeld, Y. (1986) 'Integrated information systems for social work practice', *Social Work*, vol. 31, no. 5, pp. 345–49.

Narayan, U. (1997) *Dislocating Cultures: Identities, Traditions, and Third-World Feminism*, Routledge, New York.

Nash, M., Wong, J. and Trlin, A. (2006) 'A new field of social work practice with immigrants, refugees and asylum seekers', *International Social Work*, vol. 49, no. 30, pp. 345–63.

National Aboriginal and Torres Strait Islander Ecumenical Commission (2007) *Make Indigenous Poverty History*, available at: http://www.ncca.org.au/natsiec/indigenous_poverty (accessed 10 January 2009).

Nelson, P. J. and Dorsey, E. (2003) 'At the nexus of human rights and development: New methods and strategies of global NGOs', *World Development*, vol, 31, no. 12, pp. 2013–26.

Ngugi wa Thiong'O (1981) *Decolonizing the Mind: The Politics of Language in African Literature*, James Currey, London.

Nimmagadda, J. and Cowger, C. (1999) 'Cross-cultural practice: Social worker ingenuity in the indigenization of practice knowledge', *International Social Work*, vol. 42, no. 3, pp. 261–76.

Norris, P. (2001) *Digital Divide: Civic Engagement, Information Poverty and the Internet Worldwide*, Cambridge University Press, Cambridge.

Noyoo, N. (2004) 'Human rights and social work in a transforming society: South Africa,' *International Social Work*, vol. 47, no. 3, pp. 359–69.

Oguibe, O. (2002) 'Connectivity and the fate of the unconnected' in Goldberg, D. T and Quayson, A. (eds) *Relocating Postcolonialism*, Blackwell Publishers, London, pp. 174–83.

Omaswa, F. (2008) 'Health workforce migration. Addressing causes and managing effects', *Global Social Policy*, vol. 8, no. 7, pp. 7–9.

Organization for Economic Cooperation and Development (2007) *Immigrant Health Workers in OECD Countries in the Broader Context of Highly Skilled Migration*, available at: http://www.oecd.org/dataoecd/22/32/41515701.pdf (accessed 5 December 2008).

——— (2006) *Sickness, Disability and Work: Breaking the Barriers-Norway, Poland and Switzerland, Vol. 1*, available at: http://www.oecdbookshop.org/oecd/

display.asp?sf1=identifiers&lang=EN&st1=812006091p1 (accessed 5 December 2008).

Oxfam (2008a) *Double-Edged Prices: Lessons from the Food Price Crisis: 10 Actions Developing Countries Should Take*, Oxfam Briefing Paper 121, available at: http://www.oxfam.org.uk/generationwhy/cgi/process_comp/photos/2008/10/bp121_double-edged-prices_-final_-13oct08.pdf (accessed 9 February 2009).

———— (2008b) *Climate Wrongs and Human Rights: Putting People at the Heart of Climate-Change Policy*, Oxfam Briefing Paper 118, September, available at: http://www.oxfam.org.uk (accessed 7 January 2009).

Page, S. (2007) *The Potential Impact of the Aid for Trade Initiative*, G-24 Discussion Paper Series, no. 45, April, United Nations, available at: http://www.unctad.org/en/docs/gdsmdpbg2420073_en.pdf (accessed 2 May 2009).

Pariso, S (2005) Comment on 'the real digital divide,' *The Economist*, available at: http://808.pariso.com/archives/2005/03/the_economist_t.html#comments (accessed 18 January 2008).

Parker-Oliver, D. and Demiris, G. (2006) 'Social work informatics: A new specialty', *Social Work*, vol. 51, no. 2, pp. 127–34.

Parrott, L. and Madoc-Jones, I. (2008) 'Reclaiming information and communication technologies for empowering social work practice', *Journal of Social Work*, vol. 8, no. 2, pp. 181–97.

Parton, N. (2008) 'Changes in the form of knowledge in social work: From the "social" to the "informational"?,' *British Journal of Social Work*, vol. 38, no. 2, pp. 1–17.

Patel, V. (2008) 'Mental health in the developing world: Time for innovative thinking', *Science and Development Network*, Opinion, 28 July, available at: http://www.scidev.org/en/opinions/mental-health-in-the-developing-world-time-for-inn.html (accessed 5 December 2008).

Penna, S., Paylor, I. and Washington, J. (2000), 'Globalization, social exclusion and the possibilities for global social work and welfare', *European Journal of Social Work*, vol. 3, no. 2, pp. 109–22.

Peterson, V. S. and Parisi, L. (1998) 'Are women human: It's not an academic question' in T. Evans (ed.) *Human Rights Fifty Years On: A Reappraisal*, Manchester University Press, Manchester, pp. 132–60.

Piachaud, J. (2008) 'Globalization, conflict and mental Health', *Global Social Policy*, vol. 8, no. 3, pp. 315–34.

Pincock, S. (2007) 'Vikram Patel: Promoting mental health in developing countries', *The Lancet*, 370, p. 821.

Pogge, T. W. (2004) 'The first UN Millennium Goals: A cause for celebration?', *Journal of Human Development*, vol. 5, no. 3, pp. 381–85.

Polack, R. J. (2004) 'Social justice and the global economy: New challenges for social work in the 21st century', *Social Work*, vol. 49, no. 2, pp. 281–90.

Polaski, S. (2005) *Agricultural Negotiations at the WTO: First, Do No Harm*, available at: http://www.carnegieendowment.org/files/PO18.polaski.FINAL.pdf (accessed 10 October 2008).

Pollack, D. (2007) 'Social workers and the United Nations: Effective advocacy strategies', *International Social Work*, vol. 50, no. 1, pp. 113–19.

Poole, D. and Negi, N. (2007) 'Transnational community enterprises for social welfare in global civil society', *International Journal of Social Welfare*, vol. 17, no. 3, pp. 243–46.

Pratt, M. L. (1992) *Imperial Eyes: Travel Writing and Transculturation*, Routledge, London.

Prince, M., Patel, V., Saxena, S., Maj, M., Maselko., Phillips, M. and Raham, A. (2007) 'Global mental health 1: No health without mental health', *The Lancet*, vol. 370, no. 9590, pp. 859–77.

Prior, M. (2007) 'Citizenship and mental health policy in Europe', *Social Work & Society*, vol. 5, no. 1, available at: http://www.socwork.net/2007/festschrift/esp/prior/Prior.pdf (accessed 29 May 2009).

Pugh, R. and Gould, N. (2000) 'Globalization, social work, and social welfare', *European Journal of Social Work*, vol. 3, no. 2, pp. 123–38.

Punathambekar, A. (2005) 'Bollywood in the Indian-American diaspora: Mediating a transitive logic of cultural citizenship', *International Journal of Cultural Studies*, vol. 8, no. 2, pp. 151–73.

Quarantelli, E. L. (1985) 'An assessment of conflicting views on mental health: The consequences of traumatic events' in Figley, C. R. (ed.) *Trauma and Its Wake: The Study and Treatment of Post-Traumatic Stress Disorder*, vol. 1, Brumner/Mazel Publishers, New York, pp. 173–218.

Queiro-Tajalli, I., Campbell, C. and McNutt, J. (2003) 'International social and economic justice and on-line advocacy', *International Social Work*, vol. 46, no. 2, pp. 149–61.

Raijman, R. Davidov, E., Schmidt, P. and Hochman, O. (2008) 'What does a nation owe non-citizens? National attachments, perception of threat and attitudes towards granting citizenship rights in a comparative perspective', *International Journal of Comparative Sociology*, vol. 49, no. 2–3, pp. 195–220.

Raju, S. (2002), 'We are different but can we talk?', *Gender, Place and Culture*, vol. 9, no. 2, pp. 173–77.

Ramesh, R. (2008a) 'India will pay poor families to have girls to end foeticide,' *The Guardian Weekly*, 4 April, p. 4.

——— (2008b) 'India's worst flooding in decades swamps Bihar', *The Guardian Weekly*, 5–11 September, pp. 1–2.

Rani, S. (2003) 'Call centre maladies', *Dataquest*, available at: http://dqindia.ciol.com/content/dqtop202k3/bpo/103102104.asp (accessed 10 May 2009).

Reichert, E. (2003) *Social Work and Human Rights: A Foundation for Policy and Practice*, Columbia University, New York.

Reiger, K. (2002) 'Understanding the welfare state' in Beilharz, P. and Hogan, T. (eds) *Social Self, Global Culture*, Oxford University Press, Oxford, pp. 171–80.

Ritzer, G. and Lair, C. (2007) 'Outsourcing: Globalization and beyond' in Ritzer, G. (ed.) *The Blackwell Companion to Globalization*, Blackwell Publishing, Malden, pp. 307–29.

Robertson, R. (1992) *Globalization: Social Theory and Global Culture*, Sage Publications, London.

Robertson, R. T. (2003) *The Three Waves of Globalization: A History of a Developing Global Consciousness*, Zed Books, New York.

———— (2004) 'The historical context and significance of globalization', *Development and Change*, vol. 35, no. 3, 557–65.

Rosenberg, J. (2005) 'Globalization theory: A post mortem', *International Politics*, vol. 42, no. 1, 2–74.

Rosenzweig, C., Karoly, D., Vicarelli, M., Neofotis, P., Wu, Q., Casassa, G., Menzel, A., Root, T. L., Estrella, N., Seguin, B., Tryjanowski, P., Liu, C., Rawlins, S. and Imeson, A. (2008) 'Attributing physical and biological impacts to anthropogenic climate change', *Nature*, vol. 453, 15 May, pp. 353–7.

Roudometof, V. (2005) 'Transnationalism, cosmopolitanism and glocalisation', *Current Sociology*, vol. 53, no. 1, pp. 113–35.

Rutter, J. (2006) 'Reviews: Social work, immigration and asylum: Debates, dilemmas and ethical issues for social work and social care practice', *Journal of Refugee Studies*, vol. 19, no. 1, pp. 131–2.

Sachs, W. (2004) 'Environment and human rights', *Development*, vol. 47, no. 1, pp. 42–9.

Said, E. (1978) *Orientalism*, Routledge and Kegan Paul, London.

———— (1981) *Covering Islam*, Routledge, London.

———— (1993) *Culture and Imperialism*, Alfred A. Knopf, New York.

Sapey, B. (1997) 'Social work tomorrow: Towards a critical understanding of technology in social work', *British Journal of Social Work*, vol. 27, no. 6, pp. 803–14.

Sartorius, N. (2007) 'Stigma and mental health', *The Lancet*, vol. 370, no. 9590, pp. 810–11.

Saunders, P. (2005) *The Poverty Wars*, UNSW Press, Sydney.

Saxena, S., Thornicroft, G., Knapp, M. and Whiteford, H. (2007) 'Resources for mental health: Scarcity, inequity and inefficiency', *Lancet*, vol. 370, no. 9590, pp. 878–89.

Schembri, A. M. (2008) 'www.why-social-workers-need-to-embrace-Web2.0.com. au', *Australian Social Work*, vol. 61, no. 2, pp. 119–23.

Scholte, J. A. (2008) 'Defining globalisation', *The World Economy*, vol. 31, no. 11, pp. 1471–502.

Seglow, J. (2005) 'The ethics of immigration', *Political Studies Review*, vol. 3, pp. 317–34.

Seipel, M. (2003) 'Global poverty: No longer an untouchable problem', *International Social Work*, vol. 46, no. 2, pp. 191–207.

Sen, A. (2000) *Social Exclusion: Concept, Application, and Scrutiny*, Social Development Papers No. 1, Office of Environment and Social Development, Asian Development Bank, available at: http://www.adb.org/Documents/Books/Social_Exclusion/default.asp (accessed 10 October 2008).

Sen, G. (2008) 'Poverty as a gendered experience: The policy implications', *Poverty in Focus: Gender Equality*, no. 13, January, International Poverty Centre.

Sewpaul, V. (2006) 'The global-local dialectic: Challenges for African scholarship and social work in a post-colonial world', *British Journal of Social Work*, vol. 36, no. 3, pp. 419–34.

———— (2007) 'Challenging east-west value dichotomies and essentialising discourse on culture and social work', *International Journal of Social Welfare*, vol. 16, no. 4, pp. 398–407.

Shaffer, P. (2008) *New Thinking on Poverty: Implications for Globalisation and Poverty Reduction Strategies*, DESA Working Paper No. 65, available at: http://ideas.repec.org/p/une/wpaper/65.html (accessed 10 October 2008).

Sharma, D. (2003) 'Zero tolerance to farm subsidies', *India Together*, February, available at: http://www.indiatogether.org/2003/feb/dsh-zerotolr.htm (accessed 17 February 2009).

Sheppard, M. (2002) 'Mental health and social justice: Gender, race and psychological consequences of unfairness', *British Journal of Social Work*, vol. 32, no. 6, pp. 779–97.

Sinha, C. (2005) *Effects of Mobile Telephony on Empowering Rural Communities in Developing Countries*, IRFC Conference on Digital Divide, Global Development and the Information Society, 14–16 November, available at: http://www.irfd.org/events/wf2005/papers/sinha_chaitali.pdf (accessed 23 February 2008).

Sivanandan, A. (1999) 'Globalism and the Left', *Race and Class*, vol. 40, no. 2/3, pp. 5–19.

Skegg, A.-M. (2005) 'Brief note: Human rights and social work: A western imposition or empowerment to the people?,' *International Social Work*, vol. 48, no. 5, pp. 667–72.

Sklair, L. (2004) 'Sociology of the global system' in Lechner, F. J. and Boli, J. (eds) *The Globalization Reader*, 2nd edn, Blackwell Publishing, Oxford, pp. 63–9.

Sparks, C. (2007) 'What's wrong with globalization?' *Global Media and Communication*, vol. 3, no. 2, pp. 133–55.

Spivak, G. C. (1988) *In Other Worlds: Essays in Cultural Politics*, Routledge, London.

—— (1990) *The Post-Colonial Critic: Interviews, Strategies, Dialogues*, ed. S. Harasym, Routledge, London.

Stanley, J., Tomison, A. M. and Pocock, J. (2003) 'Child abuse and neglect in Indigenous Australian communities,' *Child Abuse Prevention Issues*, no. 19, Spring 2003, available at: http://www.aifs.gov.au/nch/pubs/issues/issues19/issues19.pdf (accessed 24 January 2009).

Steinmueller, W. E. (2001) 'ICTS and the possibilities of leapfrogging by developing countries', *International Labour Review*, vol. 140, no. 2, pp. 193–210.

Suh, S. (1997) 'No easy answers: Individual supreme? Or country and community come first?' *Asiaweek*, 31 October, available at: http://www.asiaweek.com/asiaweek/97/1031/nat5.html (accessed 10 December 2003).

Swartz, L. (2008) 'Globalization and mental health: Changing views of culture and society', *Global Social Policy*, vol. 8, no. 3, pp. 304–7.

Sweeting, A. and Vickers, E. (2005) 'On colonizing "colonialism": The discourses of the history of English in Hong Kong', *World Englishes*, vol. 24. no. 2, pp. 113–30.

Tan, N. G., Rowlands, A. and Hall, N. (2007) 'Engaging in disaster relief', *International Social Work*, vol. 50, no. 3, pp. 437–40.

Tan, N. G., Rowlands, A. and Yuen, F. K. (eds) (2006) *Asian Tsunami and Social Work Practice*, Haworth Press, New York.

The Guardian Weekly in association with Traidcraft (2003) 'Trade: An insight into the way the world does business', *The Guardian Weekly*, 11–17 September, pp. 1–8.

Thomson, N., Burns, J., Hardy, A., Krom, I. and Stumpers, S. (2007) *Overview of Australian Indigenous Health Status 2007*, available at: http://www.healthin fonet.ecu.edu.au/html/html_overviews/overview.pdf (accessed 16 January 2007).

Tomlinson, J. (2007) 'Globalization and cultural analysis' in Held, D. and McGrew, A. (eds) *Globalization Theory: Approaches and Controversies*, Polity, Cambridge, Massachusetts, pp. 148–68.

Torrès, D. (2007) 'Maids for sale in Lebanon', *The Guardian Weekly*, 26 October 2007, p. 28.

Traidcraft (2005) *Fair Trade and the Crisis in World Commodity Prices*, June, available at: http://www.traidcraft.org.uk/policy (accessed 13 October 2008).

—— (2008) *Economic Partnership Agreements*, available at: http://www.traidcraft. org.uk/policy (accessed 18 January 2009).

Traynor, I. (2008) 'Europe expects flood of climate refugees,' *The Guardian Weekly*, 14–20 March, pp. 1–2.

Tregeagle, S. and Darcy, M. (2008) 'Child welfare and information and communication technology: Today's challenge', *British Journal of Social Work*, vol. 38, no. 8, pp. 1481–98.

Tyler, I. (2006) 'Welcome to Britain: The cultural politics of asylum', *European Journal of Cultural Studies*, vol. 9, no. 2, pp. 185–202.

UN-Habitat (2008) *State of the World's Cities 2008/2009 – Harmonious Cities*, available at: http://www.unhabitat.org/content.asp?cid=5964&catid=7&typeid =46&subMenuId=0 (accessed 12 January 2009).

United Nations (1948) Universal Declaration of Human Rights, available at: http:// www.un.org/events/humanrights/udhr60/declaration.shtml (accessed 10 March 2009).

—— (1996) *Report of the Fourth World Conference on Women, Beijing 4–15 September 1995*, available at: http://ods-dds-ny.un.org/doc/UNDOC/ GEN/N96/273/01/PDF/N9627301.pdf?OpenElement (accessed 30 November 2003).

—— (2000) *General Assembly Resolution 55/2*, 8 September 2000, available at: http://www.un.org/millennium/declaration/ares552e.htm (accessed 14 December 2007).

—— (2006) *World Population Monitoring, Focusing on International Migration and Development*, Commission on Population and Development, Economic and Social Council, New York.

—— (2008) *Millennium Development Goals Report*, available at: http:// www.un.org/millenniumgoals/pdf/The%20Millennium%20Development%20 Goals%20Report%202008.pdf (accessed 12 January 2009).

—— (2009) *Office of the High Commissioner on Human Rights*, available at: http://www.un.org (accessed 6 January 2009).

United Nations Development Fund for Women (2003) *Promoting Women's Human Rights and Eliminating Violence against Women*, available at: http://www. unifem.org/index.php?f_page_pid=24 (accessed 30 November 2003).

—— (2007) *Violence against Women: Facts and Figures*, available at: http:// www.unifem.org/campaigns/vaw/facts_figures.php (accessed 19 November 2008).

United Nations Development Programme (1997) *Human Development Report: Human Development to Eradicate Poverty*, available at: http://hdr.undp.org/en/reports/global/hdr1997/ (accessed 10 December 2008).

—— (2006) *Summary: Human Development Report 2006: Beyond Scarcity: Power, Poverty and the Global Water Crisis*, Palgrave Macmillan, New York.

—— (2007) *Human Development Report 2007/2008: Fighting Climate Change: Human Solidarity in a Divided World*, available at: http://hdr.undp.org/en/reports/global/hdr2007–2008/ (accessed 9 January 2009).

—— (2009) 'UNDP's response to the global economic crisis', *Fast Facts: United Nations Development Programme*, available at: http://www.undp.org/publications/fast-facts/FF-economic-crisis.pdf (accessed 27 May 2009).

United Nations Foundation (2007) 'Scientific expert group report on climate change and sustainable development,' *Confronting Climate Change: Avoiding the Unmanageable, Managing the Unavoidable*, available at: http://www.unfoundation.org/SEG/ (accessed 4 April 2007).

United Nations High Commissioner for Refugees (2007) *2006 Global Trends: Refugees, Asylum-seekers, Returnees, Internally Displaced and Stateless Persons*, available at: http://www.unhcr.org/statistics/STATISTICS/4676a71d4.pdf (accessed 10 May 2008).

—— (2007–8) *Protecting Refugees and the Role of the UNHCR* (2007–8), available at: http://www.unhcr.org/basics/BASICS/4034b6a34.pdf (accessed 27 March 2008).

United Nations Population Fund (2005) *State of World Population Report, Violence Against Women Fact Sheet*, available at: http://www.unfpa.org/swp/2005/presskit/factsheets/facts_vaw.htm (accessed 10 December 2008).

—— (2006) *State of World Population Report, A Passage to Hope: Women and International Migration*, available at: http://www.unfpa.org/publications/detail.cfm?ID=311&filterListType= (accessed 10 December 2008).

—— (2007) *State of World Population 2007: Unleashing the Potential of Urban Growth*, available at: http://www.unfpa.org/publications/detail.cfm?ID=334&filterListType (accessed 2 February 2009).

—— (2008) *State of World Population Report, Reaching Common Ground: Culture, Gender and Human Rights*, available at: http://www.unfpa.org/swp/ (accessed 20 December 2008).

Urry, J. (2003) *Global Complexity*, Polity Press, Cambridge.

—— (2005) 'The complexities of the global,' *Theory, Culture & Society*, vol. 22, no. 5, pp. 235–54.

Van Dijk, J. (1999) *The Network Society, Social Aspects of New Media*, Sage, Thousand Oaks.

Van Dijk, J. and Hacker, K (2003) 'The digital divide as a complex and dynamic phenomenon,' *The Information Society*, vol. 19, no. 5, pp. 315–26.

Veldhoen, L. (2007) 'Pulling themselves up by their keyboards', *Ode*, January/February, available at: http://www.odemagazine.com/doc/40/pulling_themselves_up_by_their_keyboards/ accessed 7 January 2009.

Vidal, J. (2008a) 'The Cinderella problem: Thousands die every day for lack of sanitation', *The Guardian Weekly*, 21–27 March, pp. 2–3.

Vidal, J. (2008b) 'The great green land grab', *The Guardian Weekly*, 22 February, pp. 25–7.

Vromen, A. (2007) 'Australian young people's participatory practices and Internet use', *Information, Communication & Society*, vol. 10, no. 1, pp. 48–68.

Wagner, A. (1997), 'Social work and the global economy: Opportunities and challenges' in Hokenstad, M. C. and Midgley, J. (eds) *Issues in International Social Work: Global Challenges for a New Century*, NASW Press, Washington, D.C., pp. 45–56.

Waldman, J. and Rafferty, J. (2006) 'Evidence from virtual social work practice: Implications for education' in Dunlop, J. M. and Holosko, M. J. (eds) *Information Technology and Evidence-Based Social Work Practice*, The Hawarth Press, New York, pp. 127–48.

Webb, S. A. (2003a) 'Local orders and global chaos in social work', *European Journal of Social Work*, vol. 6, no. 2, pp. 191–204.

—— (2003b) 'Technologies of care' in Harlow, E. and Webb, S. (eds) *Information and Communication Technologies in the Welfare Services*, Jessica Kingsley Publishers, London, pp. 223–38.

Weitzer, R. (2007) 'The social construction of sex trafficking: Ideology and Institutionalization of a moral crusade', *Politics & Society*, vol. 35, no. 3, pp. 447–75.

Welbourne, P., Harrison, G. and Ford, D. (2007) 'Social Work in the UK and the global labour market: Recruitment, practice and ethical considerations', *International Social Work*, vol. 50, no. 1, pp. 27–40.

Wharton, A. S. (2005) *The Sociology of Gender: An Introduction to Theory and Research*, Blackwell Publishing, Malden.

Whelan, J., Swallow, M., Peschar, P. and Dunne, A. (2002) 'From counselling to community work: Developing a framework for social work practice with displaced persons', Australian Social Work, vol. 55, no. 1, pp. 13–23.

Williams, L. (2007) 'Home alone' in Dominelli, L. (ed.) *Revitalising Communities in a Globalising World*, Ashgate, Aldershot, 255–69.

Witkin, S. (1998) 'Human rights and social work', *Social Work*, vol. 43, no. 3, pp. 197–201.

Wolf, M. (2004) *Why Globalization Works*, New Haven, Yale University Press.

World Bank (2005) *Environmental Matters at the World Bank: Annual Review, 34110*, available at: http:// www.worldbank.org/environmentmatters (accessed 30 April 2007).

—— (2007) *Global Economic Prospects: Managing the Next Wave of Globalization*, available at: http://www-wds.worldbank.org/external/default/WDSContentServer/IW3P/IB/2006/12/06/000112742_20061206155022/Rendered/PDF/381400GEP2007.pdf (accessed 20 June 2008).

—— (2008a) *2008 World Development Indicators, Poverty data: A Supplement to World Development Indicators, 2008*, available at: http://siteresources.worldbank.org/DATASTATISTICS/Resources/WDI08supplement1216.pdf (accessed 18 January 2009).

—— (2008b) 'Ministers, bank president, tout women's empowerment as key development goal', *News and Broadcast*, 12 April, available at: http://go.worldbank.org/76UJUVXWT0 (accessed 28 December 2008).

——— (2009) *Global Economic Prospects: Commodities at the Crossroads 2009*, available at: http://siteresources.worldbank.org/INTGEP2009/Resources/10363_WebPDF-w47.pdf (accessed 9 January 2009).

World Commission on Environment and Development (1987) *Our Common Future*, Oxford University Press, Oxford.

World Development Movement (2007) *Climate Calendar: The UK's Unjust Contribution to Global Climate Change*, available at: http://www.wdm.org.uk/resources/reports/climate/climatecalandarreport08012007.pdf (accessed 10 January 2009).

World Health Organization (2004) *The Global Burden of Diseases, 2004 Update*, available at: http://www.who.int/healthinfo/global_burden_disease/GBD_report_2004update_full.pdf (accessed 8 December 2008).

——— (2005a) *Mental Health Atlas*, available at: http://www.who.int/mental_health/evidence/atlas/global_results.pdf (accessed 10 December 2008).

——— (2005b) 'Promoting and protecting the rights of people with mental disorders,' *Information Sheet No. 1*, 7 December, available at: http://www.who.int/mental_health/policy/Promoting_and_protecting_rights_English1.pdf (accessed 17 January 2009).

——— (2006a) 'The global shortage of health workers and its impact', *Fact Sheet No 302*, available at: http://www.who.int/mediacentre/factsheets/fs302/en/print.html (accessed 10 December 2008).

——— (2006b) *Preventing Disease through Healthy Environments: Towards an Estimate of the Environmental Burden of Disease*, available at: http://www.who.int/quantifying_ehimpacts/publications/preventingdisease.pdf (accessed 25 April 2008).

——— (2007a) *Engaging Men and Boys in Changing Gender-Based Inequity in Health: Evidence from Programme Interventions*, available at: http://www.who.int/gender/documents/Engaging_men_boys.pdf (accessed 27 December 2008).

——— (2007b) 'Health of indigenous peoples,' *Fact Sheet No. 326*, October, available at: http://www.who.int/mediacentre/factsheets/fs326/en/ (accessed 10 January 2009).

——— (2008a) *Mental Health Gap Action Programme (mhGAP): Scaling Up Care for Mental, Neurological and Substance Use Disorders*, available at: http://www.who.int/mental_health/mhgap_final_english.pdf (accessed 19 January 2009).

——— (2008b) 'World Health Organization and United Nations Children's Fund: Joint Monitoring Programme for water supply and sanitation (JMP),' *Progress on Drinking Water and Sanitation: Special Focus on Sanitation*, UNICEF, New York and WHO, Geneva, 2008, available at: http://www.who.int/water sanitation_health/monitoring/jmp2008.pdf (accessed 14 August 2008).

World Social Forum (2008) *Homepage*, available at: http://www.wsf2008.net/eng/home (accessed 7 January 2009).

World Trade Organization (2008) *Understanding the WTO: Basics*, available at: http://www.wto.org/english/thewto_e/whatis_e/tif_e/fact1_e.htm (accessed 20 June 2008).

Worldwatch Institute (2003) *Homepage*, available at: http://www.worldwatch.org (accessed 1 November 2003).

Worldwatch Institute (2008) *1988 and 2008: Climate Change Turning Points*, available at: http://www.worldwatch.org/node/5799 (accessed 31 July 2008).

Wray, R. (2008) 'Electronic wasteland', *The Guardian Weekly*, 16 May, p. 43.

Wray, R. and Mayet, F. (2007) 'Upwardly mobile Africa', *The Guardian Weekly*, 2 November, p. 16.

Wronka, J. (1992) *Human Rights and Social Policy in the 21st Century: A History of the Idea of Human Rights and Comparison of the United Nations Declaration of Human Rights with United States Federal and State Constitutions*, University Press of America, Lanham, Maryland.

———. (2007) 'Global distributive justice as a human right' in Reichert, E. (ed.) *Challenges in Human Rights: A Social Work Perspective*, Columbia University Press, New York.

Yan, M. C. and Tsui, M. S. (2007) 'The quest for western social work knowledge: Literature in the USA and practice in China,' *International Social Work*, vol. 50, no. 5, pp. 641–53.

Yeates, N. (2007) 'Globalization and social policy' in Baldock, J. Manning, N. and Vickerstaff, S. (eds) *Social Policy*, Oxford University Press, Oxford, pp. 628–53.

Young, R. (2001) *Postcolonialism: An Historical Introduction*, Blackwell Publishers, Oxford.

Yu, N. G. (2006) 'Interrogating social work: Philippine social work and human rights under martial law', *International Journal of Social Welfare*, vol. 15, no. 5, pp. 257–63.

Yujuico, E. (2009) 'All modes lead to home: Assessing the state of the remittance art', *Global Networks*, vol. 9, no. 1, pp. 63–81.

Zick, A., Pettigrew, T. and Wagner, U. (2008) 'Ethnic prejudice and discrimination in Europe', *Journal of Social Issues*, vol. 64, no. 2, pp. 233–51.

Index

189

South Essex College
Further & Higher Education, Southend Campus
Luker Road Southend-on-Sea Essex SS1 1ND
Tel: 01702 220400 Fax: 01702 432320
Minicom: 01702 220642